M000119574

The Northern Queen

Kelly Evans

NORDLAND

www.nordlandpublishing.com

Kelly Evans

COPYRIGHT

The Northern Queen
Copyright © Kelly Evans 2015

This is a work of creative fiction. Names, characters, places, events and incidents are either the products of the author's imagination or used in a fictitious manner.

Any resemblance to real persons, living or dead is purely coincidental.

Kelly Evans asserts her moral right to be identified as the author of this book.

All rights reserved. This book or any portion thereof, may not be reproduced or used in any manner whatsoever without the express written permission of the publisher, except for the use of brief quotations in a book review.

Published by Nordland Publishing 2015

Edited by MJ Kobernus

ISBN Print: 978-82-8331-005-4
ISBN E-book:978-82-8331-006-1

The cover of The Northern Queen features the Albion Valkyrja Viking Sword, a beautiful recreation of an authentic viking relic found in a grave in Suontaka, Tyrväntö, Tavastland from the 11'th century. The image is reproduced and modified under the Creative Commons Attribution licensing. The original sword, discovered in 1968, is on display in the National museum in Helsinki, Finland.

Kelly Evans

ACKNOWLEDGMENTS

Although only one name goes on the cover of a novel, it takes many more people than that to create a book. I owe a huge debt of gratitude to so many people who were instrumental in helping me bring *The Northern Queen* to life.

First and foremost to Michael J. Kobernus, at Nordland Publishing, for not only the tremendous effort he put into making *The Northern Queen* ready for public consumption but also for the endless faith he had in the project, right from day one. His suggestions were invaluable and his eye for historical detail brought extra life and polish to the story.

To Allan Pringle, who patiently (and often painfully) read through each chapter as it was written and offered incredibly helpful advice. To Robyn Merckx for her support and understanding, particularly during those times when my muse abandoned me and all seemed hopeless. To my parents, who always made sure I had all the books, pencils and paper I wanted when growing up, even if it meant denying themselves something. And last, but certainly not least, to my husband, Max, who learned first-hand what it was like to live with a writer yet still maintained a sense of humour throughout. I couldn't have done this without him.

Kelly Evans

DEDICATION

For Max . . .

Kelly Evans

viii

CONTENTS

Prologue
Oxford

The smell of blood grew stronger. The church was crammed with others who'd had the same idea: sanctuary. For surely they wouldn't be harmed in the house of God? Gunhilde peered through the wooden slats that made up the outer wall of St. Frideswide's church, holding tightly to her son. Her husband had tried to fight off the attackers. She'd heard his final scream as she ran with their boy, not daring to look back.

Gunhilde gagged, covering her mouth with her hand, fighting her body's reaction to the sights, sounds and smells around her. She wanted to look away, to cover her ears and block out the screaming but she was compelled to watch, to bear witness. Her neighbours, people she had known for years, had fled in panic. She prayed they would make it to the church. After a while, all hope faded. Yet still, she stared through the tiny slit in the wattle.

It seemed that only Danes were being slaughtered, brutally attacked on all sides by multiple assailants, hacked down by sword and axe. There was so much blood that it became difficult to tell the victims from the attackers. Gunhilde was getting used to the screams, but the smell could not be ignored. The metallic scent of blood mixed with the emptied bowels of the dead and dying was too thick, too cloying. Outside, a confused child, separated from his parents, wandered straight into the path of the attackers. She couldn't bring herself to look and she turned her head away.

Gunhilde's stomach betrayed her at that moment, and she vomited, retching noisily. No one paid any attention. As she straightened, she looked up in apology to the painted image of the virgin princess, St. Frideswide, on the far wall of the church. That was when she noticed the stranger, prone on the floor, one hand holding his shoulder where blood seeped through. Grasping her son, she knelt to help the man.

The muscle was open on each side of the gash and a flash of bloodied white beneath the hacked flesh was visible. She had no water to clean the wound; the best she could do was bind the man's shoulder with her headscarf. He nodded gratefully when she was finished; it was crude, but there was nothing more she could do for him. Gunhilde stood, preparing to go back to her spot at the slats. She needn't ask how he was injured, indeed there was only one question she had at that moment.

"Why?"

"Why?"

His voice startled her; she hadn't realised she'd spoken the word aloud. The man's pale face looked up at her, emotionless, then to her son who stood close behind her.

"Why? Because the king wants it, that's why." He spat out the words.

Gunhilde's eyes widened. "Aethelred? He ordered this? " She gestured in frustration, not having the words to describe the horror around them.

"He did. I overheard one of the soldiers encouraging a Saxon boy. Told him there'd been a plot against the king's life by the Danes who had originally fought for him."

Gunhilde thought of her husband, Pallig, once a mercenary for the king. "But we're settled here. We pay our taxes like anyone else." She paused. "And we're Christians."

The man shook his head, causing the blood from his shoulder to flow once more.

"It makes no difference to a man like Aethelred. He has treacherous advisors. They fill his head with fear."

"How do you know these things?"

"My brother served with the king. I was here visiting when the attack took place."

Gunhilde was silent for a moment, the groans of the injured inside the church growing louder than the screams from outside. "But the people. They'll surely help. They know us!"

"The people are doing the king's work, turning on their Danish neighbours. They've been affected by bloodlust, are fevered with it."

There had always been an uneasy peace between the Saxons and the Danish settlers. The Danes were never fully accepted, despite their similar dress, their marrying into Saxon families and their adoption of the Christian faith. She herself had been baptised upon her arrival in England from Denmark, and had had a Christian marriage ceremony.

She felt a tug at her dress and looked down at her son, only to see him pointing at a corner of the church roof. Smoke was pouring in and it was only a moment before panic spread throughout the room. There was a rush towards the door but Gunhilde held her son back, fighting her own urge to run. She had her suspicions and was proven right when those who arrived at the door found it barred from the outside. In a cruel act of fate, those who had tried to save themselves first, who ran for the door and left others behind, found themselves being crushed by those who followed.

The smoke was all around them now, and people began to scream as flaming pieces of thatch fell, burning them. Gunhilde led her son back to their original spot at the rear of the church. Sitting, the air was clearer, but she knew it wouldn't last. Her son shivered, a whimper escaping. She held him close, running her fingers through his hair.

"Will uncle Sweyn help us?"

They were the first words he had spoken since they fled

their house, and they came out hoarsely.

"Your uncle is in Denmark, he cannot help." She knew if her brother had been here, he and his men would have cleared Oxford of the attackers. Sweyn Forkbeard ruled Denmark fairly. He would never allow such unprovoked madness in his kingdom.

The air grew hot and breathing more difficult. Her son's body slumped against her and she wailed, the smoke strangling the sound in her throat. With her last breath, Gunhilde offered a prayer to God.

Chapter One

England

Aelfgifu crossed the courtyard, a slight frown of concentration on her young face. A loud clattering interrupted her thoughts; one of the housecarls helping her husband prepare had dropped a shield, earning him a shove from a large warrior. She tried to catch her husband's eye, but he was surrounded by his men.

Sighing, she handed the bucket she had been carrying to a passing servant. "Take this to the kitchen." With a nod the servant was gone, lost in the sea of men who had taken over her manor. Unconsciously tucking a strand of hair behind her ear, she wandered over to a fence and propped up a few swords that had fallen. There was a never-ending list of tasks that accompanied running her estate. The manor, called Reodfeld, was comprised of fifteen hides which amounted to thousands of acres of land to be worked. There was also livestock, mills and wooded areas for fences and buildings to be managed. And hundreds of workers.

She couldn't decide what she needed to attend to next. The turmoil of the last two weeks had turned her usually ordered world sideways, and with all the noise, dirt and disarray, her thinking was becoming as hazy as the dust cloud that now permanently hovered over her courtyard. The men were preparing to leave, the horses were being packed and supplies loaded. Those who had formed attachments to the maids in Aelfgifu's household tried to find ways to slip away for a moment, to say goodbye and receive charms of luck and strength.

She went inside the longhouse. Most brides would enjoy a month with their new spouses but there would be no sweet moon of honey for her. She was saddened by the preparations around her, for they were the reason her husband was leaving so soon after their hand-fasting. Canute was joining his father to pursue their military campaign against the English king, Aethelred. There was just no time for the impracticality of being together every moment of the day. The only place she found peace was next to the ancient oak tree that resided on her property.

She had been taught as a child that the tree had been planted by Freya as a gift to the people in the area who worshipped her. It was still used for ceremonies, sacrifices and offerings, in spite of what those so-called priests said.

She looked around the hall, feeling the spirits of her father and brother in every corner. Most of her carls and servants slept here, in the main hall, those who didn't already had their own dwelling in the nearby village.

A maid approached. "My lady, we need candles for tonight's meal."

Aelfgifu nodded. "Come with me."

The young woman followed Aelfgifu to a cupboard in a room just off of the kitchen. Lifting the large ring of keys that she kept on her belt, she turned it until she found the one she needed. Unlocking the door, she turned to the maid. "How many?"

"Six, my lady."

Aelfgifu frowned. She trusted her staff but with so many strangers around she had to be careful, especially with expensive items like candles. "Here." She handed the candles to the waiting maid and relocked the cupboard.

As the lady of the house she was responsible for seeing that all ran smoothly, and she kept a close eye on the manor's stores. And as mistress of the manor, Aelfgifu commanded a private chamber. A small space, but cozy, with functional furniture and a small fire pit kept clean by a young woman from the village. She went there now.

The packed clay floor in her chamber was covered in rushes as well as a little fragrant lavender to scent the air. The small hearth stood in the centre of the space. Aelfgifu's bed had belonged to her parents, a heavy oak-framed structure with a feather-stuffed mattress, a luxury she allowed herself. Her linen sheets were simple, as was the remaining furniture in the room: a few wooden stools, a table near the small shuttered window and walls lined with shelves holding her belongings. A large carved chest, once belonging to Aelfgifu's mother, stood at the foot of the bed.

Brihtwyn was in the room, putting away the latest gifts that had arrived. Aelfgifu smiled at her aunt, then threw herself onto a bench and laid her head on the table, willing her father's ghost away. Passing through the hall earlier, she had seen her father's drinking horn, still hanging from a hook where he had left it all those years ago. She gulped back a sob as she remembered the last time he had used it, the day the man she most hated in the world arrived at Reodfeld. As her father left to join the other members of the household outside in the courtyard, he drained the last of the mead from the horn, shook it out and winked at her as he placed it on the hook. His memory wouldn't leave her thoughts, no matter how hard she tried to push it away. She gave up and allowed the past to invade.

"Your father was a traitor to their Majesties King Aethelred and Queen Emma." Eadric Streona, Earl of Mercia and the king's most-trusted advisor, stood before Aelfgifu's gathered household and delivered the pronouncement in his characteristic smug voice. Dressed in black, his height falling just short of average, he was not a handsome man. A defect of birth caused his mouth to wilt at one end, so everything he said was delivered with a sneer. His dark eyes, sharp nose and greasy hair reminded Aelfgifu of the rats that lived in the stables.

"But the king has decided to show your family mercy." He

leered at Aelfgifu, looking her up and down, his crawling gaze chilling her, before continuing. "The king, being a wise and benevolent man, declared that although your brother is a traitor, because of his youth and inexperience he'll be spared death."

Eadric stopped again while the household murmured its relief. The feeling was fleeting. "But a traitor, no matter how green, must still be punished. His majesty has given me the task of determining the most appropriate penalty."

He crossed his arms over his puffed-up chest, chin jutting forward. Aelfgifu would have found the man's pompous self-importance amusing under different circumstances. The muttering started again, this time with the raised pitch of panic.

Eadric drew his dagger from his belt and ran his finger suggestively over the hilt, all the while staring at Aelfgifu, until her brother Wulfheah, struggling to free himself from his bindings, was dragged before them all.

"I've decided on a suitable punishment, one that'll serve as a reminder to you all."

Her brother was forced onto the ground, then rolled onto his back. Eadric's men held him down as he thrashed in vain. A kitchen maid screamed and turned away, looking around wildly for somewhere to run. One of Eadric's chainmail-clad men stepped forward and swung the back of his hand across her face, knocking her to the ground. She struggled to stand and wiped a trickle of blood from her mouth, eyes wide with fear. Eadric watched, face contorted with rage. "You'll look, and you'll be silent. You'll learn to be obedient to your king."

Eadric handed his dagger to one of his men. The man turned the weapon over in his hand, grinning at his reflection in the steel, before he leaned over Wulfheah's body. Taking the blade point, he sliced it across the boy's cheek. The cut welled with blood.

Eadric smirked. "Let all see the shame of his actions on his face!"

Aelfgifu hadn't realised she'd been holding her breath until it escaped unbidden in relief. "It's not so bad," she thought, "we can treat it. There'll be a scar, a bad one, but around here and to all who know him it will serve as a badge of honour." But her relief was short-lived.

"Now take his eyes." Shock resonated through her household.

Eadric's man roughly grabbed Wulfheah's face before sliding the knife into the corner of his left eye. Aelfgifu moaned as blood poured from the wound, watching the guard jiggle the knife in the eye socket before making a flicking motion with his wrist. Wulfheah's eyeball came out, still attached by threads of tissue and viscous material. It landed with a sickening wet sound on his cheek.

She had been forced to watch, but it wasn't the sight that haunted her dreams; it was the screams that still woke her from sleep, the horrible awful screaming as the knife plunged into her brother's eye. She had seen the guard look to Eadric for recognition of his skill, and had nearly been sick when the earl smiled and made a motion to continue. The screams had grown worse as Eadric's man proceeded again, removing the right eye and pulling it until the tissue attaching it snapped. Her brother's agonised voice grew hoarse with pain. It was at that point that Aelfgifu had felt herself grow numb, as if the horror playing out before her was a dream.

When they were done, her brother's unconscious body had been left on the flagstones of the great manor, and no one had dared approach him until Eadric gave permission. The earl had clapped the man who had carried out the torture on the shoulder and laughed as if sharing a private joke. Rage boiled within her. That had been seven years ago and it still hurt as much now as it did then.

She felt her aunt's gentle hand on her shoulder. At eighteen, Aelfgifu was a woman, but a part of her still craved the touch of a mother. Or, in this case, her aunt. Bri was overjoyed that she was finally married, as was Aelfgifu, and not for romantic reasons. For she was no longer at risk of becoming a ward of the court, no longer worried the king would seize her land or marry her off to a stranger, as had been done with so many other women in her situation.

She had lived quietly, hoping to avoid the king's gaze, now an impossible scenario, for given Aelfgifu's choice of bridegroom, it was certain that Aethelred had already taken notice. And Eadric. Nothing Aethelred did was hidden from Eadric, so entrenched was the man in the king's affairs. Aelfgifu grinned at her own use of the word 'affair,' for it was rumoured that Eadric was the queen's lover and that Queen Emma's first son by Aethelred was not the king's at all. She didn't put much trust in rumours, but hoped this one was true, because when Aethelred finally found out, Eadric would be destroyed, and there was nothing she wanted more in the world.

She turned toward the window facing the courtyard. "If my father and brother were here, they too would be preparing for battle." She whispered the words, yet still her aunt had heard.

Bri came around and stood before her. "You must comfort yourself with the thought that your father and brother now live by Odin's side, in the halls of Valhalla."

Both Aelfgifu and Brihtwyn had been baptised in the new faith, but in private they still followed the old ways. It was sometimes prudent to keep these ancient beliefs hidden, for the tide of change was upon the land and the old ways were being pushed aside. The Christian faith had been accepted by nearly all of the country but there were still areas, particularly in the Danelaw, where families followed the old ways, and who held out against the Christian dogma that was becoming the norm.

"My father was a great man, admired by many. He was first to volunteer to fight alongside King Sweyn." She looked up at Bri. "I miss him terribly."

It was a turbulent time. Her father, Aelfhelm, and brother, Wulfheah, had made an unwise choice: they'd supported the invading king of Denmark, Sweyn Forkbeard against the reigning monarch. Aethelred had sat on the throne for many years and had shown himself to be an ineffectual ruler. When the Danes invaded England, rather than fight them and prove himself a true king, Aethelred had, year after year, paid them to go away. The Danes, realising this was an easy way to obtain gold, kept returning, increasing their demands for ransom each time until the entire country suffered from the outrageous taxes Aethelred was forced to levy.

And King Sweyn in particular wanted more than just gold; he sought revenge for his sister's death, eleven years ago. He had led several of these raiding expeditions, and it was during one of their visits that she'd met Canute. And now they were married. It was a love match; she'd known he was for her the moment they had been introduced. But it was also an astute political union, one that suited both her family and his, for Aelfgifu's father had been a wealthy landowner and an important man to have as a supporter. The country's situation was so dire that men who had formally supported the English king declared themselves for the Danes, believing that Sweyn would soon rule the country and depose Aethelred.

It was the lesser of two evils: a new, unknown ruler, yet a man who had proven himself in battle, or an ill-counselled and fearful man who would rather flee than fight. Aelfgifu's father chose Sweyn. It had proven to be a bad decision and the repercussion had come swiftly, in the form of Eadric Streona.

She felt ill when she thought of that name and the horror that came with it. Eadric was new to the court, coming from a humble family with no connections to anyone of importance. Through conniving and deceit, and his willingness to perform deeds that no one else would consider, he'd come to Aethelred's attention. With his fawning words he'd gained the king's trust and was now Aethelred's most favoured advisor, one among many who had no concern for the country, but rather advised the king to follow policies that would enhance their own position and coffers. He'd even been elevated to the Earldom of Mercia and had married the king's own daughter, Eadgyth. Eadric grinned when his men had slaughtered her father, cutting him down as he ran from the courtyard to his family. Aelfgifu never had the chance to say goodbye. But what had come next was worse, if anything could be crueller than the terror she'd already experienced that day. She shut out the images, but remembered Eadric's final words.

"I trust you've learned your lesson." This had been addressed to Aelfgifu, who was now solely responsible for the running of all her family's estates. Her brother had survived, barely, and only due to the ministrations of a local healing woman. But the following winter had been harsh and her brother caught a fever. He'd never quite recovered from the torture and succumbed to the illness, passing away in delirium.

Aelfgifu shivered and forced her thoughts to more pleasant things, for as the day of Canute's departure grew closer, her thoughts turned to her husband's fate and the danger he and his men faced.

"My hand fasting was perfect, wasn't it?" She coughed. Suddenly her throat was dry, and she reached for a cup of watered wine, numbing her fears for her husband with a long draught.

"My dear, it was a lovely ceremony."

The weather had been mild and the sunlight had filtered down through the trees surrounding the grove. She'd chosen the place for many reasons, none more important than that her mother and father were buried nearby, in mounds now grown over with grass and wildflowers, as were the rest of her ancestors. The grove itself held many pleasant memories for her; she grew up playing in these fields with her brother when she was not required at the lessons her father had insisted she attend.

Her upbringing had differed from other girls in many ways, most unusual of which was her education. She had been taught to read and write, something thought unnecessary by most, for girls would not need these skills for the running of a household. When Aelfgifu had shown a talent for numbers, her father had encouraged her further, introducing her to the estate rolls and eventually working side-by-side with her in managing his lands. *Her* lands, Aelfgifu corrected herself.

Now, two weeks later, she surprised herself, blurting out a question. "Would my father have approved?" She was still fighting the images of her husband, dead or wounded in a field, imagining the horror he would face, all the while realising the foolishness of such thinking.

She watched Bri's face soften. "I know he would." They sat in silence, until her aunt cleared her throat, her eyes wet, and hurriedly spoke of the ceremony again. "The goði who performed your joining was good, he seemed approachable but I wonder about his . . ."

Aelfgifu was no longer listening; she forced the present away, if only for a short time. Her thoughts travelled back to the ceremony and the goði.

"You've something of your ancestors?"

Canute turned and one of his housecarls handed him a leather bundle. Turning back, he carefully unwrapped the ancient covering and removed a dagger. It was broader than those Aelfgifu had seen from the southern areas of Europe, or indeed in England, and had a carved wooden handle, hewn in the shape of a stylised bear. The worn wood shone from the many hands that had held it; it was obvious this weapon had been much used.

There were runes etched into the blade, and as beautiful as they were Aelfgifu shivered when she saw them. This was an old weapon, used when trolls and dwarves and other unnatural beasts roamed the land.

"I offer this, a weapon belonging to my family for generations. Its name is Ulfban, which means wolf killer."

He handed the dagger to Aelfgifu. "Its beginnings are lost to us but it's one of the oldest items my family possesses."

She had taken the dagger with reverence, careful not to cut herself on the blade, sharp despite its age. She could feel the power and magic in the knife and shivered again, trusting that the gods would protect her from any spirits that might be attracted to the weapon.

They exchanged their vows and it was over. She had expected her new husband to release her hand but instead he brought it to his mouth and kissed it, then had drawn her to him and left a lingering kiss on her lips, one that suggested he would rather have retired to the bedchamber at that moment instead of enjoying the feast that was to come. She had smiled and bowed her head. "My lord husband."

A warm breeze blew through her hair, gently tearing Aelfgifu away from her reminiscence, for good this time. She went to the window, looking for Canute.

The last time she had had him to herself was the previous night, when he had come to her chamber in the early hours of the morning, exhausted by the preparations. Their lovemaking had been tentative, gentle, but soon their passion became fierce and all encompassing, almost desperate. For even though she knew he loved her, she had felt part of him was already slipping away, distracted by the war to come.

Now, looking out at the seeming confusion that had taken over her courtyard she remembered the warmth of his embrace, the curve of his body, the scent of him, as they had fallen asleep. She shivered at the sudden goose flesh the thought raised. Searching through the milling crowd that blocked her view, she finally saw Canute. He was surrounded by his men and looked like he was arguing. Aelfgifu wondered if it had anything to do with the news he had surprised her with during the wedding feast.

Turning from the window she crossed the room and sat again. "Canute will be made regent of England when Sweyn wins." Aelfgifu had been sworn to secrecy but Canute had agreed last night that she could share the secret with her aunt.

Bri's head turned sharply. "What?"

"It's true. My husband is more than capable. And it shows the great confidence my father-in-law has for Canute's abilities, to give him such an honour."

Bri shook her head. "I don't know what to say."

Aelfgifu waved aside the comment. "He'll have help, someone you know perhaps." She waited until her aunt held up her hands, unable to guess. "Thorkell."

"The man who betrayed Sweyn?"

Aelfgifu laughed. "The very same."

"But how? He abandoned your father-in-law last year!"

The story they'd all been told was that, after the murder of the hostage Archbishop Alphege by his men, Thorkell had been so distraught and disgusted that he turned against his own lord and joined with the king. She knew the archbishop had been instrumental in helping to negotiate the ransom payments Aethelred paid to Sweyn in return for not raiding, and that, when captured, he'd refused to allow the king to pay anything for his release. Under the protection of

Thorkell, the holy man met his fate. The warriors had been drinking and decided the torment of an old man would be a good game. They beat him to death as he prayed to his god, leaving him lying naked and bloody in the mud. When Thorkell had discovered the body he was furious. Taking his brother Heming, and any loyal men with him, he'd presented himself to King Aethelred and asked to not only be baptised in the Christian faith but also to be allowed to fight alongside the king.

"That's the story, yes. But not many know the truth, that Sweyn sent Thorkell into the enemy's midst, so he could provide the Danish invaders with information about Aethelred, his court and his army. And Thorkell also breeds dissent where he can, arguing in particular with King Aethelred's eldest son, who's been denied his inheritance by the queen and already complains to anyone who will listen."

"Isn't that a dangerous tactic?" Bri's forehead creased.

"Yes, but Thorkell is smart, and the most trusted of all Sweyn's men. He has instructions to reveal certain details about Sweyn's army to Aethelred, in order to further gain Aethelred's trust." Aelfgifu glanced at the window, hearing Canute's voice raised above the others, before turning back to Bri. "And besides, Aethelred is weak; learning more of Sweyn's superior forces will only make him all the more fearful."

Bri digested this information. "The queen believes that Thorkell has truly joined her husband's forces?"

Aelfgifu laughed. "Queen Emma is a shrew and Canute says that Aethelred has no liking for her. It doesn't matter what she believes, he won't listen to anything his wife says." Aelfgifu took her cup and drank some wine. "What a grand political alliance their union turned out to be."

It was no secret, everyone in the country knew about Queen Emma. The woman had been part of a treaty between Aethelred and Emma's brother, the Duke of Normandy. The treaty stipulated that if Aethelred agreed to marry Emma, then the Duke must not allow the Danes who had been terrorising England, to winter in Normandy, nor be allowed to sell the gold they'd stolen from good Englishmen. But the Duke had broken his promise and had continued to allow the Danes free access to his Duchy.

"By Frigg, one'd think it was a story made up by a drunken scald!" Bri hid her grin behind her wine cup.

Aelfgifu nodded. "Canute said the final insult heaped upon Aethelred, before he agreed to the joining, was receiving a gold cup as a gift from a visiting merchant – the very same gold cup that he himself had given to a retainer a few years before!"

Bri laughed, openly this time. "But why doesn't Aethelred just rid himself of her?"

"Ahh, he wishes he could. But he married her in the Christian faith, and then she proved fertile and produced an heir. A male heir." Aelfgifu grinned wryly. "She was a peace-pledge wife, sold by a man who does not value pledges!" Laughing, she drained her cup.

Their two weeks together had gone quickly and much of her new husband's time had been taken with plans of invasion. Aelfgifu had busied herself running the manor and aiding the warriors when she could, seeing that needed supplies were available and gathering notes from the men to send to loved ones on their behalf when they marched. She hated the reasons she must perform these tasks but was also grateful for any distraction, for the activity stopped her from descending into despair at the odds she knew Canute faced.

Today was the day of his departure and Aelfgifu waited patiently for Canute to come to her, eventually giving up on trying to get his attention while he was so busy. Finally, he appeared in her chamber.

"My lady, I regret not having had much time to spend with you."

She walked over and kissed his hand, holding it to her cheek for a moment before dismissing the sentimentality. Today she must be strong, stand as an oak, tall and unbending. "I won't keep you long. I wish to give you a gift." Aelfgifu signalled for a servant who was hovering nearby to bring over a bundle he'd been gripping tightly. He handed her the object then backed away. Unwrapping the linen covering, she revealed her gift.

Surprise appeared on her husband's face, a rare emotion for a boy who had come to manhood amidst the blood and terror of battle. In her arms lay a sword, the most beautiful weapon she had ever seen. Canute reached over and took the sword by the grip, stepping back and swinging the weapon, feeling the weight, the balance. "The grip, stag antler beneath the leather?"

Aelfgifu grinned her pleasure, a bittersweet moment. She hadn't expected a grand show of gratitude from the Dane, but rather a display of Canute's cleverness. "Yes."

He shifted the weapon again, swinging the blade above and behind before bringing it back again to a perfectly level position in front of him. He nodded. "A fine blade, very fine, from the forge of a skilled craftsman. The wave pattern in the steel, it reminds me of the sea." He swung it around once more, a grin widening on his face.

"The runes on the blade are to bring you fortune, to ask the All Father's blessings." She watched as he turned the weapon over in his hands.

"And the crossbar - I see the Valkyries will accompany me into battle." The noise outside had grown as the men made ready to leave. They only had a few moments, and Aelfgifu grew serious, stepping toward her husband and placing her hand on the blade.

"May the All Father bless this weapon and the warrior who bears it."

She ran her hand over his face, trying to memorise each

feature.

"Come back to me."

As Canute turned to leave her, she said one last thing to her husband.

"Avenge my family, Canute. Kill Aethelred."

Chapter Two
England

The noise in the crowded hall erupted, the men banging their cups on the tables, shouting and waving their arms. Aelfgifu was glad to see the invitations she had issued to this meeting were well-received, for all the members of the Danish burghs were in attendance, as were the major landowners from the north, including the Ealdorman of Northumbria, Earl Uchtred, known as 'The Brave' for his many exploits in battle. She fanned herself with her hand; the heavy air, filled with the smell of men and stale ale, was overwhelming.

It was the earl who now struggled to raise his voice over those of the other noblemen.

"But . . . but what if?" It was no use, his voice wouldn't be heard. Angry and frustrated, he shoved his large frame through a group of men, climbed on a chair and jumped onto a table. "What I want to say to you is this: what if Aethelred wins?"

This time there was no shouting, for Uchtred had spoken aloud the words that all in the hall were thinking. Now there was worried murmuring. Aelfgifu had heard enough. She stepped forward, her red linen dress swirling around her like a fiery haze.

"What if indeed! Shall we continue to live our lives asking 'what if?'" She'd been accompanied by Brihtwyn and her housecarl, Wulfred. Bri handed her a cup of mead and she drank before continuing. "*What if* Aethelred decides to levy another tax? *What if* he decides to further hurt his countrymen, those he's sworn to protect, by taking our livestock and our crops and our property, as he has done so many times in the past?" She took another drink, the alcohol fuelling her anger. *"What if* we and our families starve because of his taxes?"

The noise rose again, accompanied by many nods of agreement. Most of the men were of Danish blood and while forced to support the king, made no secret of the fact that they favoured Sweyn. By now someone had found a chair for her and Aelfgifu sat amongst these powerful men, many of whom her father had called friends. They knew where her allegiance lay; these same men had been invited to attend her hand fasting to Canute. They also knew of her father's wisdom and abilities, and that she was, if nothing else, her father's daughter.

She sat and was served mead by one of the maids. Wulfred cleared his throat. He was her husband's man but had, when given the choice by Canute, remained behind to ensure Aelfgifu was safe. It showed the great trust that Canute had in the man and Wulfred performed his role admirably. Smaller of stature than many of the men in Canute's service, he made up for it through sheer force of presence. His voice boomed. "Sweyn has the superior force. Aethelred will fall." It wasn't a question, as the other men had been suggesting all night, but a statement of fact. And his words carried weight, for only he among them had seen the numbers, had sailed across the channel with them and had witnessed the Danish strength first hand.

The raised voices confirmed doubts still lingered, especially about the force that both sides had available. Aelfgifu realised that she must do more to persuade them. She stood and the room stilled respectfully.

"I've heard that the king is ill-prepared for battle. It's said that he argues with the Athelings, his sons by his first wife, and with his new queen." Judging by the raised noise, she had said the right thing, for while the queen had gained supporters in the south of the country, those in the north were still suspicious of her. Aelfgifu continued.

"Emma would have her own children rule, but they're yet too young. So she goads the king, encourages the discord between him and his older sons." She strode to the middle of the hall, aware that all eyes were upon her. Wulfred made a move to accompany her but she stopped him with a wave of her hand.

"And meanwhile Eadric Streona, whose name we all know means the 'Grasper,' continues to whisper flattering words to the king, persuading our *leader*," her sarcastic use of the word raised a few chuckles from the room, "to pay more gold and coin to the invader, a bribe to make Sweyn sail away."

It was clear from the noise around her that many had not known this. They'd all experienced misery at the hands of Eadric and at the mention of his name the faces of the men around her grew dark.

"But Sweyn wants no gold! He wants no silver or coin! He has asked for nothing and will take nothing less than the crown! Yet Eadric still persists in pushing the king to raise more taxes, thinking it will keep him safe from the battlefield!"

The room erupted in laughter; all were aware of the man's aversion to fighting and appreciated the jab. "And the Athelings, Aethelstan and Edmund. The king's sons encourage him to fight to keep his throne, and they *say* they'll fight by his side, but all know of the enmity between the eldest and his father. Why, Aethelstan would just as easily swat a fly as push his father from the throne!"

There were more nods of agreement around the room. Even the earl was looking more confident.

"Aethelred is ill-met and ill-advised, a man who would rather offer his country's wealth to attackers and turn a blind eye than fight." She waited a moment for effect, encouraged by the men's rapt attention. "But Sweyn Forkbeard, this is a man who has already proven himself, both as a ruler and as a warrior. He governs Denmark like a true king, protecting his citizens and bringing them glory and battle stories to share in their taverns. He has sons, and a clear line of succession, unlike Aethelred!"

The hall burst into laughter and cheers. The men were feeling the effects of the mead and were getting rowdy. Wulfred took a step toward her once more and this time she let him. Not that she thought she was in any danger but she knew how men who were agitated could act, even ones as respected as these.

A man stepped forward, aged and bent. He held significant plots of land in Bedford, and had travelled far to be here. "But we've all sworn an oath to Aethelred."

Aelfgifu turned and looked at him, considering her words. She turned back and addressed the crowd. "Yet while Aethelred sits and argues with his son and wife, and Eadric hides behind the throne, Sweyn gathers his men and marches. Which man would you rather have as your liege lord?"

Aelfgifu was still feeling the effects of the meeting and the mead when they arrived home. Even the hard ride on horseback had not dampened her spirits. Bri quickly set about putting a plate of food together for her.

"Do you think I convinced any of them?"

Bri put a plate of sweetmeats on the table in front of Aelfgifu. "I believe you did, yes. You spoke well, and true. With much conviction."

She sighed. "It's easy to speak words, all men do. But to convince others?" She shook her head.

"Those men trust you. As they trusted your father."

"I hope you're right, Bri."

Wulfred entered the kitchen as they spoke. "Lady, all of the doors and windows are bolted." Brihtwyn offered the

Dane a cup of wine. He'd refused mead at the meeting but now gladly accepted.

"My husband will be arriving at Gainsborough, I think."

Wulfred took a long draught of wine and wiped his beard with the back of his hand.

"Yes, lady, he accompanies my king. I helped Sweyn plan his attack. He plans to sail from Sandwich up the Humber in his own longship to Gainsborough. From there he'll move north."

Aelfgifu had never seen Sweyn's ship but she'd heard it described. One of the larger longships, a drekkar, it was decorated with war symbols and the foreign runes of the Danes, the prow a fierce dragon painted in red. She could only imagine the fear people felt as they witnessed those great and terrible ships sailing within a stone's throw of their homes. Shuddering involuntarily, she reached for the plate in front of her.

"And what of Canute? Will he be in the fight?" Bri spoke as she helped herself to more cheese.

"Of course he'll fight!"

Her mind went to the stories of battle she'd been told by her brother when she was a child, and the horrible details with which he tried to frighten her. She shut out these memories, unwilling to think of her husband in the same circumstances. Unconsciously she shook her head, as if the action would remove the tales. Wulfred saw the motion and put a fatherly hand on her shoulder.

"He will be well, lady. Canute is a strong fighter; he was schooled by a Jomsviking after all. None other than Thorkell himself."

Aelfgifu was aware of this and yet it did little to calm her. She'd known the life she was going to lead when she agreed to join with Canute. She also knew there was no point in worrying. A man lived only as long as he lived, as Canute was fond of saying. But she still fretted.

Two weeks after the meeting with the northern landowners, Aelfgifu was in her chamber when a visitor was announced. Surprised, for she'd not expected company, she tidied away the charters she'd been reviewing and stood. She heard before she saw her visitor, a small mercy that allowed her to prepare herself, and thus was able to offer her hand without it shaking.

"Ealdorman Eadric."

He hesitated a moment before taking her hand and raising it to his lips. "Lady Aelfgifu."

Damn him, what did he want? Why was he here, unannounced? "Ealdorman, please sit." She indicated to a nearby chair. "Sir, have you eaten?"

"I haven't, as a matter of fact." He smiled sweetly but underneath there was impatience. And disdain.

She looked at a waiting maid. "Bring some of the stew. And ale." The maid bobbed her head and left the room as swiftly as she could; it seemed no one was happy when the Grasper was present. Sitting across from him at the table, she smiled back at him.

"Ealdorman, what brings you here?"

He waved a hand in the air magnanimously. "Call me Eadric. For we're very nearly equals, are we not?"

"Indeed. Eadric."

He laughed, as though delighted to hear the sound of his name. While the food was served he made casual comments about her manor and the number of servants and animals she had. It was only after complimenting her on the quality of the meat, despite living so far to the north, that she began to realise why he was there.

"What have you been doing while your husband is away?"

"My usual duties. Running Reodfeld and seeing to my lands takes most of my time, sir."

She wouldn't give him one word of information that he didn't directly ask for.

"But a woman alone? Aren't you frightened?" He smiled again and she felt her stomach lurch. "There are many perils for a woman, these are dangerous days."

They were, and she knew exactly where the threat lay.

"I've my own housecarls, and my husband has left one of his most faithful men with me." She pointed at the closed door, trusting that Eadric would realise Wulfred was outside it. "I'm well-protected."

As they continued their meal, Eadric turned the conversation to events around the borough. "I hear there was a meeting here a short while ago."

She thought it would come to this. "Yes."

"I hear that you attended this meeting."

She replied cautiously. "Yes." Did he know she had arranged it?

He sneered. "Why would a woman want to go without her husband to a meeting of men?"

She picked up her ale and sipped slowly, giving herself time to reply. "I had nothing of import to oversee that evening, I thought I'd go and listen." She laughed, careful not to betray her true feelings. "It was an evening's pastime, nothing more."

He snorted. "My informants tell me your involvement was more than listening." He glared at her, his eyes challenging.

"I fear your sources are faulty, Eadric."

This time he scowled when she said his name. "No, lady, my sources are sound. Are you sure you only listened? Perhaps you spoke and don't remember?"

Aelfgifu could feel beads of perspiration forming on her forehead and was nearly ready to call Wulfred. Instead she sat taller in her seat and took a breath.

"Hmm, you may be right. I *did* have some wine before leaving the manor." Smiling innocently, she continued. "But what harm are a woman's words, my lord? What could a woman say that a man would listen to?" She tilted her head slightly to the side, wondering how he would react.

He leered, the movement emphasising his facial deformity. "Oh, women have many words that can sway a man. Your words, for example. Treasonous words."

His tone was no longer friendly, it was accusatory. "You spoke out against your king."

There was no point in denying her involvement; even if his information was false he wouldn't believe what she said.

"I made a few comments, only to play a game with the men. But I spoke no treason." Taking advantage of Eadric's doubtful silence she shifted, smoothing out her dress and leaning back in her chair. She had her drink in hand and was doing her utmost to control the shaking. Casually she waved her cup.

"My lord, why would someone as important as yourself, one who advises the king, fear a woman's words?"

She was satisfied to see the startled look on his face, albeit briefly, before it was replaced with arrogance.

"Your king fears nothing. Nor do I."

He'd answered too quickly, there was something in his tone. She saw that he'd unconsciously begun to play with a large gaudy ring on his finger, spinning it around, first one way then the other.

"Then why did he see fit to send you to visit a harmless woman?"

He snorted again, this time not so elegantly as before. "He didn't send me. I was visiting my estates in Mercia and decided to investigate these rumours."

"So you admit they may be false, as rumours often are?" The ring spun, his fingers working faster and faster, driven by the anger that was plainly visible on his face. She knew she should be more cautious but couldn't stop herself.

"And why aren't you visiting the dangerous men who attended this supposedly treasonous meeting? These men who only want to live in peace?"

He stopped twirling the ring and pounded both fists on the table.

"And they think they'll get that under a foreign king? A heathen?"

As if remembering his dignity he calmed himself, leaned back in his chair and laughed.

"Oh, I'll be visiting each and every one." He stood suddenly. "You've angered people in high places."

He looked at her smugly, and she sensed there was something more to his words.

"I trust his majesty has better things to think upon than a humble northern woman." She hoped he would take the bait.

"Oh he does have more important things to occupy his time; it's not the king whose notice you've come to."

She couldn't hide the surprise she felt and was glad Eadric wasn't looking at her, couldn't see that his words had thrown her. She stood while he retrieved his cloak before turning back to her.

"Do you know the full story of the death of your father?"

Aelfgifu felt her legs go weak but steadied herself. He wouldn't dare bring up this topic, not in her own home! She saw by the look on his face he'd seen her react at the mention of her father.

"No, I don't suppose you do." Pausing to fasten his cloak, he continued. "While it was King Aethelred who ordered your father's death and your brother's blinding, he had to be persuaded this was the right course of action."

Aelfgifu grimaced; she couldn't help it. She wanted nothing more than to see him gone, yet she needed to hear what he had to say. Grinning widely now, he laughed.

"Yes, it's true. The king counselled mercy for the traitors, spoke of renewed loyalty but his wife didn't agree."

This time Aelfgifu couldn't hide her reaction. She

grabbed the edge of a table to keep herself steady.

"Queen Emma?"

"Yes, the queen. She saw mercy as a sign of weakness, as did I. Together we were able to persuade Aethelred to pursue a more—he stopped, considering his words carefully—"memorable course of action.""

She was suddenly afraid. "Wulfred!"

It was immediately obvious her carl had been ready. The door swung open and he appeared, hand on the hilt of his sword. "My lady?"

Eadric waved a hand in the air. "No need for such dramatics. I'm on my way."

He strode through the door before turning back to address her in a low voice. "I'll be visiting the men who attended the meeting. And, my lady, if I discover anything I don't like, you and your entire household will share in your father's fate. I'll see to it personally."

He slammed the door behind him as he left and Aelfgifu sat down heavily in her chair. How was it possible that her head was filled with a thousand thoughts but her body felt so empty? Worry and fear over what she'd just learned clambered for her attention. Of one thing she had no doubt: Eadric Streona was in earnest.

Chapter Three

England

Although she had denied it to Eadric, many of the men reported that Aelfgifu's words had affected them. When Sweyn returned to the north, there was a large contingent of men waiting.

"Hail, Sweyn Forkbeard!" Those gathered all bent on one knee, heads down. Earl Uchtred, the most powerful of the northern lords looked up from his kneeling position and spoke for them all.

"Sweyn Forkbeard, King of Denmark, we yield to you our swords, our shields and our loyalty."

Many in the group had been with Aelfgifu at the meeting, weeks earlier. All were dressed in their finest clothing, linen draped with gold and silver chains and pendants, displays of wealth and power, proof to their new king that he was acquiring capital as well as loyalty. The noblewomen were also dressed in their best, but they remained behind the men, peering over shoulders and around arms, curious to see the foreign king.

Aelfgifu, with Brihtwyn and Wulfred beside her, had chosen a spot off to the side where they could watch the entire exchange. Her loyalties were not in doubt. There was no need for her to swear allegiance.

Sweyn stepped forward and placed a hand on Uchtred's shoulder. "I accept your allegiance, you and the northern lords." He grabbed the man and lifted him from his knees. Sweyn stood a head taller than Uchtred, and all present could feel the power he exuded. But to his credit the earl didn't shrink from the Dane's stare. Nodding at the Englishman, Sweyn continued. "I welcome your loyalty and as a show of good faith and gratitude for your future service my men will do no harm to any man, woman, child or beast from these lands, nor from any of the lands owned by men who willingly give themselves to my rule."

Whenever an army marched, whether on the land belonging to friend or foe, they took what they wanted, and did what they wanted. So there were murmurs of relief at Sweyn's words, for many had feared that the force he brought with him would mean pillage and destruction.

Their surrender nearly complete, the men began to stand. All were silent, knowing that the most difficult part of the ceremony was yet to come. Uchtred spoke again.

"We thank you for the great leniency and benevolence you've shown us." He turned his head to look behind him, the sign a young man in the crowd had been waiting for.

"It would be a great honour if you would allow my eldest son, Ealdred, to be educated in your court."

Both father and son bowed before the king. All present knew these words for what they really were: that the boy was a hostage, held by Sweyn to ensure that the nobles kept their word. All of the lords would be 'allowing' their sons to depart with the king when he left to travel south and they had all said their goodbyes the evening before. It would be inappropriate to show any signs of attachment or emotion at their leaving; any sign of weakness in front of their new ruler would put them and their families at further disadvantage.

Sweyn smiled and squatted down in order to better greet the terrified boy. Ealdred approached slowly, and started to glance back towards his father before seemingly remembering some warning, snapping his eyes straight ahead. When he reached the Dane he bowed deeply. Sweyn's face was motionless for a moment, than a grin appeared and he laughed, a deep jovial sound that reached even those at the back of the crowd.

"Ealdred Uchtredsson, I welcome you to my court."

Ealdred looked up, startled, and Aelfgifu guessed that he'd never been addressed this way, using the Danish convention. Sweyn had stopped laughing but the grin remained on his face. "How old are you, boy?"

Ealdred swallowed. "I can count ten years, my lord."

Sweyn humphed at this. "A child."

Turning from Ealdred he addressed the men. "You'll all provide a male family member to be guests at my court. Your kin will be well-treated and protected from all harm, provided no news of treachery or dissent reaches my ears."

The mood had gone from light to dark in a heartbeat and Aelfgifu could see the nervous looks return to the men's faces.

"Now we will feast, and toast our alliance!" Sweyn strode towards the great hall where already the smells of roasting meat could be detected, as were the beginning strains of music.

The benches were quickly filled, all sitting in order of importance. Sweyn and his most trusted retainers sat at the main table at the top of the hall and were served by the hostages the noblemen had presented to the new king. Aelfgifu sat at the end of a long table with the other women and Brihtwyn, and both could see those around them struggling to keep their sadness hidden, for most were mothers and were losing a son or brother this day.

A large leather-clad man approached Aelfgifu when the meal was over and whispered in her ear. She stood and motioned to Wulfred, who had been watching her, to remain seated. She followed the shaggy man to the top table. Curtseying gracefully before her father-in-law she suddenly became aware that the room had grown quiet, the conversations of the men around her muted. They knew who she was. "My lord."

Sweyn pushed his chair back and came around the table to embrace her. "Daughter, how do you fare?"

"I'm well, my lord."

The Dane nodded his head. "You'll let me know if you've need of anything." It was a courtesy and while Aelfgifu was sure he would grant her any boon she asked, she also knew that one of his servants would be delegated the task.

"I only wish the gods to bless your endeavours, my lord, and to see my husband again."

Sweyn grunted his acknowledgement. The hall was noisy once more. Those who had been eavesdropping realised that the king's conversation held nothing of consequence for them personally.

"My son remains in Gainsborough, on my orders. I've given him command of the city and the men there. When I march south, he will remain at Gainsborough and ensure that my new guests," he gestured to the hostages sitting at one table, "are well looked after." Then, looking her up and down, he nodded. "But yes, my son needs heirs. To do this he will need to visit your bed, yes?" He laughed, the booming noise startling some of the men nearby.

Aelfgifu's face flushed; she desired Canute's presence as much as Sweyn did but didn't like having the fact announced in front of a hall full of people.

"Yes, my lord."

The king turned his attention back to his table, the conversation was over. Curtseying and backing away, she returned to Bri.

"What did Sweyn want?" Her aunt spoke before Aelfgifu had a chance to sit, so eager was she.

"To wish me well."

Aelfgifu waved away any further enquiries. "And to see to my needs."

Bri clearly didn't believe her but she thanked the gods her aunt had the grace to remain silent.

News arrived almost daily at Reodfeld; Aelfgifu had given orders that any messenger who appeared was to be brought to her immediately. Sweyn had taken the northern hostages back to Gainsborough and had then forged south. True to his word he'd stopped his men destroying people, land and animals until they reached the borders of the Danish burghs, those who had sworn loyalty to him first, and without violence. Then he unleashed his army. If the attack was on a smaller town, the warriors would circle it and, banging their shields with their swords to instil terror; they'd march in and cut down any who stood in their way. Afterwards they'd take what they needed from the empty households and set everything alight. If the town was larger, with defences, the Danes would climb walls or traverse ditches to reach their goal, once again destroying and burning. No one was spared in the slaughter, save those who surrendered before Sweyn approached. From these towns he took more hostages to ensure the citizen's continued loyalty, and supplies for his men. The captives were sent to Canute in Gainsborough.

The distinctive sound of a horse approaching at speed caught Aelfgifu's attention one chilly afternoon in October. Glancing out of the window she saw a stranger dismount from a large black horse and gesture to one of her servants. Soon there was a knock on her door.

"My lady, a messenger is here." At her nod, Wulfred ushered in the man.

He knelt before her. "My lady, I'm Oswulf. I'm here with news from King Sweyn's camp."

Aelfgifu called for her aunt. "Bri, see that mead and food are brought." She waited until the older woman left the room before addressing the man. "Oswulf, you're welcome here, no matter your tidings. Sit with me."

She pointed to a chair at her large work table and quickly gathered up the various papers and receipts that she'd been reading before taking her seat. The food arrived quickly.

"Bri, you and Wulfred will stay to hear this news. I'm sure my housecarl is yet lingering outside my chamber door." She raised her voice slightly and a moment later Wulfred was standing in the doorway, looking embarrassed.

"Both of you, sit." When they were ready, she gave the messenger leave to speak freely.

"My lady, as you know Sweyn marched south from the main camp at Gainsborough once he'd obtained the loyalty of the northern lords." He stopped to take a drink of the mead Aelfgifu poured for him. He nodded gratefully and continued. "With a mighty force and the will of the gods behind him, he swiftly subdued the Five Boroughs."

Aelfgifu leaned forward in her chair. "He's taken them? So soon? This is great news indeed!" She slapped her hand on her leg and, smiling, sat back in her chair. The Five Boroughs, Derby, Leicester, Lincoln, Nottingham and Stamford, were large cities spread across the north-south divide of England, and were important tactical wins for the king.

"Yes, my lady, and this victory has given Sweyn not only hostages and supplies but secured his northern base, providing him with more strength and support."

There was exhaustion on the man's face but his enthusiasm showed through and was contagious. "And? There is more?" Aelfgifu asked eagerly, leaning forward, her gaze boring into Oswulf's.

Taking another quick draught of his mead he wiped his hand across his mouth. "Yes, my lady. After the Boroughs, Sweyn moved further south, down Watling Street, his army destroying any who opposed them!" He stopped to take a breath. "As he approached Oxford, the gates of the city swung open before him, allowing the king and his men free access to the town without a sword raised, so fearful of Forkbeard were the citizens." He paused again but by his look, she knew there was more. "My lady, he has also taken Winchester."

He let the words hang in the air. Aelfgifu flew from her seat, unable to contain herself. "Can this be true?" She rushed over to the startled messenger and shook his shoulders. "Say you speak the truth!"

The man looked directly at her. "Yes, lady," he said with a grin. "Winchester has fallen to King Sweyn."

Aelfgifu stepped back and laughed, clapping her hands together. Brihtwyn looked astonished and Wulfred frowned.

"You doubted my father-in-law?" Laughing again at their disbelief, she sat and poured herself a cup of mead.

"No, no . . ." Bri shook her head.

"I jest, I jest." Leaning back in her chair once more she sighed contentedly. "Winchester, the seat of the great kingdom of Wessex, and favourite of Aethelred." She took a drink and laughed again. "I wish I could have seen the *lombungr's* face when he heard this news!" She saw Brihtwyn wince at her use of the profanity but didn't care. "And what of my husband?"

"My lady, he remains in Gainsborough, in charge of hostages from across the realm. And the king has given him a most singular honour, that of keeping all of the north secure!"

Aelfgifu felt a swell of pride. She'd heard that the Christians forbade this feeling and decided it was foolish. How could she *not* feel proud of such a man as her husband?

"I pray to the gods every night and I see that my words have not been ignored." The messenger nodded his agreement, waiting for further questions. "What of the royal family? Aethelred, his wife and their children?"

"They have all fled to London, my lady. Aethelred plots with Thorkell, who has risen in favour and now advises the false king."

Aelfgifu nodded and kept her face calm. Only a few knew

that Thorkell was still loyal to Sweyn and she would say nothing to reveal this secret.

"I hope they all live in fear within their stone walls, wailing to their Christian god." She took another drink and snorted. "They can pray all they want, it will do them no good."

The messenger nodded. "There is yet more, my lady." At Aelfgifu's gesture he continued. "King Sweyn has sailed from Winchester with fresh supplies to attack London."

Sweyn stood on the prow of his longship, watching the shore, the ships that accompanied his, the men. The ships were laden with supplies, taken from towns they had attacked, including the jewel of his growing empire, Winchester. He smirked; while attacking the cathedral he'd overheard one of the holy men cursing them, shouting that this place was the king's favourite, and that he would avenge the destruction. Monks, all they did was complain. Sweyn shook his head in disgust. Not one among them was able to fight. Weaklings, like all of these Saxons. And now he was heading east, where Aethelred and his family were cowering behind the walls of London.

They had camped upriver the previous night and the mood had been positive, almost festive. But all were still alert to signs of attack from Aethelred's men, none more so than Sweyn. Despite the fact that his most trusted friend, Thorkell, was deep within the enemy's camp, there would still be a fight come the morning. He knew Thorkell must aid Aethelred, otherwise the king would become suspicious.

"There! I see it." Bolli, peering into the distance, yelled to the ship. Sweyn shielded his eyes from the mid-morning sun and stared, instincts honed by a lifetime of battle.

"Do my eyes lie?" Bolli's bushy red eyebrows raised up.

"Slow your rowing!" Sweyn held up a hand. His ship crept

forward but slowly, the pace kept by the others in the fleet. The men who were not oarsmen made their way to the front of the ship, as surprised as the rest by what they saw.

"It seems the Londoners have prepared themselves." Sweyn spoke through a clenched jaw.

The plan was simple: sail east on the Thames to London, ease beneath the huge timber bridge and attack the city. The first part had been easy. They had encountered only mild resistance, farmers throwing rocks or whatever came to hand as Sweyn and his men passed. Women cast fearful glances as they herded their children and livestock into buildings. Men threw stones and lumps of mud, anything they could part with. One man threw a chicken at them and it landed in one of the ships. After scrambling over each other they had finally caught it and wrung its neck.

"The Saxon spirit is clearly not to be underestimated!" Someone held up the dead bird, laughing. "Based on the strength of their warrior chickens!"

The boat erupted in cheers and laughter. Everyone but Sweyn joined in, throwing insults to those who cowered on shore. For this event showed him how much these people loved their land and how little protected they were. He would remember this.

But now they were before the bridge. "Is that the army?" A voice came from somewhere to Sweyn's left. He still faced forward.

"No, they are common men, look at their dress." The men who lined the bridge wore nothing more substantial than linen, with heavy farming gloves on their hands.

"Are those sticks they're holding?" Sweyn momentarily regretted the pride they had felt the night before and whispered an apology to the All Father.

"Yes. And look, some have arrows and shields. They mean to defend the bridge." He heard his men muttering around him.

"My lord, let me take a few ships." Gunnar, a trusted man and good warrior, stood beside Sweyn, waiting.

Sweyn nodded and the man set out for the side of his ship, hailing neighbouring vessels. Halting the rest of the fleet Sweyn watched them approach the bridge. As soon as the four ships were near enough, they were met with a hail of arrows.

"Shields!" Sweyn heard Gunnar's voice and saw the men cover themselves and continue on their course. A few were left to launch their own arrows but the Londoners had protected themselves, hiding behind planks that they had attached to the bridge's railings. Boiling oil poured down on the first ship to try to cross. Most of the men were protected by their shields but the oil splashed and Sweyn heard angry cries as his men were burned. The ship turned back but before it was able to get clear more arrows appeared, tipped with flame. Soon the retreating longship was on fire and men were jumping into the river to escape.

Of the four ships that attempted to pass, two returned. Gunnar's ship was still smouldering from numerous small fires and Sweyn could smell the oil as he pulled alongside.

"You saw?"

Sweyn nodded. "Can it be done?"

"We lost two ships. And men." He shook his head. "No. They will get more oil."

Sweyn finally turned to face the men on his ship. "Then we will find another way through."

Gunnar had been sceptical but lost the bet he had made with Sweyn. "My lord, I should know by now not to doubt you. Please forgive me." The bet had been in jest, as were the comments he had made to his king, and Sweyn knew this. But the gods valued respect.

"The men did well, they'll be rewarded." Sweyn again

stood at the prow of his ship, his usual place for the last week. The entire fleet had been waiting for this day.

The idea was simple, the execution less so. But thanks to the marshy soil on the south side of the river, the idea was now a reality. Sweyn's men had dug a shallow canal into the bank of the river and curved it around the bridge. The V-shaped channel, dug using shovels and axes, was deep enough to allow the keels of the longships to navigate the marsh but was not so deep that hastily hewn planks couldn't hold back the sides.

"These cursed Saxons, don't they ever run out of arrows?" Bolli held his shield higher, protecting the man digging in front of him. Despite the excavated earth being piled into a ridge for protection against the Londoners' projectiles, there were still gaps and those who volunteered to dig were in constant danger.

By working with the tides and swapping men in and out from the safely assembled fleet downstream, the work went quickly and within a week was nearly completed.

Gunnar ducked behind his shield as an arrow hit. "They're like flies, annoying as hell!" The large man laughed, narrowly avoiding another arrow.

Bolli glanced out from behind his shield at the men digging. A few more feet and the trench would be done.

"How will the ships manoeuvre? There's no room."

"Ropes. A ship will be tied and pulled by men on either side of the trench."

"All while avoiding these damned," he broke off as another shaft bounced from his shield, "arrows."

"I'll sail first. Gunnar, you follow. Be cautious. These Londoners can no longer reach us with oil but they will continue to attack."

They set off. Sweyn's ship was pushed from the river to the channel and ropes thrown to waiting men on each side. Together they heaved the longship until it moved through the trench. Those not pulling formed a long shield wall to protect those who were. After a few stumbles in the marsh a rhythm was established and the ship moved quickly through the canal.

Sweyn heard the cheers of the men behind him and his mouth twitched slightly before forming itself back to his usual stern countenance. He continued further along the river, until well clear of the bridge before stopping and waiting.

One by one the entire fleet was moved, with the Londoners watching. Many of them, now afraid for their lives when presented with the ingenuity and sheer determination of their attackers, and seeing that Sweyn could bypass the bridge and now take the city, fled. When all were through, they regrouped in the open river and prepared to face their enemy.

A fleet of ships, more than Sweyn had anticipated, built by Aethelred, waited before him. The battle would be on water. "There. We'll move there, join the ships and wait." Sweyn moved into position first, with ships drawing up on either side and lashing their gunnels to his. The rest of the fleet did likewise until there were a number of floating platforms. They waited.

"Why won't they attack?" Bolli stood, tense, axe in hand. "They are doing nothing."

Sweyn held up a hand, silencing the man. For Aethelred's ships were finally moving, approaching and picking up speed. "Shields!" The deafening noise of shields being raised and pressed together into service as protection echoed across the water. Soon Aethelred's arrows were hitting them and they fought in kind, egging their attackers forward. "If we can get onto the ships, we have a chance!"

Bolli nodded and yelled to be heard over the chaos. "I have heard this king has no experience fighting on water."

Sweyn turned to avoid an arrow and looked out from

between his and Bolli's shields. Aethelred's men were still coming. Searching the main ship, he saw no sign of the king but he did spot Thorkell. As if by some force between them, his friend saw him at the same time. The briefest of nods then a look and a shake of the head told Sweyn all he needed to know: they would not win this battle. He didn't begrudge Thorkell's involvement; the man was acting under Sweyn's own orders. But he knew that Aethelred would have relied heavily on his friend for advice on how to defeat the Vikings.

"We must retreat."

"But my lord . . ." Bolli's forehead furrowed.

"There are too many. They are better prepared than we believed."

Bolli began to speak again but was stopped by Sweyn. "This is the path the gods have chosen today. Better to leave now while we are still able." He looked directly at Bolli. "We will return. These Londoners and their foolish king are only delaying their fates. I seek vengeance and not even the gods can stop me taking it."

Bolli nodded and passed the word that they were leaving. Sweyn would not give his enemies the satisfaction of hearing him yell to his men to flee. They untied the ships, all the while protecting themselves from the still-falling arrows. The best shipmen in the world, under oar they could reverse direction without even turning by merely repositioning themselves in their seats. They were soon heading west beneath London Bridge.

"They're letting us through." They were still cautious and suffered the indignity of rotten fish and human waste being thrown at them, but no oil fell, nor arrows.

"Stupid men." Sweyn looked back as they passed beyond the bridge. "They let us live."

A ship came alongside Sweyn's and Gunnar jumped aboard. "What now?"

Once again Sweyn took up his place at the prow of his

ship, glancing up at the dragon figurehead before looking ahead. "I have heard that the king's wife, Emma, has favoured the city called Bath." He turned to Gunnar. "Burn it. Take what you want, kill every inhabitant. Do what you will with the women. Destroy their homes and steal their possessions. Take their children for slaves. Make them suffer."

The sacking of the city was brutal. When news of the city's fate spread, the remaining towns fell, their leaders kneeling before Sweyn and offering hostages. The barbarities perpetrated on Bath were such that the Western thegns gave homage to Sweyn without further resistance.

"These people are weak. A nation of sheep." Sweyn spit the words. His army was camped outside London once more. "Their king has fled to the Isle of Wight, his family sent away. He leaves nothing but a trembling mass of cowards." He turned to Bolli who, even on land, was never far from his lord. "I told you I would return."

In a matter of weeks it was all over. Sweyn Forkbeard, King of Denmark, was now King of all England by right of conquest.

Chapter Four
England

Aelfgifu had always held a place of importance in the north, not only by virtue of the lands and estates her father had left her, but also because of her reputation for being fair and even-handed with the men and women she ruled. Since her father-in-law had been proclaimed king however, the visitors to her manor had escalated to such a point that her resources were now strained. Lavish gifts arrived daily with notes praying for her good fortune and soul. She usually laughed at these; she'd been baptised in the new faith, as had her brother, because her father had thought it an astute political move, but in truth she loved the old gods. With all of these strangers visiting, she was grateful for the gifts of food and drink that also arrived regularly. At first the attention was flattering but when people began to ask her for favours, or to intervene for them with King Sweyn, she soon grew weary, cynical and suspicious of every new person.

She was considering a trip to another of her estates further north when a messenger arrived from Canute: she was to join him in Gainsborough and together they would travel to London to attend the coronation of King Sweyn.

Guests were ushered out of the manor and grounds as politely as possible and all haste made preparing for the journey. Despite the lateness of the year, they would journey north on horseback, staying with families loyal to Sweyn along the way. Wulfred had planned their route, and advised them to dress warmly for the week-long trek through the cold, snow and ice.

It was only their third day out and Aelfgifu was bitterly tired of the freezing temperatures and dullness of their trip.

She gazed out over the barren landscape, fields of broken stalks dusted with snow, the leaden sky and the wind carrying the scent of more of the same. The cold had seeped into every bone.

"My lady, drink this." Brihtwyn handed her a skin of wine. Aelfgifu could feel the warmth spread into her chest as she drank. Handing the skin back to her aunt she shivered as the heat reached deeper inside her. Bri evidently sensed her boredom. "Tedious, isn't it?"

Aelfgifu turned on her horse, wincing at the pain in her legs as she did so. "Yes." She gestured at the land around her. "I'm from the north. I know these lands are beautiful in the summer but there's little to recommend them during winter." She sighed and smiled grimly. "I am tired of this too."

"We'll be there before you know it, have faith." They rode in silence for a while, the wind whipping the drifting snow into their faces. "You'll see your husband soon."

Aelfgifu smiled broadly at that; her aunt always knew how to help lift her mood. "I can't wait, it's been," she frowned and thought for a moment, "three months, perhaps a little longer?"

"He'll be happy to see you again, I'm sure."

More silence as another gust of icy wind blew through them, taking their breath with it. When there was calm, Brihtwyn continued. "I wonder what Aethelred's doing at this moment."

Aelfgifu snorted and sat straighter on her horse. "I'm sure he's still on the Isle of Wight, cowering within the walls of his lodge, fearful that Sweyn will come for him."

Brihtwyn laughed. "I warrant he wakes in the night, crying and shrieking!"

The younger woman laughed, the colour returning to her face. "He dreams of my father-in-law, no doubt." She beckoned for the wine skin again and this time took a long draught. Wiping her mouth on the rough sleeve of her heavy coat she laughed again.

"The last message I got related that Canute still has his supporters in the south, watching and reporting all. And Thorkell yet remains with Aethelred. He states that the old king is preparing to flee the country, to follow his wife to her homeland with his tail between his legs like a beaten dog."

She sighed again, the sound nearly lost to the wind. "But that was many weeks ago, I've heard nothing since."

"She left before him, then?"

"Yes, and it doesn't speak well of the lady. She reveals herself by such actions; it shows she has no real faith in her husband."

"And what of her children?"

"I can only hope they know nothing of their father's cowardice. How could any child live with that?"

"I wonder how 'Queen' Emma fares?" Aelfgifu had shared with her aunt Eadric's revelations about Emma's involvement with her father's death.

Aelfgifu's reply was lost on another gust of wind, but the disapproving look on Brihtwyn's face told her that her aunt had heard words better suited to a more common woman.

"She must be terribly ashamed, how could any lady not be? One day a queen, the next a begging relative, depending on the generosity of an indifferent brother with no access to income from her lands in England. Sweyn is seeing to that."

It was common knowledge that Emma's brother Richard, Duke of Normandy, had sold his sister off to the highest bidder, and cared little for her or her problems once his gold had been delivered. She smiled, suddenly amused.

"No more sitting in her decorated palaces, doing nothing but ordering expensive tapestries and plate for her chambers."

She thought Duke Richard's deal with Aethelred for Emma indecent; the gold given to the duke obtained by King

Aethelred from some of the poorest of his people, in exchange for a bride and a promise. The bride he'd received. The promise, that of closing the ports of Normandy to any Danish invader, had been broken soon after Emma had arrived in England.

"They have a political marriage, nothing more. Our informants tell us Aethelred hates his wife, cannot bear to be in the same room as her, never mind bed her." She shook her head. "No, their union is no partnership."

"I hear she's a devout Christian, and that this was one of the reasons she was so acceptable to Aethelred."

"It's all an act to win the goodwill of the people." She paused as another gust of wind blew between them. "She's acquired much land and gold since she's been here, she's shown that she's just as greedy as Eadric."

"It's also said she's given many gifts to monasteries and churches."

Growing irritated, Aelfgifu wondered why her aunt continued to talk of these things. "Then she must've needed something, some favour from the establishment."

"I've heard she's a hard one, has been since childhood."

Aelfgifu thought of what Eadric had told her. "Yes, and a practiced manipulator." These were the last words she managed to say before the winds grew angrier, making further conversation impossible.

When they arrived at Gainsborough, the battle-town was busy with activity, as was to be expected. But there was something else. Anger? Panic? She couldn't tell but something was amiss. They were met by one of her husband's carls, the same man who had delivered many messages, Oswulf.

"Lady Aelfgifu, Canute bids me greet you, and to show you to your lodgings."

"Where's my husband?"

"My lady, Canute can't attend you at this time; he's busy with"—the carl hesitated, choosing his words carefully—"pressing business."

She was puzzled by this, and after their long trek, angry. "He couldn't tear himself away for a moment to greet his wife?"

Oswulf's face was surprised. "You've not heard the news?"

"What news? We've had no communication for weeks."

The carl shook his head, his long braided beard swaying stiffly with the movement. "My lady, King Sweyn is dead."

Chapter Five
England

Aelfgifu's party was shown to a large wooden hall, where her belongings were already being unpacked from the carts that had accompanied them on the journey. Aelfgifu had barely heard any more of the carl's words, and she asked no questions; she wanted to hear the details directly from her husband. The activity grew more frantic as they approached the hall, and now that she knew the reason, she understood the worry on the men's faces.

A basin of warm water had been laid out on a dressing table, along with food and drink on the central table. Aelfgifu cleaned herself as best she could and sat with Brihtwyn, waiting for more news. "It would appear that the handover of the kingdom from father to son is not going smoothly." She waved her hand in the direction of the door, outside of which the sounds of the preparing army could be heard.

"I heard some of the men cursing, but couldn't say what had angered them." Brihtwyn's face revealed her confusion.

Aelfgifu thought for a moment, washing the last of the shock from her mouth with wine before speaking. "It must be the witan, the council. The north is loyal to Sweyn, and therefore to his son, as is the west."

"But the witan proclaimed Sweyn king!"

"And now that he's dead they think only of themselves, and how they can benefit." Aelfgifu shook her head. "They're fickle and arrogant men who do only what's best for them, not for the country that gave them their wealth." They were silent, each thinking. Aelfgifu broke the quiet. "Eadric is a member of the witan, although why they seek his foul counsel is beyond my understanding. I'm certain he's the one stirring up trouble even as we sit here."

She felt exhausted after their long travel, and both her body and head hurt as she'd eaten little that day.

"Bri, I'm going to lie down. Wake me the moment Canute calls for me." She got up and went to her bedchamber. She saw that Canute had ordered the room to be decorated as wonderfully as the hall, despite the fact she was in the middle of a military camp; there was a soft mattress of goose feather with a matching pillow and linen sheets. She sank wearily onto the bed and closed her eyes, but try as she might, sleep eluded her. Thoughts of her husband and what this latest news meant ran endlessly in her mind.

She heard the heightened noise coming from the hall and groggily woke before Bri came to tell her Canute was there. She'd expected an invitation, perhaps to the chamber where he planned with his soldiers, or the public hall, and was pleased that he'd come to her in her own rooms.

She excused Bri and the servants while Canute waited, standing by the door. When they were gone, she rushed to him, happy to see his arms unfold to hold her. They stood like that together for a few moments before Canute untangled himself and led her to the table, sitting across from her. She grabbed his hands and held tightly. "I'm sorry to hear about your father."

He lowered his head, hiding his face from her, before looking up again, releasing her hands. Pouring himself a flagon of ale, he nodded. "Thank you. Did you hear of his death before you left?"

She was horrified that he might think her foolish. "No! If I'd known I never would've left Reodfeld. I received no message." He nodded his head. She got up and went over to him, pulling him to his feet and leading him to a chair closer to the fire. "What happened?"

Canute raked his hand through his hair to capture the strands that had escaped the leather thong he used to tie it back. She'd seen him do this before, but only when he was under pressure or had a big decision to make.

"He was out on his horse, supervising the strengthening of the city's fortifications. He'd decided to rule England from here in Gainsborough, rather than from Winchester or London as English kings have always done."

He looked around for his cup and Aelfgifu went to the table and brought back their ale. After a nod of thanks to her and another drink he continued.

"The horse he rode, an accursed English beast, shied suddenly at a rabbit and threw my father." He took a breath. "The ground was frozen and he hit his head." He waved a hand wearily. "His wound was stitched by our physicians but my father didn't regain his senses, just lay as though asleep. A few days afterwards he contracted a fever. It got worse until it was plain that our healers couldn't do anything. I was called in the early morning to my father's rooms where he was already dead."

Aelfgifu shuddered, despite the warmth from the fire. There were few details in Canute's story, as she'd expected, but she knew the king must have suffered. She suspected there was more to the story but didn't ask. Her husband had been treated like a warrior from the day he let go of his wet nurse's teat, and emotions were a nuisance, rarely to be indulged.

She stared at her husband's face, lit by the dancing flames of the fire. He looked older, was that possible? How long had it been since she'd seen him last? Surely he couldn't have aged this much? And tired. There were dark smudges beneath his eyes and she wished she could lay him down on her bed and take away his cares, if only for a night or two.

"And there's trouble."

She thought as much. "The witan?"

He nodded, showing no surprise that she'd guessed. "They haven't yet sworn the oath of fealty."

Her eyes widened. How could she have not realised? Canute was now the new King of England; it was his father's will.

"They're weak, all of them. They'll soon realise their delay will cost them." Receiving no reaction, she continued. "You must gather your forces and march south, show these *hrafnasueltir*, these cowards, how a true leader behaves." She could feel her face growing warm.

He took her hand and brought it to his cheek, holding it there for a moment before dropping it again, a rare show of tenderness from her warrior husband. "It's more complicated than that."

She moved her chair closer to his. His exhaustion was beginning to show itself in his voice, which grew lower and softer. "My informants tell me the council has decided not to support my claim to the throne."

Aelfgifu stood suddenly, knocking her chair over. "How can they not? How can these curs deny that you're their lawful king? You must march, and soon! Don't give them a chance to rally behind a king of their choosing."

Canute rose slowly and took her hand, righting her chair with his other. He led her back and waited until she sat before returning to his own seat. His next words were barely a whisper. "I fear the gods have abandoned me."

She rushed to him, kneeling before him. "No, no, don't say that! Never say that! It's not true!"

He threw up his hands. "But how can it be otherwise? How do you explain these happenings? First my father, then this?" He leaned back in his chair heavily. Grabbing his cup, he found it empty and threw it across the room, where it smashed against the wall, breaking into pieces.

Aelfgifu quickly fetched another cup and filled it with the dark beer. "Canute, it's a test, surely it's a test." She sat again, and watched as he drank, silent. "Doesn't Odin challenge his own children? The All Father sets difficult tasks so his children may prove themselves worthy; this is what he does now, with you."

He looked at her with hope in his eyes, a desperate need to believe. "Your words carry weight, but how can I know for sure?"

She shook her head. "It's not for us to know the minds of the gods, Canute, but the very fact that you experience such difficulty is a sign that you're already deemed worthy." She took his hand. "The gods don't send us trials they know we're not capable of bearing. That these times are arduous means they already believe you're a strong warrior and that you have the right."

He nodded, still looking uncertain. "The manner of my father's death sits ill with me. He was an excellent horseman."

Taking both of his hands in hers, she pulled him to standing. She stood on her toes and raised her lips to his, feeling him reach down and pull her closer. She looked up into his face. "Your father was a great man and a great king. But his time is past. It's your time now, Canute. Those fools will pay for their decision. You must march south. Burn London to the ground if you have to."

Aelfgifu oversaw Bri and the Danish women who travelled with the army in helping to prepare King Sweyn's body for the funeral. Although suspicious of her at first, the Danish women gradually grew to trust Aelfgifu, finding a strength and temperament that matched their own. There was no doubt in anyone's mind that so great a man would be welcomed in Valhalla, nevertheless, those that still lived needed to mourn his passing, to say goodbye. The funeral was as much for them as for their king. Together they would ensure the body remained cared for until it could be returned to Denmark for a royal burial. Despite the work of the healers she could see the back of his head where it had hit the frozen ground, the collapsed indent at the left side. She'd heard men speaking in hushed voices of a murder, something sinister that had killed their lord. An agent of Aethelred, some said. Aelfgifu could see no evidence of foul play, just the tragic outcome of an unfortunate accident. Men died, and it was painful when it happened before a man had his chance to live a rich life. The gods saw that life continued, forcing those who remained to follow their path, particularly in the case of warriors.

"Canute asks that I prepare to leave Gainsborough and return to my estate." The preparations to the king's body were complete and they were washing their hands in the large golden water basin that had been provided. A servant stepped forward with a square of linen.

"When will we leave?" Bri was rubbing water from her hands that the linen had missed.

"I'm not sure, as soon as we're able." Aelfgifu hadn't started packing her belongings, never mind the numerous gifts from those loyal to her husband that had been arriving daily since she got here. "There's so much to do."

Bri nodded agreement. "Shall I start right away?"

Aelfgifu sighed. "I can't see any reason why not. My lord husband is busy with matters of running the country. I'm afraid he would rather see me out from under his feet."

"No, lady, that's not so! He loves you very much and trusts you above all of those close to him, but he has a great many issues to address. He's a new king."

"Yes, and I'm a new queen." She stopped Bri's eagerly nodding head. "No, don't agree with that, I don't feel like a queen. A darkness hangs over my head that won't allow a crown to sit comfortably." She stopped to wrap her cloak around her more tightly. The winds that plagued them as they travelled here would also accompany them home. "I'll do as Canute asks and see to the northern thegns. With the trouble in the south, many may start to question their loyalty. My husband has tasked me with ensuring these men understand that their continued support will yield them reward."

"It's a great challenge you've ahead of you, my lady."

"Not as great as the king's." She shivered and pulled her cloak even closer. "I'm also to inform Canute of any dissent I learn about."

"I'm sure there'll be no discord. These are good men we speak of, not like those in the south."

She glanced at her aunt. "I hope you're right."

A messenger arrived as Aelfgifu was in the hall with Canute, having a last meal before she was to leave for home. They'd spent the previous night together, neither of them sleeping much, both saddened by their pending separation. Their lovemaking had at first been slow, a luxurious gift amidst the chaos that surrounded them. But towards dawn their passion had an urgency to it, a final attempt to consume each other completely before the sun rose and they had to part.

"Here, to me." Canute stood and waved the man over. Snatching the parchment, he dismissed the messenger before tearing through the seal. As he read, Aelfgifu could see her husband's face growing darker, like storm clouds gathering on the horizon. When he'd finished he was silent for a moment, then strode over to the table, a great roar of rage erupting as he swept food and dishes from the surface. As his housecarls rushed in, daggers drawn, Canute was still shouting, sometimes words Aelfgifu recognised but mostly ancient curses from his homeland.

"Do you know what they've done?! Do you?" He waved

the letter, then threw it from him with a look of distaste. "Those *ormstunga*, those serpent-tongued sons of *hōra*?!"

By now Wulfred had arrived, weapon ready. He was quickly by her side. Unable to speak, Canute gestured at the letter which lay on the table. Aelfgifu read it and was appalled.

"They've written to Aethelred? How could they?"

"Because they're traitors, all of them!" He rushed over to the table and picked up the letter again. "They've also sent a delegation to Normandy, inviting the old man to return and rule over them." He laughed. "And they've made demands! Do you believe it? These men, who are nothing, will allow Aethelred back if he agrees to rule them more fairly and justly." He paced the room for a moment; Aelfgifu could see the emotions warring on his face. "Who are these men, these *hundr* who would order a king to do their bidding? Who would make such demands of their ruler?"

Aelfgifu knew her husband hated Aethelred and would kill him, had the man been here in person, but a king was sent by the gods to rule his people, anointed in the blood of those who resisted his claim, and it upset the natural order when subjects made demands of their lord. Bewilderment prompted Canute's anger, for if these men could so bend Aethelred to their will, what of his own reign?

With a great cry of anger and frustration, Canute sat heavily in his chair and banged both fists on the table. "What is wrong with these fucking Englishmen?"

The town was eerily quiet, despite the constant activity of the soldiers around her: weapons and armour were being repaired, shields and axes being made, blades sharpened to a cutting shine, and while this produced a lot of noise, somehow it was subdued. The usual ribaldry and enthusiastic voices of the men was missing. There were daily arrivals of food, drink, supplies, horses and messengers, so the town was in constant turmoil. Sweyn's army, now loyal to Canute, had been severely depleted during the fight to win the crown, and the refurbishment of the force was slow. Despite the fact that winter had finally released its iron grip on the land and warm breezes now blew through the town, there was no joy, relief or happiness; the mood remained cold, heavy and grey.

Aelfgifu remained in Gainsborough and received regular updates from her stewards. She knew she should probably return home as there was much to do at this time of year and her presence would be missed, but staying with her husband, now that the future was so uncertain, was more important to her. Even Bri's comments about the manor and her sighs as she looked out the window wouldn't change Aelfgifu's mind. Canute continued to manage the country as if there were no concerns, and the details of rule kept him busy. Aelfgifu had taken over management of the army's basic needs: laundry, food, drink, plate, anything that didn't involve battle. It took her mind off the pall of apprehension that hung over them all and allowed Canute to concentrate on only the most important matters.

Easter was fast approaching and some of the men had begun to make noises about a feast. The camp was filled with both Christians and those who followed the old ways and this time of year was a celebration for both groups: for one, the rebirth of their new god and for the other a renewal of the earth, the awakening of all things. As she walked through the street, muddy with the runoff from melting snow, looking at those who passed her, she saw a weary, unhappy people, both men and women. The town of Gainsborough was loyal to Canute and would do anything for their king, but it was difficult to support so many people, especially these large Danish warriors.

She was announced by Oswulf, who nodded at her as she

passed and entered the room. Curtseying before her husband, she sat in the chair opposite his and served herself a cup of wine. It was tart, and she grimaced as she drank, making a mental note to obtain a finer stock.

"My lord, are you well?"

He refilled his own cup. "Yes, yes." She knew he didn't like to discuss anything to do with his physical being.

"You look tired." None but she would dare suggest that the king was anything but virtually immortal.

He waved away the comment. "I'm busy, that's all." She waited for him to continue, knowing from experience that he'd elaborate. "This realm is infuriatingly complicated, and these people, these English, they're . . ." He threw up his hands. "I don't know what they are, but they're not like us." She was gratified that despite her birth in England, her husband considered her one of his people. But she was born in the north and had always found the ways of southerners strange. He sighed and looked at her. "How does the town fare?"

"Very well. I check all deliveries myself and see that any merchants who try to cheat us are punished appropriately. I'm also overseeing the laundry and other tasks that are far too lowly for you to concern yourself with."

Canute smiled his appreciation. "Aelf, you're a better warrior than many of my men, and a great deal more organised. I've no complaints, indeed it's almost as if we're back in Reodfeld and not in a muddy war camp." Gainsborough was, in fact, nothing like a war camp. It boasted one of the largest manors in the north, with high ceilings, carved beams and fine wall hangings. But still she appreciated her husband's praise and he need not have thanked her; it was her duty to ensure these things were seen to.

"Is there anything important to discuss with me?" Canute continued. "Do you need anything?"

"No, my lord, your stewards help me where necessary, they're worthy men." She took a sip of her wine. "But, if I may suggest something?"

Canute raised an eyebrow. "Of course."

"I've been watching the town and the people who are here for you. The mood is sombre and there's anxiety in the air." She looked at him, waiting to see if her husband would acknowledge the fact. He merely looked at her expectantly. She continued. "The new season is finally upon us, as is the Christian holy day of Easter. We've those who follow our own faith and those of the new religion; I believe a feast to honour both would benefit everyone."

Aelfgifu knew a feast was the last thing Canute had been thinking about. In fact when it came to food he had to be reminded to eat these days, he was so busy. But it was a sound idea, and one he seemed to like more and more as he thought on it. It would cheer the camp, give the men something to celebrate, perhaps calm some of the tensions that had begun between the differing faiths. "Aye, a feast. Arrange it and let me know if you need anything."

She stood and grasped his hands in hers, bringing them to her lips. "Thank you, I'll arrange something worthy of a king." She curtseyed and hurried from the room. There was much to be done.

As she'd expected, news of the feast was welcomed by all. There was suddenly a lightness to the air; women started to hum as they did their chores and men's laughter could be heard more often around the town. Tasks seemed easier and errands shorter. Even her husband's mood improved. He still carried much weight on his shoulders but his carls had convinced him to forget his troubles and enjoy himself, if only for the day.

By the time the day of the feast arrived, all was ready.

Men and women made an extra effort with their appearance: the women wore pale-coloured spring dresses with lighter furs and the men tidied their hair and cleaned their boots. Even the mightiest of Canute's carls washed and braided their beards. After the Christians had worshipped at their church and the Norsemen had made a sacrifice to Idunn, goddess of Spring, they all poured into the huge hall, where heavy oak tables were set in rows, each with a long wooden bench. The tables were decorated with plain linen cloth and garlands of early seasonal flowers, and simple but well-made pewter plates and tankards were ready for use. Many of the more affluent of those attending brought their own drinking horns and from her hiding place, Aelfgifu could see the fine workmanship of many of them: various animal horns, carved with scenes from stories and decorated with silver and gold.

Peeking through a door at the side of the hall, she was pleased with how it had turned out: the torches were burning brightly and, along with the light from the fire pit in the centre of the room, illuminated the shields that hung every few feet along the walls and from the carved wooden rafters above. The smell of roasting meat and bread hung enticingly in the air, making her mouth water. Aelfgifu was certain she wasn't the only one who hadn't eaten that day, saving space for this evening's celebration. She smiled and hurried around to the front of the building to meet her husband.

The room filled with the sounds of drums and pipes, with the occasional howling dog and the crackling of the fire accompanying the musicians. When all were seated, the music stopped and everyone turned to the entrance of the hall in expectation. Quietly at first, then growing in tenor, a drum beat out a steady rhythm. Canute stepped through the doorway, Aelfgifu proud to be on his arm. He'd listened to his carls' advice and dressed in his best clothing, his long hair tied at the back with a leather thong that had been braided into intricate designs through his blond locks. Aelfgifu was wearing her best, a dress made from exquisitely decorated linen that had been a gift from her husband, the gold circlet that she had received at her wedding controlling her braided hair. Canute wore his wedding gift too, the magnificent sword she'd presented him. Together they made their way to the high table at the top of the hall where Aelfgifu was helped into her chair by Canute.

Canute held out his drinking cup, a ram's horn decorated with filigrees of slender silver. A servant moved to serve the king and when the horn was full, Canute raised his arm high. "May the gods of all men bless this feast and join us here tonight, that we may feed and entertain them and gain their favour." The room waited until Canute had taken a long drink before doing the same themselves, and then shouted their approval with thunderous enthusiasm.

Aelfgifu watched the hall while she ate, content that she had been able to do something to contribute to the well-being of Canute's followers. The food was clearly appreciated, going by the number of bones being thrown onto the woven floor mat and by the way the men tore into their meat. The noise in the room was deafening; clattering plates, laughing, shouting and barking dogs all causing her to have trouble talking to Canute, their efforts at conversation finishing in smiles and shoulder shrugs. As the evening wore on, less of the fish and pork was served and more of the ale was demanded. The men grew more and more merry, and as the light of the torches and fire grew dimmer their jokes took on a more ribald quality.

Aelfgifu was puzzled by many of the insults she heard; while those in the north and the Danes often shared a common ancestry, there were still cultural differences between the two groups.

"I hear Geirr has a new favourite servant, a beardless

young man with locks like those of Freya!" The men all roared with laughter and pounded their hands on the table. The poor man whose masculinity was being questioned looked angry but said nothing. The joker, a clumsy man named Ingolf, took a large draught from his drinking horn, held it up for more and wiped his beard. "Aye, I hear he lavishes the boy with gifts and sits back to enjoy the man enjoying them." Again the table exploded into laughter.

Geirr stood and knocked the dishes from the table. "You filthy lying *bacraut!*" He reached for the dagger at his waist before a restraining arm from a friend stopped him. Aelfgifu wasn't sure about the exact meaning of the word he'd used but she could tell by the delivery that it wasn't respectful.

Ingolf, expecting the retaliation, had jumped up and was also reaching for his dagger. Seeing Geirr restrained, he instead held out both of his arms and laughed. "Friend, it was only a joke! Here," he motioned for a maid, "let's drink together." When both horns had been filled, he raised his arm. "May the gods bless both you and your family." As Geirr nodded his head and lifted the horn to his mouth, from behind his own horn Ingolf whispered, "and your beardless friend." Those gathered waited for Geirr's reaction. When he smiled and laughed everyone joined in, some thumping the older man on the shoulder.

The conversations were similar throughout the hall, involving the men as well as some of the women. Many of those who practised the new religion frowned with distaste at the crudeness of the comments but Aelfgifu couldn't see the harm, as long as tomorrow all remained friends and allies. She waved a hand at the musicians, who had been playing quietly, to perform something more lively. When they started, a few of the women began dancing, with more joining the faster the music got. Aelfgifu looked over at Canute, who smiled at her and nodded. She gathered her dress and stepped from the dais, joining in the dance, the rushing steps and heady music making her laugh. She glimpsed her husband while mid-twirl and saw that he too was laughing. But the next time she turned and saw him a frown had replaced his smile. Stopping, she saw a messenger approaching the king, holding out a letter. By the time she reached Canute he was already standing, his face red. He bent over to speak directly into her ear, so only she could hear him.

"Aethelred is back in England, and marches north as we speak."

Aelfgifu stood on the deck, the sway of the ship beneath her feet making her feel slightly dizzy. Her belongings had been loaded from the carts, as was the body of Sweyn Forkbeard. She shivered and pulled her cloak around her, the cold night air still finding its way in. Brihtwyn stood beside her, silent, looking out over the dark water.

Things had happened quickly after they'd heard the news, and one of the first decisions Canute had made was to send his queen to Denmark, to accompany his father's body to his homeland. It had been a hard conversation, her final effort to persuade her husband to allow her to stay.

"But why must I flee? Surely your army will . . ."

Canute interrupted. "My army is ill-prepared!" She remembered the frustration in his face. "Aethelred gathers forces as he moves north. It isn't safe for you, or for my father's body. Who knows what evil they'll do should they get their hands on him!" He was nearly in tears, so great was his rage. She'd reached for him, taken his hand and looked up at him. He sighed. "You're the only one I trust with my father. And I'd see you somewhere safe." He'd gathered her into his arms and she yielded completely, melting into the warmth and security of his body. She'd held him for as long as she was able, knowing that time was short. Then, looking up at him, she spoke. "I'll do as you ask. I'll help in any way I can."

So here she stood, watching the lights from shore fade from view the farther out they went. Leaving her home, not knowing when she would return. She'd written to her stewards at Reodfeld and had spent the night saying goodbye to her husband. He'd sworn on his honour that she would be by his side again soon but the promise did nothing to lessen the ache in her heart.

Chapter Six

Denmark

There was no question that King Sweyn would have a Viking burial, and a beautiful longship had been built for the ceremony. Sweyn had been baptised in the new faith, but after his sister had been killed while seeking sanctuary in a church during the St Brice's Day massacre in 1002, he'd gone back to the old ways of worship. The massacre had been Aethelred's solution to the supposed disloyalty of the Danish in England, and had quickly escalated; thousands of Danes had been slaughtered. Not even those who had converted to Christianity had been spared and Sweyn, while alive, had often been heard to question why he should pray to a god that had allowed his good Christian sister to die so horribly.

The longship had been lavishly decorated; the sides hung with shields painted with scenes from Sweyn's battles, and on the deck a small pavilion had been constructed. A cradle held the ship upright on land, with wood and brush packed between the boards. Sweyn's embalmed body had been carried onto the ship by his housecarls, all dressed in their finest, some with silk from Persia. The sun was slipping into the sea, the light failing as darkness gathered. Even so, Aelfgifu could see an ancient woman waiting by the ship until the king's body had been placed in the pavilion. When the carls were done, the crone summoned a slave girl from the waiting crowd.

Because she was Sweyn's daughter-in-law, Aelfgifu had been given a place of prominence and stood with Sweyn's first son, Canute's half-brother, King Harald. Canute was still in England and had not been able to leave his campaign for the funeral. Harald, as eldest, had inherited the crown of

Denmark and had stepped into the role easily. His first duty as ruler had been to arrange his father's funeral, a task he had performed efficiently and with the expected grace and sincerity of a strong ruler. She had no doubt he would be a good king. "My lord, who's the old woman there?"

Harald, standing at least a head and a half taller than his sister-in-law, leaned down to explain.

"She's a seer, an ancient one. Some say she is a Norn, and can see the fates of men. The women with her are her daughters and will help her. But it's the crone's role to ensure the slave girl performs her duty."

Aelfgifu shivered, wishing for the hundredth time that her husband was here. She had an idea of the slave girl's role in the funeral. Harald took her silence as permission to continue.

"The slave girl volunteered to accompany her master to the gods. She has been bedded by all of Sweyn's carls, who all ask that she pass their messages of respect to their lord."

The girl was clad only in the lightest of dresses. She removed her gold torc from her arm and gave it to the Norn. She then took off two golden cuffs and passed these to the old woman's daughters, payment for their services and to ensure a smooth passage to the afterlife. Aelfgifu understood the slave girl would give her life but this hadn't affected her until she saw with her own eyes the state of the poor creature. The girl had obviously been drugged with something powerful because she staggered and swayed as she turned to face the mourners. Two large men stepped forward and grasped the girl beneath her arms, lifting her into the air. When she was raised up, she called out words that Aelfgifu could only partially understand. While she had learned much of the Danish language in her time with Canute, the funeral was performed using a more ancient Norse tongue.

"Do you know what she says?" Harald's voice startled

her, so close to her ear.

"I think so, my lord." She listened, the crowd deathly silent so all could hear. "She says she looks upon her parents, her father and mother." She listened again. "And also her brothers and sisters and aunts and uncles." She tilted her head to better hear the last words. "She sees her?" What was the word? "Master? She sees her master, with his men, and they call to her." She watched as the girl was lowered and escorted onto the ship. "I don't understand this last part."

"The girl sees into the Halls of Valhalla. She still lives, yet has a foot placed in two worlds, ours and that of the afterlife." King Harald explained carefully, as if speaking to a child.

Aelfgifu nodded, slightly irritated by the king's tone, then chided herself. This was not the place for anything but sorrow and respect. The slave girl was helped into the pavilion where Sweyn's body waited. She struggled to enter it herself, and had to be helped by the Norn, who grasped her arm and guided her. The Norn followed the girl, withdrawing a dagger with a broad blade from beneath her sleeve. The moment they both entered the tent, the assembled carls began to bang their swords on their shields and shout loudly. Aelfgifu flinched at the noise; it was such a contrast to the silence that had blanketed them only moments before. Some of the women, the shield maidens, screamed, making her scalp prickle. Aelfgifu had not needed to ask about the noise; she knew it was to conceal the screams of the dying slave girl as the Norn plunged the blade into her chest.

When it was over, Harald took her arm and together they moved through the crowd to the ship. Aelfgifu stared straight ahead but could feel the eyes of the crowd upon her. They arrived at the longship and the king took a burning torch. He handed it to Aelfgifu and, taking another for

himself, approached the dragon-headed vessel. Harald
threw the torch onto the ship. It landed on the deck and
caught the side of the pavilion, sending flames running up
the tent. He looked down at her and nodded. Nervous,
knowing she could never hope to match his throw, she
stepped forward a few feet and threw her own torch into the
dry brush that surrounded the ship. She held her breath as
the flames sputtered then glowed, more and more brightly
as the dry wood caught. Returning to their places, they
watched the other nobles and carls do the same, until the
entire ship was alight with flames, sending streams of fire
into the night sky.

As they returned to the palace, Harald explained more of
the ritual to her. "Christians bury their dead in the ground,
waiting for a day when their loved ones will be reunited with
their god. Does it not seem better to honour the dead in the
old way, where their spirits will be returned to the gods in a
mere hour or two?"

She'd at first thought it a barbaric practice, another of the
differences that separated the Danes from the English, but
the way the king explained it she had to admit that it made
sense. She knew her own impatience at times, and could
understand wanting to forego waiting to achieve a goal,
especially one as important as one's reunion with the gods.

"What will happen to your father's remains now, my
lord?"

Harald spoke without looking at her. "The ashes will be
gathered and placed in the church here."

She frowned. "A church?"

Harald smiled at her reaction. "My father was no fool, he
was baptised and commissioned the building of a Christian
church." He waved his hand in what she assumed was the
church's direction. "By placing my father's ashes in his own
church, I'm able to placate those in my land who follow the
new faith."

Ah, she thought, so Harald was of his father's ilk; clever at playing the political game, but something else, a certain deviousness to him. She nodded her head. "It's a fitting tribute to so great a man, my lord."

For the next few weeks Aelfgifu kept herself busy while waiting for Canute to arrive from England. Sometimes her mind took her to dark places, and worries for her husband overwhelmed her so she occupied her time writing letters to the northern lords in England, advising them to stay true to their oaths, that Canute would prevail and be a good master to them. She sent gifts, small items to remind the men of Canute's favour and the potential rewards to come.

It was deep into spring when Canute finally arrived, late one night. The sun had set long ago and Aelfgifu should have been in bed for hours, but she found that sleep eluded her more and more. Canute appeared in her rooms unexpectedly, announced by one of the carls that Harald had assigned to her.

When she saw him she was overjoyed. She rushed to him, heart pounding; he'd removed his outer travelling cloak but still wore stained and battle-worn clothing.

"Canute! You're here!" She threw her arms around him, smelling ocean and horse sweat. Breathing in the scent of him, she squeezed tighter as he enfolded her and they stood like that for what seemed like an age before she reluctantly let him go.

"Sit there." She pointed to a wooden bench beside which stood a heavily carved and decorated table. She served him wine and waited until he'd drained the goblet before pouring him another and joining him at the table.

Brihtwyn, hearing her niece's voice, had risen from her bed and entered the main room. She stopped and curtseyed when she saw Canute. "My lord." She asked no questions, although Aelfgifu could see that her aunt was as desperate for news as she was herself.

"Bri, instruct the maids to fill one of the large tubs, my husband needs a bath."

Bri nodded and hurried from the room. Grasping her husband's arms from across the table, she looked deeply into Canute's eyes, trying to guess at the Dane's state.

"I was so worried, we've had no news for weeks, I didn't know what to think!" She tightened her grasp on his forearms. "Were you wounded?" She didn't dare ask about the fighting; it was a fact that he'd had to flee England, but she wanted to know everything. "And your men? How do they fare? And do you know anything of my lands? My servants?"

Canute withdrew his arm from hers, stopping to squeeze her hand. "I'm well and uninjured." He took another long drink and was silent, staring off into space as though she weren't in the room.

She rose from her place and knelt before him, placing her hands on his knees. She saw him start at her touch and look down at her. "My lord, what happened?"

He sighed and she could hear the frustration and grief in the sound. "We were attacked. At Gainsborough. We were preparing to march south, to meet with Aethelred's forces, when we were surprised by his men." He reached for the cup again, and, finding it empty looked around the room. Aelfgifu stood and pulled her husband's chair closer to the fire. Although it was spring, the air in Canute's homeland had a permanent chill, especially at night. Getting them both more wine, she handed Canute his and sat beside him, waiting. He took another drink and wiped his mouth before speaking again.

"We had no warning! Our scouts had not reported back with any news, I don't know why!" There was sorrow in his sky-blue eyes before he closed them, bowing his head. "We weren't ready." She waited in silence; confident that, now he'd started, he would continue. Her patience was rewarded. "I had no choice." He looked back up at her, his eyes boring into her. "I had to do it. They had to be taught a lesson."

"What did you do?" Her voice was barely above a whisper.

"We sailed away, and took all of the hostages given to my father as guarantees of loyalty." He breathed deeply. "We sailed to Sandwich." He shook his head, unable to speak. With an effort she could physically see, he continued. "I did what my father promised the nobles would happen should they betray us."

Aelfgifu's hand flew to her mouth in shock. She knew what was coming. "My lord?"

"We took the hostages to the beach." He stopped and Aelfgifu could see raw emotion on her husband's face before it hardened again. "I ordered that the hands and nose of each hostage be cut off." His voice had gone flat; the admission had done nothing to soothe him. He turned to her, seeking her approval. "It had to be done! To not do so would have shown weakness! It's their fault, these English nobles! They care not for the peace of their country, only for the prosperity of their own purses!" He scowled. "And they'll follow anyone who they think will reward them best."

The maids arrived at that moment, making them both jump. A tub was carried in by two carls which was filled with steaming water by a steady flow of maids. Each bobbed a curtsey at Aelfgifu and Canute as they entered and exited. When the tub was half-filled, Canute, tired of the people and the waiting, stopped the next maid who entered. "Enough, that'll do."

Aelfgifu watched as Canute undressed and lowered himself into the tub. She took a cloth and started to wash her husband's back, feeling the stiffness in his shoulders as she lathered the soap. It gave off a scent she recognised; herbs that Bri had shown her, and instructed in their use. She smiled; it'd surely been Bri who had ensured this was here, for the herbs were known to relax.

As she rinsed the soap she felt the tight knots in Canute's back relax; the hot water and herbs were playing their part. He was silent as she washed him and waited until the water had lost most of its warmth before speaking.

"I lost many men, good men, warriors all. We had no choice but to flee and live to fight again, or else die at the hands of those miserable whoresons." He rose from the tub, the dripping water dancing in the light of the fire. She led him to her bed and climbed under the covers with him. Curling her body around her husband, she felt the tension leave him as he succumbed to sleep.

They'd been living in Denmark with Canute's half-brother, Harald, for nearly a year and Aelfgifu was growing impatient. It seemed there were many meetings and dinners and discussions but nothing ever happened; she was still away from her home and living off the generosity of another. She knew that Canute was becoming frustrated as well. She could sometimes see it in his face and by the way he spoke to people after an audience with his half-brother. In late spring of 1015, a year almost to the day Canute had fled England, King Harald invited both Aelfgifu and her husband to dine with him alone.

The first time she'd dined in the king's private chambers, she'd been surprised by the lack of decoration. Everything was well-made and the materials of the highest quality, some even from far to the east, but there was nothing extraneous in the rooms; everything was functional, there wasn't an object or piece of furniture in the suite that wasn't used. The kitchen had worked late, providing a feast of fish and sea food dishes for the diners.

"The meal is delicious. Thank your grace for inviting us to dine with you." Even if Canute was in a foul mood this evening, she would at least observe formal etiquette. It became easier as the evening wore on and Harald asked her about trivial matters.

"You're very welcome, sister. I trust you've been enjoying your stay in my country."

From the corner of her eye Aelfgifu saw her husband tighten at his half-brother's claim to the country of his birth. "Yes, my lord, it's a beautiful land. I've taken the opportunity of making short trips, in order to see more of," she stopped herself just in time from saying 'your country', "Denmark."

"Good, good. And you're treated well? As someone kin to the king should be?"

"Oh yes, your majesty. The Danish are a very welcoming people. Sometimes it seems I only need think of something and one of your carls or servants displays it before me."

The king laughed, his face showing the pleasure he felt at the compliment. Turning to Canute, he spoke. "And you, brother, it must be good to be home."

"Aye, Harald, it is. And I hope to remain here for a long time."

Aelfgifu glanced up from her meal, watching Harald's reaction. The startled king dropped his knife while it was half-way to his mouth, spattering white fish on the table.

"For a long time." He repeated the words, as if trying to determine their exact meaning. "Do you not intend to restore your army and take back the throne our father left for you in England?"

The room was silent, save for the shuffling of servants and crackling of the fire. Then with a glance at Aelfgifu Canute replied. "I've half a mind to abandon that quest, brother. It's a mad country, full of mad people." He shook his head and speared a bit of fish on his knife. Placing it in his mouth, he waved the knife in the air as he chewed. "I was

73

thinking I'd remain here, in Denmark, and rule with you."

The mood in the room suddenly turned. King Harald's face reddened, his glowering eyes staring at his brother. Aelfgifu focussed on her food, suddenly finding her knife fascinating. Canute sat, seemingly unaware of the reactions his last comment had elicited, and ate more fish. Harald was fighting to keep his composure. Turning to Aelfgifu, he smiled grimly. "My dear sister, I've enjoyed your company immensely but now I've business to discuss with your husband, and I fear it would only bore you."

Aelfgifu rose from her chair, aware that she was being politely but firmly asked to leave. There would be words, harsh ones, and the king was being chivalrous. She curtseyed at the king. "Your Grace, thank you again for allowing me to share your table." Harald held her cloak for her and swept an arm toward the door.

Bri was waiting outside, ready to accompany her back to her room. It was late and Aelfgifu knew her aunt wanted to retire for the night but she paused, lingering in the hall close to the door, using any excuse to remain: shifting her cloak, adjusting her boot, smoothing imaginary wrinkles from her dress. "My lady, will you not come?" Bri was already half way down the corridor.

"Stay a moment. I wish to hear what's going on with Harald and my husband." She assumed that the older woman had overheard Canute's earlier comment about ruling Denmark jointly with his half-brother.

"My lady, if we linger, we'll attract the attention of the housecarls, and they'll want to know why we're standing in the hall."

"We'll only be here for a short while, I need to know what is said between them." She pointed at the closed door.

Their closeness just outside the king's chambers hadn't been necessary, for the shouting that issued from within could surely be heard by most of the court.

"Has fighting these English driven you mad? You must be making some jest I don't understand. Your suggestion is preposterous! I won't share rule! Not with you, nor anyone! Denmark is mine!" Harald's voice was hoarse; he wasn't used to having to raise it.

Canute fired back. "You were our father's favourite, you should share in the good fortune he left you!"

The king laughed. "Me? It was you he took raiding, and you he gave a green country!"

"A country of old men, women and children."

"Our father took all of the capable men with him when he went raiding. They yet remain in England. I've little left to protect my own borders." Harald paused. "But you! To you he gave a new land, one with untold wealth!"

"Aye, and populated by dogs!"

There was silence after that. Aelfgifu waited as long as she could but heard nothing more. She returned to her own rooms with Bri, her head swimming with confusion. What could Canute be thinking? She returned to her own rooms with Bri and readied herself for bed. She lay awake long into the night, waiting, but her husband didn't join her

Canute sought her out late the next morning as she was strolling in the garden. The first blooms were out and Aelfgifu enjoyed the smells and quiet of the walled enclosure. His body language and expression indicated he was worried, and assumed it was due to the conversation the previous night.

"Canute, you never came to me last night. Where were you?"

They sat on a stone bench. "I'm sorry, my love, but I had tasks to see to." He took both of his hands in hers. "I've news of your family in England. It's not good."

Kelly Evans

She was grateful he'd tried to protect her with the warning but she'd already known something was amiss. "My family?"

"Yes, your cousins, Sigeferth and Morcar. They're dead." She slumped onto the bench, knowing there was more to this story. Canute continued, watching her face as he spoke. "They were murdered. By Eadric Streona."

At the sound of that name she flew from the bench and walked away, forgetting herself, anger overwhelming her. Canute caught up and pulled her back around to face him. He took her in his arms and she was grateful for the comfort. Taking her shoulders, he guided her back to the bench and waited. After a long silence she asked the question. "How?"

Canute sighed. He didn't want to provide details. "Your cousins travelled to an assembly of Aethelred's men in Oxford, to beg forgiveness of the 'king' for their support of my father. Before they could submit their case to Aethelred, Eadric somehow tricked them into coming to his quarters, perhaps pretending to offer friendship and support. When they arrived he ambushed them and killed them both, claiming they were trying to steal from him." Aelfgifu tried to rise again, so blinding was her fury but Canute held her down. "Aethelred then had Sigeferth's wife taken and sent to a convent."

Aelfgifu nodded at this, understanding. "He can then lay claim to her lands, those left to her by her husband!"

"Yes, but calm yourself, there's more. The king's son Edmund disagreed with this, and rode out to rescue the widow, taking her in secret as his own wife. All her lands are now his." Canute shook his head. "And they are many."

"Aethelred must have been furious." The anger had subsided and she was able to think more clearly. The king's eldest son, Aethelstan, had died the previous year and now Edmund was in line for the throne.

"Oh yes. There was apparently much shouting and

76

throwing of tableware. The widow's lands, now Edmund's, are in the East Midlands. Edmund gets all her estates and, more importantly, all her supporters."

"It was a clever thing to do."

Canute nodded his head, reluctantly agreeing with her. "Yes, and very honourable." His voice held a grudging respect. "I'm sorry, Aelf, if I'd only been able to keep the country, this wouldn't have happened." He took her chin in his hand and tilted her head to look into her eyes. "I'd do anything to stop this pain from entering your life." Drawing her close he held her, and she felt as though he could physically do what he'd just said.

She knew he meant it and was grateful. "It's not your fault. It's Eadric's." She spat out the name, feeling bile rise as she said it. He offered no argument and together they sat, world-weary and tired.

"I've news of my own." Aelfgifu said, her voice barely above a whisper. Canute turned to look at her, frowning. "I didn't want to say until I was sure, and didn't want to worry you when you've so much else to concern yourself with, but I want to temper your news with my own." Canute's frown deepened, accompanied by a curious glint in his eyes. "I'm with child."

Chapter Seven
Denmark and England

A few days later, while Aelfgifu and her women were sewing in her chamber, Canute rushed in without being announced, a frowning Wulfred following close behind. She rose and nodded a thank you to her carl, before dismissing her ladies.

"What is it?" she asked.

"Sit, sit, I've got news!"

He led her back to a chair and sat across from her.

"Your idea worked. We're returning to England!"

She leaned forward eagerly. "Is it true?!"

"When I asked to rule jointly with him over the people of Denmark my brother was very," he thought for a moment, "*disturbed.*" Canute laughed. "Harald has always been this way, even when we were children."

"I don't understand."

"My brother is used to entitlement. His mother made sure he wanted for nothing, creating a selfish child who grew into a selfish man. One who would share nothing. When you suggested I propose he share his kingdom with me I knew full well how he would react. So I've been pushing the idea and by the time I relented," he emphasized the word with a grin, "and agreed he should rule our homeland alone, he was only too happy to grant me money and men, if only to see the back of my ships sailing from his harbour for good!"

Aelfgifu jumped up squealing, decorum forgotten. "Then it's true? We're really going home?"

Canute stood, grinning. "Yes, we're really going home. As soon as we can."

She glanced around her chamber, seeing for the first time how much she had accumulated in just one year. Looking up at her husband, she smiled.

"I'd best get busy then. I've got a good many letters to write and much to prepare for our homecoming."

It was early in the autumn before they were finally ready to sail. Canute's fleet was glorious; over 200 longships, each manned with the finest fighters in all of Scandinavia. Indeed the variety of men who made up Canute's force could be seen by the differing shields that adorned the sides of the great vessels. The prows sported beasts that would terrify an enemy upon sighting them: bulls with golden horns, dragons breathing gold-tipped fire and snakes with long silver teeth. Aelfgifu sailed in the midst of the fleet, in a smaller ship carrying her small retinue, including her aunt.

It was late in the season for a crossing but a sacrifice made before departure and the seers had determined that it was a good time for Canute's attack, and so far they spoke the truth, for the sea was calm and the wind favourable. Aelfgifu stood at the prow of the ship, watching the horizon as if by staring out to sea she could will her homeland to appear. Bri stood by her side. They were so nearly home and Aelfgifu's heart ached to see Reodfeld again.

The gods were with them the entire crossing, an auspicious sign, and one that both the Christians in the fleet and those who practised the old religion could give thanks for. Soon the flapping of the sails was accompanied by the screams of sea birds that let the fleet know they would soon sight the shore. They arrived at Sandwich, where Aelfgifu was to continue overland.

Canute stared out at the beach, his face blank but there was something in his eyes. Aelfgifu watched him but dared not interrupt his thoughts. He closed his eyes, head hanging down. Like a penitent man, she thought. Then the realisation struck her: he's reliving the horror of mutilating the hostages. She reached out a hand, but he shrugged it off, the flash of anger in his eyes a warning. She nodded slightly in appreciation of his mood. Good. Better rage than indifference. She needed him to be strong. Strong enough for both of them.

"It was their fathers who betrayed you, husband. They made their oaths. You were honour bound to do what you did."

"You're right, of course. And now I'm going to make them pay again. And again." He shook the darkness from his head. "You'll need someone to accompany you to Reodfeld."

"I'll be fine travelling on my own," she said.

Canute frowned. "No, I won't allow it. I'll provide a few men to go with you to the manor." He held up a hand as she started to protest. "Nay, I'll brook no argument." They were interrupted by the arrival of men on horses. Most of the fleet was still offshore; only Aelfgifu's ships and a few of Canute's had docked, those that had contained his most trusted men. All who were on land readied their shields, preparing to create a shield wall should it be needed. Aelfgifu looked at the tree line for a place to hide but stopped when she heard distant laughter. The ripple of greeting and cheers finally reached them and she could now see why.

"Thorkell, my friend and teacher!" Sliding his sword back into its scabbard, Canute approached the largest man Aelfgifu had ever seen with arms held wide.

The huge Dane's legs brushed the ground as he rode. He stepped more than jumped from his horse and embraced Canute. "My former student." They laughed together before Thorkell grew serious and kneeled before Canute. "And my liege lord."

Pulling him to his feet, Canute led the man to Aelfgifu. "Thorkell, this is my wife, Aelfgifu."

She curtsied awkwardly; her pregnancy had advanced to the stage where movement she had found easy only a few months ago was now difficult. "My lord, it's a great honour

to finally meet you, I've heard many tales of your bravery."
Standing straight again, she saw that Thorkell was at least a
head and a half taller than her husband, whom many agreed
was a giant.

Thorkell laughed and nudged Canute. "And I hope none
of my less noble deeds, my lady."

She smiled, enjoying the deep bass of his voice. He was
dressed for travel, and from his appearance it seemed he'd
travelled far. She looked around and saw many men in the
same state; tired, dirty and thirsty. A makeshift pavilion had
been set up not far from the beach, to use as a resting stop
before continuing their respective journeys. At Aelfgifu's
suggestion, they moved to the tent, but not before Thorkell
signalled to his men to dismount and rest.

When food and ale had been presented they sat. "What
happened?" Canute shook his head. "Why are you and your
men here?" He frowned, as if remembering something and
looked around. "And where's Heming?"

Thorkell leaned back in his chair and drank the entire
goblet of ale. Wiping his mouth he placed the cup back on
the table. "My brother's dead, at the hands of Aethelred."
Before Canute could answer, Thorkell added, "as are many
of my men."

Canute jumped up, shoving the table away. Aelfgifu rose
quickly to avoid being hit by the table edge. "How can this
be? What happened? What did that bastard *gargan* do?"

Thorkell waved Canute back down; Aelfgifu saw from his
face that he'd already had time to adjust to the incident.
"After you left, Aethelred grew suspicious of me and my
men. I don't know why except to guess that words were
dripped into his ear by his most trusted advisor."

Aelfgifu shivered; a man she hated advised by the man
she despised. Unconsciously she whispered the name.
"Eadric."

Thorkell nodded. "Aye, Eadric. He's close to the king but

81

wishes to be closer, to perhaps aid in the king's rule. But he became jealous of my role as advisor. My brother often came to me with stories of Eadric sneaking into the queen's chambers at night for secret discussions."

"You don't think . . . ?" Aelfgifu was too shocked to continue.

"That Eadric shares the queen's bed?" He shook his head. "No, she wouldn't be that stupid. She despises the king but she knows better than to make so obvious a fool of him. To do that would mean her complete downfall. And none of her children would ever inherit the throne."

Aelfgifu signalled for a servant to refill their cups and patiently waited until Thorkell had further refreshed himself.

"This is all speculation, for I didn't have the time to determine the truth of anything I heard in those last few days." He stopped and his shoulders slumped slightly. "Aethelred struck fast. He attacked my men, saying that we were Danes and no Danes could be trusted. This despite the fact that we fought on his side." Thorkell made a disgusted noise in his throat. "His men came for us as we slept, just before the sun rose."

Aelfgifu didn't have knowledge of battle etiquette but she recognised shameful and deceitful behaviour.

"We fought but not many survived, only those who accompanied me. The rest were slaughtered as they slept or tried to flee." His great head dipped, his long white beard reaching his lap. "My brother Heming had saddled his horse and went to help others when he was surprised by one of Aethelred's men."

The silence in the tent was oppressive, the wind and the distant sound of the waves crashing on the shore the only sounds infiltrating their anger and sadness. Aelfgifu could see that Thorkell had been very close to his brother and the pain of his death was still an open wound. Canute spoke.

"It's good to have you back, by my side. But by the gods, if these damned English wanted to further fuel the flames of our discontent then they have succeeded."

"Hold my hand, my lady, I can see the babe's head!" Aelfgifu had her aunt's hand and saw Bri grimace as she squeezed with the effort of delivering her child. She shrieked as the contraction tightened and fought the urge to hold her breath against the pain. As if reading her mind, Bri spoke again. "You must breathe, my lady, inhale deeply then blow out the air in short stages. It will ease the passage of the child."

She did as commanded and tried to concentrate on the massaging motion of the woman before her. The maid had covered her swollen belly with oils containing sage to help her labour, and the exotic jasmine her aunt had procured in Denmark for dulling pain. Bri had tried to explain the other ingredients but at that point Aelfgifu didn't care about plants; she only wished that the pain would stop. "The child! It's coming! Push, my lady, push!"

With a final effort, and with every bit of energy she had remaining, she opened her mouth and screamed. She was only vaguely aware of the sudden flurry of activity around her until she heard a small cry. The sound immediately forced her senses and she looked down as Bri placed the naked mewling child upon her belly. "You've a son, my lady."

She picked up the baby, still wet but warm from her own body and held him in wonder. His eyes were open and of the darkest of blues. His small face was screwed into an angry frown and his tiny fists clenched in defiance at having been forced from his home of nine months. Laughing and feeling the tears rolling down her cheeks she started when her son began to wail. The sound was tentative at first then became a full cry, his small face turning red. She looked up at the women around her, all eyes glistening, all faces smiling. "My son has a loud voice, doesn't he?"

Brihtwyn stepped forward, looking down at the child. "He does indeed, my lady, the voice of a future king." She reached over and touched one of the baby's hands, feeling the tiny fingers instinctively curl around hers. "And a strong grip too!"

Aelfgifu couldn't stop laughing and smiling, her previous pain all but forgotten. Reluctantly she handed the child back to her aunt so the other women could help her clean herself. She was then led to her bed from the birthing stool and helped to a comfortable position. Despite the cold of the dark November morning, she ordered that a few of the windows be unshuttered so the crisp breeze could clear the chamber of the reminders of the birth. A maid had wrapped her in furs against the cold but she didn't need them; she felt only warmth. Her child had also been taken away, in order to be cleaned and swaddled. Before long the room was freshly scented and the windows closed again. Only when the cold air had gone was the baby brought back to her. Bri laid the boy in her arms then sat on the edge of the bed.

"What will you name him?"

Without looking up from her son, Aelfgifu replied. "I'll let my husband name the child, as is his due with a boy." She was disappointed that Canute couldn't be with her now, but he was fighting for the very crown this child would one day wear. She tore her gaze away from the baby. "It's a good sign, is it not? The gods must be pleased with my husband, and to show it they have sent us a boy. I will arrange a feast of thanks to Freya."

"Any child is a sign of the gods' pleasure with us, but a male at this time is indeed a great sign." Bri nodded her agreement.

Aelfgifu nodded too, her gaze returning to her baby. The joy she felt now was tempered with the knowledge that her husband might well be fighting for his life this very instant. A stab of concern speared her and she wondered if he would ever see his son.

Less than a month after the birth, Aelfgifu received two surprises: one, a letter from Canute detailing the submission of all of Wessex to him and his men. The second, only a few days later, the appearance of the man himself.

"Canute, what are you doing here? I had no notice that you were planning to visit!"

He waved the comment aside. "Not many know I'm here. I don't intend to stay long but I had to see my son!"

She smiled and took his arm in hers, leading him to her chambers. His face broke into a wide smile as he gazed down at the baby, asleep in his simply decorated wooden cradle. Reaching down, he picked up the child, laughing at the boy's displeasure at being woken. Holding him up in the air, he grinned. "He's a strong child, just like his father. He'll become a great warrior!"

Aelfgifu didn't want to think of her son as a grown man, fighting. She changed the subject. "He has no name yet. You must choose one."

Canute pursed his lips, staring into the boy's eyes. "If you agree, I'd like to name him Sweyn, after my father."

It was a traditional practice to name sons after fathers and grandfathers and didn't surprise Aelfgifu. "It's a perfect name." She reached over and took the squirming child. Rewrapping him in his swaddling, she held him until he fell asleep once more and gently placed him back in his cradle. Leading Canute out of the room they went to the main hall.

Sitting at the table, Aelfgifu signalled for mead and waited for her husband to speak. She saw the joy of meeting his son fade and knew there was more to his visit.

He'd never hedged around any news before, good or bad,

and this time was the same. "I've allowed Eadric Streona to submit to me and join my forces."

Although she'd recovered physically from the birth of her son, her emotions were still volatile. She flew from the table, picking up and throwing first one then the other of the cups of mead, spraying a nearby servant with the contents. "You've done what? You allowed that *hrafnasueltir*, that murderer, into your camp?" She couldn't ever remember being so angry, her fury taking her words away.

Canute stood and went to hold her. She shrugged out of his grasp and walked a few paces. Again her husband came to her, gently taking her arm. She allowed herself to be led back to the table but wouldn't look at Canute. "I wanted you to hear this news from my own mouth, instead of rumour or false reports." She stared straight ahead, past Canute. He sighed. "It was necessary."

She exploded again. "Necessary? How can keeping the man who killed my father, brother and cousins alive be necessary? What can the . . ." once more her anger overwhelmed her and she struggled to find a word foul enough.

Canute finished for her. "What reason do I have for not killing him on the spot? What can I obtain from such a creature?"

She pursed her lips and remained silent, arms crossed over her chest.

"Eadric . . ." Aelfgifu knew he saw the look of disdain on her face. "He deserted his liege lord, Aethelred, on some pretext of being played false. The old fool probably demanded Eadric's lands to support his fight against me, and Streona took it badly. I couldn't have him roaming the country causing trouble and while I know the pain this causes you it would be better to know where he is at all times." His face softened. "And I do have a use for him. He has important information about Aethelred and his army, where his soldiers camp, how many and how well-armed they are. All information that will help in my campaign."

"But he's my enemy!" A vision of Queen Emma floated before her but she pushed the portion of her hatred reserved for that woman to the back of her mind. "And yours also! Was it not he who persuaded the king to attack Thorkell and kill his brother?"

"It's better to always know where my enemy is and what he does." He bent to the floor and retrieved the cups. Fortunately the jug had remained standing and he poured them both a drink. "It's also well-known that he cannot stand the king's son, Edmund. I may perhaps learn something of the Atheling from Eadric." Aelfgifu's stomach lurched every time she heard the name said aloud. "You'll be pleased to know that Edmund and his men have already seized all of Eadric's lands, razing villages and taking all that they wanted as punishment for his disloyalty."

"But the man himself still lives."

"And as I now have control of him, I needn't fear his harrying of you and your manor."

She looked up, startled. She'd been so focussed on her son she hadn't considered the possibility that Eadric would come after her. The thought chilled her.

"You'll know at all times the whereabouts of the monster?"

Canute nodded his head. "Yes."

"And if he does one suspicious thing, no matter how small, you'll kill him?"

He nodded his head once more. "Yes."

"Will you swear this to me?"

Canute came to her side of the table and, taking her hand, pressed it to his heart.

"I swear to Odin the All Father that I will kill Eadric Streona should he do anything to displease or dishonour me, my men or my family." He raised her hand to his lips and kissed it. "That especially means you and our son."

She'd learned very soon in their marriage that her husband was a great leader, his political as well as battle instincts strong. And she learned to trust his judgement. She nodded her acceptance but the taste of bile wouldn't leave her mouth.

Canute left her again to continue his campaign and Aelfgifu remained as before, waiting for news of her husband and his soldiers. The months passed and she was glad she had Sweyn to keep her darker thoughts at bay. She loved her son more than anything in this world, more than she thought possible. He was a lovely, good-natured baby who provided her many an occasion for a smile and a laugh when a part of her wanted to weep. Canute and his advisors sent her regular news, often via the capable hands of Oswulf. He'd become a trusted friend, but Aelfgifu still found it more and more difficult to smile when he came, knowing the news he potentially carried. She learned details of all of the battles her husband fought, those he won as well as those he lost. It seemed strange to her that many of the battles resulted in no one winning. She was always grateful to Oswulf for bringing her these reports in particular; any messenger who confirmed that Canute was still alive was welcome in Reodfeld.

Spring had finally taken hold of the year 1016 and Aelfgifu could usually be found outside, directing planting activities in some of the gardens that her manor relied on. As a result of their time in Denmark, Brihtwyn had additional herbs to plant from samples she had brought back with her. Aelfgifu was there when one of her servants delivered a note, given to him by a monk who was travelling north. She wiped her hands on her apron and hurried into the house, her aunt following quickly behind her. Sitting in a window seat in the main hall, she opened the letter. Reading quickly she said nothing as she refolded the small piece of parchment.

"What is it?" Brihtwyn's voice was tight with worry. Aelfgifu handed the paper to her aunt and waited until the older woman had finished reading. "Can this be true?"

Aelfgifu nodded. "The monk swore he received the note from Thorkell himself."

Bri stood, her arms held high. "Then gods be praised, for they surely favour your husband's quest!" She heaved a sigh of relief. "Aethelred is dead!"

Further news was received over the next few weeks, mainly telling of the chaos Aethelred's death had caused. Many of the nobles had grown weary of the fighting and hoped to persuade the new king, the Atheling Edmund, to offer Canute and his men gold, enough to stay their attacks. But they soon discovered that Edmund was not his father; he would rather fight to the death than pay an ounce of gold more to the attackers. As a result of his army's discontent, the new king often found that upon winning a battle, he then had to flee south to gather more troops, as many of his men fled or surrendered to Canute. But still he fought, and the battles continued.

"I wonder if the queen has scurried back to the precious homeland I hear she so often speaks about?" They were in Bri's herb garden, Aelfgifu watching as her aunt tended to the young plants.

"Nay, she remains at Westminster in London, protected by her own housecarls and servants." Aelfgifu knew how beloved Emma was in London. "And no doubt the townspeople would come to her aid, if need be."

Brihtwyn clapped the dirt from her hands and straightened. Wincing and placing her hand on the small of her back, she rolled her shoulders. "This fighting, these battles, how much longer do they think they can hold out against your husband?"

Aelfgifu shook her head. She'd known before marrying that being the wife of a king would include living in ignorance much of the time. "I don't know. But when he wins this country, Queen Emma," the words dripped from her mouth like acid, "and her wretched sons will be exiled and *my* son will one day be king." She made this statement with as much force as she could muster but there was no forgetting that Emma was a dangerous woman.

Later in the year, Aelfgifu learned of the battle of Otford, fought between Edmund and Canute's forces. After an unsuccessful siege of London, Canute had been forced south-east until he stood ground and fought Edmund in Kent. It was as unremarkable a battle as any of the minor skirmishes she constantly read about, with one difference: Eadric Streona had abandoned her husband and had sought out Edmund once more, begging forgiveness and re-pledging his loyalty. Canute had known nothing of the man's defection until it was done and the stories that reached Aelfgifu told that her husband's anger was so great that he destroyed the contents of an entire room before his carls managed to calm him. When Aelfgifu heard the news she ran to her son and held him, yelling at any who came close to leave her. How could she ever let him go when her enemy was once more free to roam, to seek her out if he wanted?

Canute had a wide network of contacts, men who would spy and report from the enemy's court for a few coins. One had reported that Edmund, upon agreeing to take Eadric back to his court, was heard to say "No greater folly was ever agreed to than that one." It may have been something as insignificant as a mere folly for the king but it was a direct threat to Aelfgifu and her family.

"Niece, you must let someone else do that!"

The sharpness of Bri's words made Aelfgifu wince. As she stood her hand went to her back to support herself. A moment later Bri was by her side.

"Why do you insist on doing these things yourself? Let one of the servants pick the apples. You should be resting."

"I'm fine." She knew Bri could spot the lie; this pregnancy wasn't as easy as her first had been.

The tone made her aunt stop and stare. "I'm sorry but a woman with child, especially the king's child, should take more care."

Aelfgifu wiped her forehead. She *was* tired and a break would be welcome. "My husband is not yet king."

"He's the rightful king." Bri dismissed the comment and returned to the earlier subject. "Will you rest awhile? Lay down in your chamber, I'll bring you weak mead."

Knowing that this was an argument she wouldn't win, Aelfgifu nodded. But they were interrupted by a servant, announcing the arrival of Oswulf.

She invited him in, immediately noticing that his usual calm composure had abandoned him that day. When Oswulf had removed his travelling cloak and they were seated, barely a second passed before her husband's carl spoke. "My lady, I've come to tell you that Edmund has gathered his forces and will soon march on Canute."

Aelfgifu thought for a moment. "What do you know of Edward's forces?"

"Edmund, his men, he. . . "

"What? Tell me." Her throat tightened.

"Edmund's forces are great. Superior to Canute's." He reached over and took her hand. "You'll want to prepare yourself."

She stood and held her swollen belly. "Thank you for your advice. Go, get food and ale." Aelfgifu turned and walked slowly from the room, still cradling her stomach.

Canute surveyed the landscape, his most trusted men by his side. The sun hadn't quite risen and they could see the fires from the enemy's camp in the distance.

"A lot of men." Thorkell stared straight ahead as he spoke.

"A lot of dead men." Canute spat the words. His scouts had returned late last night to deliver news he already suspected: Edmund's forces outnumbered theirs by three to one. "A challenge worthy of my warriors."

Canute turned to his carls. "If you have any words to say to the gods, now is the time."

The horn blasted, echoing across the field and Canute paused in his speech to glance towards the enemy before continuing. The sun had risen and burned off the dew left behind by a damp night. "We will take this land! As my father did! Their *kamphundr* king will perish beneath our might! Else we will celebrate in Valhalla tonight!" He walked past the rows of men, seeing their eyes flit from him to the enemy. "The gods are on our side, they have blessed our effort!" He stopped and faced the warriors. *His* warriors, weary, wearing battered leather and bearing scars of previous battles. Canute raised his axe. "For Odin!" The men cheered, banging swords and axes on their shields.

He watched the enemy forming their shield walls and ordered his men to do the same, joining Thorkell at the front. Archers were sent to the rear, protected and ready to strike on command. Canute's stomach tightened, a moment of uncertainty gripping him. His father had told him it wasn't a lack of fear that made a warrior but the conquering of fear. Those men who claimed to have no fear were dangerous fools. "Hold your positions!" The men around him tensed, the entire structure taut and solid. Moving his shield slightly to create an opening, he saw Edmund's forces advancing. "Now!" They surged forward as a wall, a single unit bent on a single purpose: kill.

The air thundered with screams and the clash of shield against shield as the two forces met. The noise was deafening and could be heard in the next town over. Their survival depended on how closely they could hold the wall, and how quickly unexpected problems were handled. The walls remained intact as men on both sides reached over the shields with axes to hack at anything in their way. Thorkell moved to his left, leaving space enough for Canute to thrust his sword at one of Edmund's men who had left himself exposed.

"Thorkell!" A Saxon spear appeared over the top of their shields. Thorkell ducked in time but the man behind him wasn't fast enough and fell, trampled beneath the feet of the wall. It was a battle of strength and agility. And perseverance. Canute could feel the shield of the man behind him pushing, forcing him to shove his own shield harder. The second row were important; if any in the front fell, the man behind would have to rush forward and take his place.

Thorkell brought his axe down and split a Saxon shield in two. "He should have gone to a better shield maker." The large man grinned and turned back to the battle.

The trumpet sounded and the Saxons withdrew, still in formation. Canute ordered his men to do the same. They retreated slowly, backing away over the churned field, avoiding the bodies of the slain and injured but watching the enemy, fighting their instincts to rush forward and attack. The only way they would survive was to maintain order.

"These Saxons are more aggressive than I thought." The comment from the back of the wall was met with grunts of agreement as the men caught their breath. But there was little time to recover as Edmund's forces regrouped and advanced once more.

For the entire morning and most of the afternoon the battle continued. At times it seemed Canute would win, but the Saxons fought on, always protecting the path to their king, who watched the battle sitting on his horse atop a hill a short distance away. Canute guessed he had lost a few hundred men, and it was difficult to see how many of Edmund's men had fallen. But it had to be at least twice the number the Danes had lost.

"They have too many men! They replace their dead as quickly as they fall!" Thorkell shouted to be heard over the clash of steel against wood.

Canute had noticed this but said nothing. They could not retreat, not now. They had to keep fighting. After another withdrawal of the shield walls they prepared themselves.

"Something is happening."

Canute followed the direction Thorkell's axe pointed. He saw a large number of Saxon men disengaging from their walls, the dust they kicked up as they fled the field obscuring his vision. Finally he saw the banner of the leader of the defection and looked at Thorkell. "Is that. . ."

"Yes." Thorkell's lip curled as he spoke.

Canute looked back at Edmund's forces, now in disarray as half of the army fled the battle, led by the Earl of Mercia, Eadric Streona. "That fucking coward." Edmund recovered and reformed his shield walls but the lines were uneven and the shields held too low. "They are tired! Weary of fighting us! And half of their army has fled in fear of us!" He took a breath. This was their chance, their enemy in disarray, their numbers more evenly matched. "I should be grateful to the Grasper," he thought, then shook his head to rid himself of the bile that had risen. His voice hoarse, he shouted, "Odin!"

They rushed forward, surprising the Saxons. This time there was no one to replace the dead and the ground grew slippery with blood, treacherous with bodies. Thorkell, using the shoulders of a few larger men, leapt into the air and over the failing Saxon shield wall, axe slicing as he landed.

"There's fear in their eyes! They know they're defeated!"

It was true. Canute saw the panic in the eyes of a young warrior as he thrust his sword into the man's belly, spilling his entrails. He swung again to the right as another of Edmund's men attacked, sword raised high. Bending low, he avoided the sword and shoved his own through his attacker's neck. All around him individual battles were occurring. He looked for the king but at that instant the Saxon horn sounded again. "Retreat!"

Edmund's army fled, exposing themselves as they ran. Canute's men didn't need to be told, they followed the Saxons, cutting them down as they ran. Soon there were few enough left fleeing and Canute turned to look back over the field. Fallen warriors from both sides littered the area, detached limbs and spilled organs fouling the plain.

A hand on his shoulder made him turn. Thorkell, bloodied and dirty but alive, stood beside him. Looking back at the carnage, he grasped his Mjolnir pendant and gave thanks to the gods.

Oswulf was back at Reodfeld, delivering supplies and, more importantly, news. Aelfgifu prayed each day at the old tree since his last visit, barely eating or sleeping while she waited for reports of Canute.

"My lady, your husband is alive."

Aelfgifu slumped in her chair. There was only Oswulf here and she was able to abandon the stoic façade she had adopted lately. "Thank the gods." She straightened in the chair once more.

"But there is news."

She held her breath, unable to read any clues in Oswulf's face. "Go on."

"After a mighty battle fought near Assandun, where many men were lost to both sides, Edmund and your lord husband came to terms and have signed a treaty!"

"A treaty?" She was puzzled; this was not what Canute had quested after. "What kind of treaty?"

Oswulf, unaware of Aelfgifu's concern, continued. "Edmund offered peace in return for splitting the county into two, to be jointly ruled by both him and Canute."

Aelfgifu thought on this news in silence. Surely there must be a mistake? Why would her husband, who had spent years trying to gain the crown of England, settle for half a crown? "You're certain of this?"

"I am my lady."

"But why? What can he hope to gain?" Then a thought hit her. "Is my husband injured? Was he struck during the battle?"

Oswulf hurried to reassure her. "Nay, my lady, he's well, in fine form."

She saw a sly grin on his face as he spoke. "What? What else?"

He laughed, ignoring the impatience that grew on her face. "My lady, your husband was not hurt. But Edmund was."

Edmund, injured? She wondered how badly. Oswulf read her thoughts.

"It's said his injuries are dire, although the man himself never shows any sign of weakness or infirmity."

"Do we know the extent of the injuries? Are they mortal?"

"Our informants tell us his physicians fear the worst."

A suspicion arose in her mind. Her husband was no fool. "And the terms of this treaty?"

Oswulf knew which of the terms she most wanted to hear. "If one of the rulers should die, the country passes in full to the other."

This made sense to her, as both Canute and Edmund's

sons were too young to wear a crown, and no one would countenance an infant king, particularly after so many years of upheaval. "So King Edmund . . ."

Oswulf finished her sentence, "is not expected to live out the year."

Chapter Eight
England

Aelfgifu learned later that, although the English had had superior forces, they had lost the battle at Assandun and Edmund had been forced to sue for peace. The two leaders met on a small island near Deerhurst, in Gloucestershire where Edmund presented his terms. She already knew about the succession; that if either of the men should die the entire kingdom would pass to the other. But he had also been specific about the division of the country: Edmund would retain Wessex and Western Mercia; Canute would rule over Mercia and Northumbria, including the Danelaw. Having two kings rule the country seemed odd to Aelfgifu, but she remembered her history lessons and knew that England had, not so long ago, been ruled by seven kings simultaneously. The memory brought a grim smile to her face; how soon the past was forgotten!

As predicted, although not spoken of aloud, Edmund's condition grew worse and he passed away in agony at the end of November. He'd ruled for such a short time, and that time taken by constant battle, that he left no lasting impression in the minds of the English other than that of being the son of Aethelred. Canute was now the undisputed ruler of all England, and his accession was welcomed by a battle-weary country. High and low-born alike had become tired of the constant raiding and fighting, the growing taxes and financial burdens that they'd suffered, and a tentative hope was once more felt across the land.

Aelfgifu welcomed the news of Edmund's death, but couldn't celebrate, as her labour had started and she was nearly delivered of her second child. This time Canute was in the manor with her, waiting in the main hall with his carls and discussing plans for the country. The messenger who had delivered the announcement earlier that day was carried around the room on the carl's shoulders and rewarded with gold and silver after being given as much mead as he could hold. Bri had whispered the news into Aelfgifu's ear, then backed away as another contraction gripped her. There was a flurry at the end of the birthing chair and, knowing from her first time what this meant, Aelfgifu took a breath and pushed as hard as she could. She flopped back into the chair as a cry, weak at first then growing stronger, echoed around the room.

"A boy, my lady," the midwife proclaimed. "Another fine boy!"

Aelfgifu smiled and held out her arms for the child. He was very like his brother although with more hair. She shook her head, knowing his features would change as the weeks went by, but she thought she could see Canute's eyes staring back at her and, even knowing new born babes didn't smile, swore she saw Canute's grin there as well. Handing the baby to her aunt, she allowed herself to be helped up and to a waiting basin of warm water. She and her son were washed and dressed, and the room freshened before her husband was allowed to visit.

He approached her bed cautiously, an act that made Aelfgifu laugh. "Why do you creep so? I'm used to seeing you come to my bed with more enthusiasm!" Canute looked sheepish and sat on the edge, peering into the bundle in her arms. She smiled and moved the blanket away, teasing him. Seeing his frown she laughed again and showed him the child. "You've another son."

Her words were rewarded with a great smile and a gesture that indicated he wanted to hold the child. Cradling the boy in one arm, he unwrapped the swaddling and looked at the hands and feet. When the babe, feeling the cooler air, began to squirm, he quickly rewrapped and returned the child. "We need a name."

She looked up at him. "It's your job to name a son."

Canute frowned, thinking. "Have you any suggestions? Any names that please you?"

Aelfgifu suspected he might ask. "I'd like to name him Harold, after your grandfather."

He nodded his agreement. "It's a good strong name. The gods will be pleased." He smiled widely. "As they already are, for have they not shown me their favour many times already?"

She settled the child in her arms and looked up at him. "The birth of a son is a good omen."

"As is the death of an enemy."

Together they gazed at their son, shutting out the rest of the world for a short time.

At first Aelfgifu could only feel the drums in her feet, the vibrations making their way from the tiled floor through her leather shoes. As the procession grew closer to the chapel the beating grew louder until she could feel the booming in her chest. She shivered, unsure if the cause was the drums or the January air. The abbey was filled; chairs had been brought in for the most important guests, everyone else stood, packed in tightly, necks straining to see the activity. The most influential men and women in all of England were in attendance, displaying their wealth and power by their clothes and jewels. Every woman wore her best circlet, and Aelfgifu was astonished by the variety and workmanship. She tried to stop feeling self-conscious and squeezed Bri's hand for reassurance, focussing on the dancing flames of the torches that hung every few feet on the stone wall around her. They'd discussed her feelings while she dressed for the coronation that morning.

"You're beautiful, more so than most of these fancy women." Her aunt had been unimpressed by the sights and sounds of London, where Canute's coronation was to take place, thinking the people soft and the food ill-prepared. "And a good sight more talented. Do you think any of these city women could run a manor? Or kill a wild hare with a single arrow?"

"I don't believe any of them could, no. But I'm not in the country, I'm in London, and I'll be judged by London standards." She looked at herself in the mirror, turning. "Are you certain this dress is suitable?"

"It's not just you and your husband who have spies. I know many of the servants here, and have been receiving reports of what the other women will be wearing. Trust me, your dress is perfect." Aelfgifu still wasn't convinced, so she added, "You're the wife of the king, what do you care of other's opinions?"

She swirled around and threw her arms up in despair. "It's because I'm Canute's wife! All eyes will be upon me today! Most have not seen me, only heard my name mentioned, and all will be curious to see what manner of woman their new king married."

Brihtwyn grabbed her niece by the hand and brought her back to the full-length mirror. Together they gazed at the reflection. "Your dress is perfect. Your hair is perfect. Your jewels are perfect." She moved to touch Aelfgifu's circlet, but stilled her hands in mid-air for there was nothing to straighten. Putting her arm around Aelfgifu's shoulder, she added, "You, my sweet, are perfect."

Aelfgifu smiled at her aunt and masked her nerves. When Bri smiled and nodded at her in the polished silver mirror, she knew she'd succeeded. She still couldn't stop the jumping and turning of her stomach nor the hammering of her heart against her chest. Smoothing the dress a final time, she turned to Brihtwyn. "I'm ready."

The drums suddenly stopped and the murmuring at the back of the abbey grew louder, the procession had arrived. Peering down the central aisle from her place at the front of the church, Aelfgifu was grateful that everyone's attention was focussed on her husband. Dressed in his new royal robe and wearing his crown, he stopped just inside the heavy wooden doors and stood with his arms held out to his sides. Two men stepped forward from the shadows behind Canute: Lyfing, the Archbishop of Canterbury and Wulfstan, the Archbishop of York. She'd been told just that morning that the Archbishop of York was also known as 'Lupus' and suppressed a smile at the thought, for here was a thin, wiry man with a hawkish nose and small dark eyes, nothing at all like a wolf. Lyfing looked like a man who enjoyed a good meal, and she was certain that one in such an exalted position would be able to indulge a large appetite on a regular basis. She watched as both men proceeded to disrobe and decrown her husband, leaving him standing in nothing but a linen shift. They removed his boots too, replacing them with a pair of simple leather sandals. Aelfgifu had been told that this represented some element of the Christian faith but she was unsure what.

Holding his arms, the archbishops led Canute up the central aisle, all three men looking straight toward the altar and ignoring the stares of the congregation. As they passed Aelfgifu, she saw a twitch in his neck, and knew that he was fighting the urge to turn and look at her. Following behind were the men who had been selected to participate in the coronation, the men whom her husband trusted most in the world. She watched as Thorkell went by, dressed in the English style and looking as uncomfortable as she in these surroundings. Then came Oswulf, whom both she and Canute had relied upon so greatly to relay messages and news between them while her husband had been fighting. Her chest swelled with pride when Wulfred passed by her;

he'd become such an important member of her household that she considered him almost family. Finally, one of Canute's newer men walked past. Eirik of Hlathir, whom they'd met in Denmark, was the ruler of Norway and had offered his men and ships. He'd been promised land and gold for his aid and had become one of the king's closest advisors, known for his hatred of Christians.

She waited while Canute and the others arranged themselves on the dais. Now that the drums had stopped, along with the whispering, she could hear the chanting of monks somewhere within the huge chapel. She took a deep breath, smelling incense and beeswax and the scent of people in close proximity. The incense and chanting made her feel drowsy and she blinked her eyes a few times, refocusing her attention. Canute had prostrated himself before the altar. She had objected to this act when they discussed it a few days ago.

"I don't understand why you have to lie on the floor?"

Canute had frowned. "I was taught these things when I was a child but I've forgotten most of it. The altar is sacred, like our altars to the All Father. But instead of sacrificing animals to their god, they sacrifice themselves, or their pride, by prostrating themselves and mortifying themselves." When she shook her head, he tried again. "Nakedness is a shameful state for them. It's part of the ritual humiliation their god requires."

"But you enjoy shedding your clothes." She smiled at him, teasing. She couldn't understand why her own people were so upset by a man without his shirt.

He waved a hand. "It's these monks, they're fearful of their own shadows." He grinned. "And I only enjoy removing my clothes when requested to do so by my wife." He went and put his arms around her. "She's a very demanding woman." He laughed at Aelfgifu's mock anger and stayed her struggles by holding more tightly. "Oh yes,

I'm sometimes frightened of her." He silenced her shriek of feigned rage by covering her mouth with his. His carls and servants discreetly left the room, leaving the new king and his wife alone.

She wondered if Canute now thought of that moment and smiled, unconsciously tightening her grip on Bri's hand. Her aunt looked at her, puzzled. She shook her head and continued watching. Or rather listening, because as her husband lay on the floor, a choir erupted in song, a *Te Deum*, a blessing for the new king. When it was over the monks continued their solemn chanting while Canute was raised to his feet by the archbishops. His robe was draped over him once more but the crown was still retained by Lyfing.

Archbishop Wulfstan stepped forward. "Canute Sweynsson, do you swear to the Almighty God that you'll do all that is in your power to ensure peace is observed throughout the kingdom of England?"

Canute's voice was deep and clear, reaching those at the very back of the chapel easily. "I swear."

"And do you swear that you'll uphold the laws of the land, forbidding robberies, murders and all other evils?"

"I swear."

"And do you promise to treat all of your subjects with equity and fairness, and ensure that all of your judgements are tempered with mercy?"

"I swear."

"With the might and wisdom of Almighty God beside you, may you keep to your promises and rule justly as our king." Lyfing stepped forward at that point and stood in front of Canute. The Dane bent slightly so that the archbishop could reach him and place the circlet of gold on his head, then straightened again and looked out over everyone in the chapel. Aelfgifu heard a ripple of whispers around her and couldn't help but feel pleased by the awe that her husband inspired.

The room became silent again as first a heavy gold ring was placed on Canute's finger and then a belt with a new sword was fastened around his waist.

"In nomine patri et fili et spiritu sancte. Amen."

The room was filled with people reverently repeating the archbishop's last words.

Canute was led to a stall at the side of the altar while Lyfing addressed the congregation. "The scripture I have chosen for today's mass are the commandments. For who among us does not need to be reminded of the guidance of our Lord."

Aelfgifu frowned. Did the archbishop deliberately look at Canute as he spoke these words? She shook her head. She was tired and imagining things. The archbishop droned on but she barely listened.

". . . have no other gods before me . . ."

There, again. Did he look at Canute? He'd warned her that there would be a Mass said after his consecration but she wasn't here for the religion, she was here for her husband.

". . . shalt not . . ."

Aelfgifu sighed and relaxed in her chair. These holy men certainly could go on. Canute was looking at her. He shrugged and smiled, a twitch of his mouth only she would notice. She glanced down to keep from laughing but for the rest of the Mass, they indulged each other and shut out the rest of the hall.

Aelfgifu enjoyed the coronation feast, as much for the food, drink and entertainment as the looks of shock on the faces of many of the English nobility. It was the first time that most of these privileged people had encountered the Danes in anything other than battle and they quickly learned that their differences when fighting were not the only ones that existed between them. The English, particularly the ladies, sipped gracefully from glass goblets and daintily picked at their food with elegant bejewelled knives. The Danish women, on the other hand, drank great gulps of wine and used rough knives similar to the men's to spear their food. It seemed to Aelfgifu, sitting at one of the higher tables, that the English, her people, ate only for the sake of appearance, while the invaders enjoyed their food and drink, thanking the gods for such a feast. And while both groups wore silks and other expensive materials, the design of the clothing was completely different. The English noblemen looked like they were used to haunting the halls of their great manors, while the Danish nobles, dressed in as much or more finery than their Saxon counterparts, still had the look of warriors about them, of men and women used to spending most of their time outside, sailing the sea and farming the land. She knew that wasn't the case, given the lavishness of the Danish court, but there was a look about the Danes, like they were made of tougher material.

Fortunately the two groups spoke a similar enough language to communicate and Aelfgifu was glad to see conversations starting up between them all over the great hall. She reached her hand subconsciously under the table, used to the wet nose of a dog snuffling around for scraps of food. Frowning, she looked around. These southern English apparently didn't allow their hounds into the hall.

There was a stir from the tables at the back of the room; the music, flutes, drums and some sort of stringed instrument she'd never seen before all stopped mid-song. Conversation fell to hushed whispers, making the hall uncomfortable, the feeling almost ominous. Aelfgifu glanced over her shoulder as Thorkell, his men following, marched up the aisle between the tables, stopping and kneeling at the head table in front of Canute. She noticed that he wore no weapons, an unusual occurrence, and she suspected the large Dane must be feeling exposed and vulnerable at that moment, despite the alarm his physical appearance caused some of the nobles.

"I, Thorkell Strutharaldsson, pledge my body and steel to Canute Sweynsson, King of England, and promise to be faithful and true, to love all that he loves, shun all that he shuns and to never do what is loatheful to him. I swear these words by the All Father and upon this sword." At these words, Canute stood and unsheathed his sword, the one that Aelfgifu had given him as a wedding gift, and offered the blade to Thorkell. The large man leaned forward and kissed the blade, quickly leaning back to right himself. At Canute's nod he stood and, over the table, the two men grasped each other's forearms in a show of friendship. It was understood that Thorkell's oath applied to his men as well, each of them having already pledged themselves to Thorkell himself. He then bowed and, sweeping his cloak dramatically around him, left the room with his men.

The next man to take the pledge was Eirik of Hlathir, also known as Haakonsson, the King of Norway. It was odd to Aelfgifu that one king would swear allegiance to another but Eirik and Canute had sworn to protect each other's interests and she knew that, in England, Eirik was Canute's man. Numerous other nobles followed Eirik, many of whom she'd been introduced to but most of whose names she'd forgotten. Each man repeated the same words, the only difference being that Christians would swear by their god and on a holy relic, a nail from the hand of Christ, rather than by the gods and on the sword the Danes used. Aelfgifu grew weary of the parade of people who swept past her and her mind wandered, thinking about the coronation, and the trek from her manor in Northampton to the great city of London and of her two small sons who were currently sleeping in a room adjoining her own. Smiling at the thought of her boys her reverie was interrupted by increased noise at the end of the hall. Before she could look around a figure dressed in dark ermine, a colour for royalty, hurried passed. He had a few men with him, none of whom she recognised. He knelt before Canute, his face turned away from her. When he started to say the oath, her blood froze.

"I, Eadric of Shrewsbury, do pledge . . ." She heard no more of his speech; her head was pounding in time with her heart, filling her senses with white fog. Staring straight ahead as he left the hall, she saw him glance her way, a look of triumph on his face. She knew that Eadric still held the titles to most of his Mercian lands for despite his treacheries, no charter had ever been drafted that legally removed them. But when she saw that Canute wouldn't meet her eyes she also knew he'd kept Eadric's presence at court a secret from her.

The rest of the banquet passed in a blur. After the pledges had finished Aelfgifu found she no longer had any desire to be in the hall. The candle holders she'd so admired held lights that were now too bright, and the music to which she'd clapped her hands suddenly became too loud.

"My lady, are you unwell?"

Aelfgifu wondered why her aunt was looking at her so anxiously before she realised she was rubbing her forehead. "I'm fine, Bri, just tired."

Bri frowned. "I don't doubt you're tired. Today has been exhausting. Triumphant and wonderful but tiring all the same." She reached to put an arm around her niece but pulled back. Aelfgifu had warned her against shows of familiarity, in case they breached some rule of court etiquette. She instead opted for a discreet pat on the hand and a nod. "And with Eadric here, who wouldn't want to be elsewhere?"

Aelfgifu sighed. "I wish I could speak with my husband." She gazed at the head table, and at her husband sitting with his advisors, wearing his robe and hard-won crown. He was surrounded by food and people, nobles, thanes and important men of business, all clamouring for his attention.

Brihtwyn still didn't understand why her niece couldn't sit with her husband, never mind not speak to him. She leaned closer so her voice could be heard over the rising din of the hall. "Can't you just go up to him, as others are?"

She shook her head. "No." She turned her gaze from the table to focus on Bri, explaining once more what she knew. "Many of the English nobles aren't content with their king's wife. Although I've been baptised they question my faith." Both she and Bri knew this to be an understandable, if hurtful, concern for they'd always followed the old religion. But the world was changing and personal beliefs were more and more often held to ransom. "They feel it's not meet that the king of a Christian country be joined to a heathen wife." She felt her frustration rising as she spoke. "Some even say that our marriage is not real, because there weren't any of their holy men present." She clenched her goblet then forced herself to calm down. This was not the place, nor the time. Taking a drink, she looked back at her husband, still surrounded by strangers and not even aware of her gaze. "Canute will find a way to sway them, don't worry." As she spoke, she wondered if she was trying to convince Bri or herself.

Chapter Nine
England

It was mid-Summer before Aelfgifu finally began to feel comfortable in the London palace. She'd been busying herself where she could: helping with household staff, taking charge of deliveries and trying to understand the already efficient system that ran the court. A very small part of her was gaining respect for Emma, although begrudgingly. The ex-queen, who had fled to her home of Normandy when Canute was crowned, had devised the current system and Aelfgifu had to admit that there was little she would change. Everyone at court had a role and all were determined to perform to the best of their ability.

"Perhaps they're trying to impress their new king," said Bri, shrugging. The motion causing her to poke her finger with the sewing needle and she frowned in irritation

"Maybe. But they all know what to do, there are never any questions. I know there are overseers watching everything but not one has come to me with an issue."

"Isn't that a good thing?"

Aelfgifu nodded slowly. "I guess. But at Reodfeld there were always decisions to be made. Here, I feel as though I'm not needed."

Bri stopped sewing and turned to face her, a puzzled look on her face. "You are queen now, you understand that? Queens do not make decisions about which sheets to use or what to serve for meals."

"Well then, what *do* queens do?" She heard the exasperation in her own voice.

"Their purpose is to provide an heir to the throne. A male heir. And you, my lady, have already done the most important thing you can do, you've given Canute a son."

Aelfgifu couldn't keep the derisive noise escaping her lips but kept her words to herself. "You've only been here for a few weeks, everyone is still settling in and getting used to things. It's only a matter of time before you'll be more involved."

Aelfgifu wasn't convinced. "I hope you're right Bri, because right now I feel like an ornament, something to be looked at and talked about but not to be bothered. It makes me uncomfortable."

"Be patient, love. Things will change soon, you'll see."

A few weeks later Aelfgifu began to notice messengers arriving at court more frequently. She ignored it; surely such a place as London would need many more couriers than elsewhere as the business of running the entire realm was accomplished here. But then she began to see strangers in the halls whispering and looking at her, turning away as she passed. Many a time she came across a conversation that stopped as she walked by, only to resume again when the speakers supposed she was out of earshot. Frustratingly she couldn't catch the words but heard only muffled voices and, sometimes, laughter. After many weeks of this she was on her way to her chambers to ask Bri what she knew when a great noise from the courtyard below stopped her. Peering down through a second-storey window, Aelfgifu saw armed men standing to attention as someone was helped out of a litter. The traveller had a heavy wolf-skin cloak and despite the obvious weight of the fur they stood straight, wearing it with confidence. Stopping to look around, the newcomer glanced up into the sky, shielding their eyes with a raised hand. The face was covered but Aelfgifu got enough of a glimpse to see who it was. She watched, silently hoping she must have been mistaken, when Emma of Normandy turned her head up and looked directly at her.

She watched Emma and her entourage leave the courtyard and, knowing where they were going, hurried to meet them. She arrived as the great doors to Canute's receiving room were closing.

"Let me through, I must see the king." She tried to force her way past two large guards who had been placed outside the room. When they continued to bar her way, she put on her most imperious tone.

"I order you to allow me to pass, don't you know who I am?" Of course they knew, everyone in court knew, but still they stood their ground, their faces impassive. Growing frustrated and anxious, her voice betrayed her worry.

"Remove yourselves from my presence, this instant, and let me through or so help me . . ." One of the doors suddenly opened and out slipped Thorkell, closing it quickly behind him. "Finally, someone with sense!"

Thorkell came over to her, having seen the guards and Aelfgifu's proximity to them. "My lady, your husband, the king, is engaged at present. Tell me your message and I'll deliver it for you."

She glared angrily at the man and could see he was keeping something from her. "Thank you but I'll speak to Canute myself."

"That's not possible just now." He offered her his arm. "I'll escort you back to your rooms, and will inform the king of your visit when he's completed his business."

Aelfgifu tried to argue but found herself being led away from her husband and down the hall. When they arrived at her chamber the huge man bowed to leave.

"A word of advice, my lady." She raised an eyebrow at him but remained silent. "It would be best if you remain here."

"Why won't Canute see me?"

"That is for the king to tell you. It's not my place."

"Damn your place! I know something is going on, it

seems that the whole court knows the details except me!"

She was satisfied to see an embarrassed look pass over Thorkell's face. And pity? "My lady, I can't help you with this."

"You don't say it directly but by your words you confirm there's something amiss." The large man remained silent. She had a sudden thought, and spoke words she never thought she'd use. "I'm the queen. You'll tell me what I want to know."

Thorkell displayed his uneasiness at her words in both his face and his stance, and it did not sit comfortably on him. He looked at her, sadness in his grey eyes. "The king has been persuaded by the council to marry Emma of Normandy, widow to the deposed king."

The last thing she saw was his face looking down at her through a haze, shouting words she couldn't hear. Then nothing.

Aelfgifu yawned, stretching out her arms. The sun was shining brightly through the open windows in her bedchamber and she could hear the twitter of the birds who nested in the tree just outside. She breathed in the smell of baking bread and, rolling over, wondered where her attendants were. There, in a dark corner of the room, she saw her husband, quietly watching her, and the memory of the previous day came crashing back.

Canute slowly made his way over to the bed, his head down the whole time, and sat beside her. After a moment of silence he spoke. "How do you feel?"

She flinched away, scrambling over the bedcovers as far away from him as possible. "Is it true?" When her husband looked down and remained silent, she repeated the question. "Is it true? Are you going to marry Aethelred's widow?"

He seemed to remember himself and stood, straightening his shoulders. "Yes, it's true."

Aelfgifu rose slowly from the bed and put on a robe to cover the light summer shift she slept in. "I hate you," she hissed. She went to her dresser and, sitting in front of her polished silver mirror, began to brush her hair. After a few moments she heard her name whispered.

Using the dresser to steady herself, she rose, anger so fierce she could barely summon her words. She paced the room, afraid that if she stopped moving her legs would give out.

"How could you? How could you betray me like this? How could you agree to this . . . this act?" She spat out the last word, unsure of what to call it. "She was responsible for the deaths of my brother! My father!" Unbidden, tears began to flow and she cursed herself for the show of weakness. Her last words had been pleading. She stopped and as she'd predicted her legs betrayed her and she collapsed in a heap on the floor. The anguish she felt came flooding out. "I can't bear this! Don't you love me? Tell me you still love me! Tell me you still want me!"

Canute came rushing over and knelt down beside her, wrapping his arms around her shaking body. "Yes, I love you, more than my own life!"

They remained like that until the sobs that shook Aelfgifu's body had subsided. Hoarse from the crying, she summoned what little voice she'd left. "Then why?"

He released her and seated himself more comfortably on the floor. Sighing, he finally spoke. "The council insisted their king be bound to a wife in the Christian way."

She'd understood that many people were upset by her dismissal of the Christian practises but never once realised how serious the issue had become, nor how hurtful the outcome. "But you can marry me again."

"I said those very words but . . ." He looked away.

Aelfgifu finished the sentence for him. "But they wouldn't have me."

He held her hands, his eyes begging her to believe him. "I tried to convince them! But there are many very powerful men in this land and I need their support if I'm to rule a peaceful kingdom."

"And I'm not good enough." She spoke normally now, the enormity of the insult done to her becoming more and more apparent. It was a slur to them both, their children and their marriage. She shoved him away and, struggling to stand, began to pace the room again, grateful he gave her space. There were muffled noises outside the closed door but she knew no one would dare disturb them.

"I've no stomach for this, it's a political move, nothing more." His voice lowered. "In my heart I desire only you. It's been that way since we met."

Aelfgifu turned to look at him and saw he was sincere, but also saw that she had little choice. Shaking her head, she thought of Emma, who had already done this to another woman. Aethelred's first wife had been pushed aside so that Emma might marry the king and share the crown of England. Now it appeared that she aimed to keep hold of it, and any power that came with it. Her husband continued.

"The union will also give me the support of Normandy." He paused before amending his words. "Will give *us* their support."

She looked back sharply at him. "Us?"

"I want you to rule the north in my name. There's no one else I can trust." He waited for her response. "There are many who love and admire Emma in the south of the country but there's little affection for her in the north."

There was nothing she could do, she realised that. And what her husband offered proved beyond doubt that he trusted and loved her. Perhaps she could use this opportunity to learn more about the woman she hated most in the world.

"You know I'll do anything you ask of me."

He drew her into his arms. "I know, my love."

Toward the end of summer, after Canute's marriage to Emma had taken place, Aelfgifu was invited to dine with her husband one last time before she returned to her own manors in the north of England. She had not attended the wedding, had not been invited and would hear no words spoken of it. But despite her efforts she still learned of the ceremony. It had been a traditional Christian wedding with the appropriate vows spoken and prayers offered to the Christian god. Canute had been forced to declare his support and love for this woman, and it was exactly these details Aelfgifu strove to avoid, for each story she heard made her heart tear open a little bit more.

It was the Yuletide season and Aelfgifu was dining with her husband, a rare moment alone amidst the celebrations. As king, Canute had more masses and religious events to attend this time of year resulting in fewer and fewer moments together. As she hurried down the long hall to Canute's rooms, the music and revelry of one of the many feasts followed her, growing fainter as she approached his door. She entered the room with a smile but stopped a few feet short of the table, her hand covering her mouth. Regaining her composure she bowed to Canute before sitting across from Eadric Streona. Throughout the meal she met Eadric's glares with a polite smile and a raise of her glass. When they had finished eating, and the dishes were cleared, Eadric settled back into his chair and waited expectantly.

"I've invited you to dine with me so that I might speak with you on a matter of great importance to us both." Eadric nodded his head and she guessed he expected further word of his lands. But Canute's face grew dark. "I've ruled this land for less than a year, however in that time I've learned a great deal about the men around me."

Eadric's face remained impassive but his eyes betrayed his puzzlement. "Indeed, my lord?"

"Oh yes. I've found that men like to talk in London, especially about each other." Still Eadric's face remained frozen but Aelfgifu saw a muscle in his cheek begin to twitch. She listened intently to her husband, enjoying Eadric's confusion. "Many have come to me, those who fought with you against me, asking forgiveness and readily answering my questions about the battle." He stopped, knowing the value of empty air. Eadric, however, also remained silent. Canute's voice grew louder. "I've been told of your part in the fighting. I've been told that you acted dishonourably and treacherously."

Here was a word that finally garnered a reaction from Eadric. "Whatever I've done, my lord, I did for you!"

Canute stood, towering over the other man. "After you had already turned against me!" Aelfgifu had never seen Eadric nervous and she relished the frightened look on the man's twisted face. Her husband continued. "I've heard of your 'deeds' on the battlefield. Many have told me how you slayed an innocent man, one who had the misfortune to look like Edmund, your liege lord, and, holding up his head, screamed that the king was dead, tricking them into believing all was lost." Aelfgifu was transfixed; this was news discussed by men, and while some of the stories of battle reached the women's chambers, they were few and far between. "You then abandoned the fight, running and hiding while others perished in the confusion you caused." She shivered, her eyes widening at this revelation. Not just the absolute treachery of the man, but the fact that he'd been roaming the land free, alone and unguarded.

Eadric quickly regained his composure, his own opinion

of himself still high, but his earlier discomfort had made him reckless. "How dare you treat me like this? It's thanks to me you gained your throne!"

Both Aelfgifu and her husband were momentarily stunned by this show of arrogance. "And how did *you* accomplish this feat?" The king's voice was quiet.

Eadric smiled smugly and crossed his arms over his chest. "By removing Edmund."

"Edmund died of his injuries."

He shook his head. "No, he was recovering." Eadric stopped to take a drink. "It was quite miraculous. Of course his injuries would have bothered him still, but he would have lived. Edmund was taking many potions for his health, it may have been one of these that helped him." He waved a hand airily. "But mayhap his potions had gotten mixed up and instead of curing him they killed him." He held his arms out to the side, as if helpless to explain how a recovering king's health might suddenly fail. Then bowing slightly, he grinned. "All this for you, my lord. I should be rewarded for my service."

Aelfgifu could see how upset Canute was with this new revelation. He was about to speak when a knock on the chamber door drew his attention. A carl entered and approached the king, whispering a brief message in his ear.

"I must attend to this, I'll return shortly." With a nod to Aelfgifu he left the room.

The silence he left behind blanketed the air and Aelfgifu found the room stifling. She looked at the rings on her hand, picked at a thread on her dress sleeve and examined the goblet in front of her; anything to avoid looking at Eadric.

"How are you coping, my dear?"

She shuddered at the sound of his voice, silken yet at the same time mocking. Superior. Aelfgifu looked up but remained silent, glaring at him from the rim of her wine cup. He continued. "How difficult it must be for you, to be cast aside like an old dog."

Aelfgifu gripped the table edge, her knuckles white. Realising her cup was empty, she began to rise but Eadric stopped her with a gesture.

"Let me."

She nodded, watching him silently as he rose to fetch wine from a nearby side table.

"Of course Queen Emma is a beautiful woman. And sophisticated. With a truly pious soul." He turned from the table, wine in hand. "A woman worthy of being a queen." He poured wine for himself before heading over to Aelfgifu's side of the table. "How can the king not have fallen for her?" He reached the end of the table and turned toward her. "And you. What will you do now? Back to your muddy manor I suppose." He sighed, the mocking light in his eyes growing brighter. "What would your father have thought? How disappointed he would have been with you." Eadric was at her side and reached for her cup. He leaned down and his closeness made her stomach lurch. "Perhaps I will visit." He straightened and she felt his eyes crawling over her like a hundred fleas. "You may be able to provide some entertainment, now that the king has no use for you."

Before she could stop herself Aelfgifu leaped to her feet. Her dagger, which a moment ago had been on the table, was now in her hand as if transferred by magic. She rushed forward, arm raised. "This is for my father and brother, you whoreson!"

Eadric had little time to react. She plunged the dagger into his eye. She pulled out the blade and stabbed him in the other eye before taking a step back. Eadric screamed shrilly, waving his arms wildly, grasping the air in front of him, blood running down his face and covering his chest. With a groan he fell, clawing at the ground as he crawled towards her.

Aelfgifu backed away, eyes wide, using the table for

support. After a few steps she stopped. Eadric slumped forward onto the floor. She waited a moment before reaching out to touch him, then stepped back as the chamber door swung open.

"I'm sorry, that took longer than I . . ." Canute stood, open mouthed, taking in the scene before him. Aelfgifu remained silent, standing with her bloodied dagger in hand, waiting for her husband to speak. Slowly he turned towards her. "It would be foolish of me to ask what happened."

"My lord." Aelfgifu approached Canute. "I'm sorry for the trouble this may cause you but I will never be sorry for the act."

Canute glanced down briefly at the body of Eadric before his eyes rested on Aelfgifu again. Smoothing strands of her hair that had escaped her circlet, he placed a kiss on her forehead. "There is no trouble. Streona was a traitor, known through the entire country as one. His death will be unmourned. And no one will learn of the true manner of his passing."

"Thank you, my lord." Leaning over she wiped the blade on Eadric's tunic before handing the dagger to Canute and slowly walking from the room.

Barely a month after her marriage to Canute, Emma's coronation took place with the expected ceremony and pomp. By that time Aelfgifu had taken her sons back to Northampton with her, wanting to be as far away as possible when 'the woman', as Brihtwyn labelled her, gained her crown. She knew the nickname was a reference to Emma's previous title as Aethelred's queen, 'The Lady', but couldn't laugh with Bri when she joked about it. A messenger had arrived from court with the ludicrous demand that Aelfgifu attend the coronation.

"My child is ill and as a good mother I cannot possibly

leave my son." It was a lie but she took pleasure in placing heavy emphasis on the words 'good' and 'mother', for it was common knowledge that Emma treated her own children by the deposed Aethelred with harshness, and she hoped her words would find their way to Emma's ears.

"The queen cares nothing for your child, you must attend."

"No."

She'd sent him away without another word. A week before the coronation, she learned that, while the witan and nobles didn't take her marriage to Canute seriously, Emma herself did. Emma had insisted that the traditional coronation oath be altered in such a way as to ensure any children resulting from the union between Canute and herself be placed before Aelfgifu's sons when it came to succession.

Canute sent Aelfgifu a golden crown with delicately engraved lions playing amidst twisted vines. She knew he meant well but she packed the object away without wearing it, never wanting to be reminded of this day or of 'the woman" who ruined it.

The months passed, pushing the seasons along with them. Aelfgifu rarely saw her husband but he visited when he was able, leaving Emma in London or Winchester with Thorkell nearby to watch her and rule for Canute. She usually had advance notice of a visit from Canute but one night he arrived unexpectedly and with a sense of urgency. Aelfgifu arranged for one of her housecarls to help him with his cloak and boots and ensured there was food and drink for him and all of his men. When they were seated in the main hall and he'd caught his breath, he revealed the reason for his visit. "My brother is dead."

She reached for his hand and squeezed it. He didn't have

a close relationship with his step-brother but they still had great respect for one another despite their differences. "I'm sorry." Death made her uncomfortable; not that she was afraid of it but as with most people she never knew what to say or how to act around people who experienced such loss, even though she herself had suffered through it. Then it dawned on her. "But that means . . ."

He nodded. "Denmark is mine."

Chapter Ten

England, Denmark

Before they left for Denmark there was still much to do in England. Canute's brother, Harald, had left a council of nobles to watch over the affairs of the country and Canute was content to let them rule until he could be there in person to claim his throne. Aelfgifu knew how precious her husband's time had become and was grateful for any moments he could spend with her and their children, even if it meant travelling for days at a time to meet him.

"Eadric had expensive tastes I see." She looked around the main hall of the manor and was astounded to see tapestries and plate to rival a royal household. She hadn't wanted to stay in the man's home, but it was the most convenient location for Canute.

Canute shrugged off his cloak as he gazed around the room. "He must have spent a fortune. I wonder how he could afford so much?"

Aelfgifu frowned. "Perhaps he was over-taxing his tenants."

Her husband nodded his agreement. "I'm certain the old king didn't see half of the money Eadric collected in his name."

She still couldn't believe he was truly gone. "Let's talk about something else. I hate that man, just hearing his name makes me ill."

Canute sat on the bench next to her. "Agreed."

Aelfgifu arranged for food and wine to be brought in; there was no lord or lady here, the lands had belonged to Eadric as Earl of Mercia and, since his death, ownership had remained vacant, with a steward in place to maintain the property. As they sat across from each other and ate, a soft breeze filled the hall with the smell of cut hay and ploughed fields. With their lord gone, many of the servants had found work elsewhere, and the few who did remain were busy performing their duties, leaving the king and his wife in peace. Despite her disdain for the location, Aelfgifu couldn't remember a more perfect day.

"I've called a meeting of the nobles; I'll meet them in Oxford in a few weeks."

Aelfgifu looked up from her meal. Fish, subtly spiced, fresh vegetables and exotic cheese and breads had been prepared for them. Eadric's tastes obviously extended beyond decoration. "What'll you say to them?" She was curious; Canute had many meetings with his council and didn't usually announce the fact. This meeting must be of some import.

"There are two main edicts I wish to present. The first won't be liked." Aelfgifu frowned at this, waiting. "I need to pay my army. Once they're paid, I'll send them home." He shrugged as if this made perfect sense to him. But she suspected there was more. "And the payment will serve as a final punishment to all who opposed me."

Ahh, here was the trouble. "How much will you ask?"

"From the country, 72,000 pounds." He paused.

"And? There is more?"

"And from the Londoners, who caused me and my father the most trouble, a payment of 10,500 pounds will be levied."

"That's a sizeable sum."

"I know, but my men must be paid. And I'll deliver news of the payment in a positive light. I'll tell the nobles that, once payment has been received, there'll never again be a threat of attack from the north."

She nodded. It was a good plan. They'd still complain about the enormity of the tax but weighted against a guarantee of future peace? What logical man couldn't agree with this? "And the other item?"

He smiled. "I've been working with Lupus and together we've determined a way forward with regard to ruling this country."

Aelfgifu recalled that 'Lupus' was the nickname of Wulfstan, the Archbishop of York. "And you're in agreement?" She was surprised; in the past Canute had complained of the arguments between the two of them, particularly in areas of religion.

"We are, for the main. We'll reinstate the laws of King Edgar."

She thought about this, trying to recall any specific laws that might impact her. "How will this affect the country?"

"Not by much. Aethelred had similar rules, passed down from his brother, but many of the laws went unnoticed. Thieves escaped justice more often than not, lords took advantage of the people they were meant to care for and liberties were taken by all in positions of power."

"And this will no longer be the case?"

He shook his head. "No, the laws will be obeyed or there will be strict penalties, more severe than under the old king. Thieves will be pursued and punished, and their victims reimbursed. And those in power will be forced to meet their tenants regularly, with the events at these meetings written down. And they'll be unable to use the law to their own advantage, especially to mistreat poorer men." She could hear the conviction in his voice, along with authority. "There'll be no more abuse of power while I'm king." He ran a hand through his hair, the grey beginning to show. The habit betrayed his feelings, but only to those who knew him well.

"Something else bothers you. What is it?"

He sighed and looked at her, his face bewildered. "It's these men! These bishops and archbishops. Their constant demands! More land, more money, exclusions from the laws that most men are governed under . . ." He threw up his hands.

"There's nothing you can do to placate them? Come to some understanding?"

"I don't know."

She thought for a moment. He must have the support of all men, including the clergy. She'd learned quickly how powerful these men were. "Perhaps you should make overtures to them?"

His head turned swiftly. "What do you mean? What overtures?"

"Is there nothing you can give them?"

Canute snorted. "They're getting enough with these new laws. Wulfstan made sure his legal suggestions were included."

"That's not what I meant."

"Then what?" She could hear the exasperation in his voice.

"Give them gifts. They may be holy men but they're still men and all men are greedy."

"Most of these men are as wealthy as I, despite their vows of poverty. And they have more plate and baubles than many a king in Europe."

Aelfgifu thought. "Then land. Not to govern on your behalf, but to own in their own right."

After a moment of silence he nodded his head. "Yes, that's possible."

"Aethelred used the ploy often enough." He frowned; she knew he didn't like being compared with the old king but his face showed he accepted the practicality of what she was suggesting. She continued. "Begin with the Archbishop of Canterbury, Lyfing. The town suffered much during your father's attacks, it would be a show of good faith to both the archbishop and the people."

He was silent for a moment. "There is a parcel of land in

Sussex, it's barely a copse of trees and means little enough to me but it borders Lyfing's own lands."

She smiled her agreement and they spoke more about the Oxford meeting as they ate. The late summer greens were crisp and fresh, the cold roast boar still tender and earthy. Aelfgifu swallowed a mouthful of local cheese and closed her eyes, enjoying the calm. An abrupt thought occurred to her. "Will Emma be there?" She studied the design on her knife, trying to appear uninterested. In private, she and her aunt still referred to Emma as 'the woman' but Canute didn't know this, or if he did he was gracious enough not to mention it.

"No, she'll remain at her estates in Exeter, where she usually stays." Aelfgifu looked up, aware that her expression betrayed her relief. Canute leaned forward and took her hand. "And where she buys plate and tapestries and gossips with her ladies."

She knew he said these things to make her feel better and today the food, wine and atmosphere had put her into a good mood. This time she believed him.

Not long after Canute's meeting at Oxford, Emma gave birth to a son. Aelfgifu had known the woman was with child but the announcement of the boy made it real. When she heard the news, her jealousy flared like an all-engulfing fire, no matter how much she tried to rationalise the event. She had recently returned to her own manor and as she stormed around the place, barking orders and making demands, more vengeful thoughts came creeping into her mind, soothing the jealousy, wrapping it in a protective cloak. She'd hoped Emma would suffer some mishap during her pregnancy, and that the child would be lost. Now she wished harm upon the boy himself. She fought the guilt these thoughts brought on but allowed herself the luxury of imagining, for a brief moment, that only *her* sons succeeded their father, that there were no other claimants to Canute's legacy. But this was no longer true and she directed her thoughts back to reality, no matter how painful. Emma's two boys by her first husband, Aethelred, had already been hastened out of the country and sent to Normandy to live with Emma's relatives, hardly surprising as all knew Emma had no love for them. But this new child was different; his birthright had been assured by Emma during her coronation, with words she herself had composed, before he'd even been conceived.

Someday Aelfgifu would have to fight for her sons, hers and Canute's, she knew that. Today was not that day. She went to their chamber and stood gazing at them. Sweyn was growing fast, he'd be a large man like his namesake; at three he already towered over the other children at Reodfeld. And Harold, who she'd delivered nearly two years ago, was a thin, thoughtful boy, his speech already surpassing that of his elder brother. Unable to bear the emotion, she collapsed next to their bed and cried, weeping silently.

"You've been avoiding me."

The creaking of the boat's planks as it bucked the waves soothed Aelfgifu. She waved a hand. "I've been busy, my lord." She stood at the stern, feeling the sting of the salt water. Around them Canute's men and her own servants and carls sat amongst her crated belongings. It was the first time she'd seen her husband since news of Emma's son had arrived.

"So busy you've had no time to speak with me since my arrival?"

She avoided his gaze, instead focussing on the shrinking shores of her homeland. "I didn't want to disturb you. I worked with Thorkell in arranging our voyage."

"Thorkell was as busy as I. He'll govern England in my stead while I'm away, yet you saw fit to interrupt him?"

She stared out at sea until he forced himself into her view. Irritated by his questioning and lack of understanding, she turned on him. "You've had a child with another woman!"

She saw the frustration on his face and was surprised he controlled his voice. "I'm the king. I must be seen to be doing my duty."

"And that includes rutting with your new wife." She noticed a few of the men turn to glance at her before turning back to their own business.

"That's unfair, Aelfgifu. It's not like that and you know it."

"Then tell me what it's like because I no longer know."

Canute put his hands on either side of her face. "It's you I love but I must keep peace in the country. Everything I do is to obtain this goal, and all will benefit." He took her chin and lifted her face so she looked at him. "Including our sons." The hood of her cloak had fallen, leaving her skin to the mercy of the harsh spraying salt water. Canute reached over and lifted the hood back onto her head. "Think of it. Our boys will grow up in a country unaffected by war and fighting. Think how prosperous and content they'll be."

She knew he was right, as usual. It didn't make these facts of her life any easier to bear. "What's the child's name?"

She watched his face redden. "Harthacanute."

She nodded. An ancestral name. Sighing she walked to the prow of the ship, where she could focus her attention forward, rather than backwards.

Their arrival in Denmark was marked with much celebration, with many Danish nobles there to welcome them. It took much longer to unload the ships this time than on their last visit when she'd only been permitted to take a single chest, a few pieces of jewellery and her favourite servants.

As if reading her mind, Bri came up beside her, breathing hard at the exertion. "It's a different scene before us this time, isn't it?"

Aelfgifu nodded and took her hand. "Last time there was no one here to greet us except for my brother-in-law's guards, and only one cart was needed for my belongings."

"And now look! People are pleased you've arrived."

"I'm certain they are. With the recent troubles they're grateful that a true leader has finally come." One reason for their visit was for Canute to claim his throne, now empty for nearly half a year. Harald's advisors had shown themselves to be as ineffectual and greedy as most, and Canute was disgusted when messengers delivered tales of their mismanagement. Because of their poor rule and inattention to even the most basic details of governing, neighbouring countries had started to cause trouble on the Danish borders. This was the second reason for their visit: to take back complete control of Canute's homeland.

Aelfgifu immediately took charge of running the Danish court, organising the cleaning of all the rooms and the distribution of chambers to all who had arrived with them from England. The palace was in a terrible state. The rushes in the dining hall contained layers of old food and bones, creating a foul odour throughout the corridors. She arranged for all of the floors to be cleaned down to the flagstones, then new rushes mixed with fragrant herbs scattered once more to keep the cold of the floor from chilling the room. The old material was taken outside and burned, the servants assigned this task wearing scarves across their mouths and noses to block out the smell. Aelfgifu stopped to think of her last visit. She'd faced an uncertain future but she was happy. It was a simpler time, or so it seemed to her, and one she missed. Now her life was filled with complications and her feelings had become unpredictable. For now, though, there was much to keep her thoughts occupied and she took advantage of the work to stop her from dwelling too much on sad topics. Besides, they were in Denmark and there was no other wife or children here of Canute's except for herself and her sons.

Aelfgifu, with Bri's help, had finally managed to restore the Danish court to a semblance of normality; all signs of the neglect left behind by the old council now gone. Every room in the palace had been aired and sweetened, clean bedding had been placed on every bed and all surfaces had been scrubbed. The kitchen had been the worst task; thankfully there were many hands to help with the cleaning and organising. Once fresh supplies had been brought in, Aelfgifu began to relax and enjoy her surroundings. Canute had been attentive since their journey over from England, ensuring she wanted for nothing.

"You had another private dinner with your husband last night?" Brihtwyn squinted her eyes to see the needle she was threading. Her focus might be on her sewing but her voice betrayed her interest.

"Yes, we dined in his rooms." Before her aunt could ask, she replied. "Alone."

"And you had a good meal?"

Aelfgifu smiled. She knew the details the older woman wanted to hear. "It was a very good meal, yes. Well prepared and pleasantly seasoned." She made her next stitch, ignoring the annoyed look that began to play on Bri's face.

"I imagine you spoke of events in the kingdom?"

She decided to end her aunt's frustration. "Yes, we did. Then my husband presented me with a beautiful ring," she lifted her hand "and took me to his bed." She found her aunt was getting less delicate these past few years and hoped this would suffice.

Bri laughed, a hoarse croaking that made her sound like a squawking bird. The noise alarmed Aelfgifu and she stared at the older woman. The last crossing had been difficult for Bri. She'd caught a fever and it had taken an unusually long time for her to recover. Even when her aunt swore she was better, Aelfgifu could see that she still struggled, sitting down to catch her breath when she thought her niece wasn't looking. "Aunt, you're ill!"

The older woman dismissed the comment with a wave of her hand. "No, no, I'm well enough." Aelfgifu wasn't convinced and frowned at her aunt, prompting Bri to continue. "Too much strange food is all, and this Danish air, it's different from England."

"Aunt . . ." Aelfgifu could see there was more.

Brihtwyn deflected further questions by asking about the rebels. "I hear tell there are a group of men who defy your husband's rule."

Aelfgifu nodded; although still worried about Bri she knew there was no arguing with the woman, a quality she herself had inherited. "Yes, Canute leaves tomorrow with his men, they're prepared to fight if need be." Her stomach knotted as she spoke.

"He'll succeed; he's favoured by the gods."

She sighed. Her aunt was right but she couldn't help her feelings.

Bri, as she was always could, guessed Aelfgifu's thoughts. "You needn't be fearful, Canute's a good ruler and a skilled fighter. All will be well."

"I wish I could be as confident as you. Every time he goes to battle I worry I'll be left without him. And now . . ."

Her aunt finished her sentence. "And now there are two of you, two queens."

Yes, there were two of them: herself and Emma. And they both had borne Canute's children. But only one of their marriages had the approval of the most important men in England.

"Emma's children would inherit everything. My sons, and myself, we'd be abandoned." She dropped her head.

Bri turned in her chair and Aelfgifu felt her aunt's gaze. "It's you here now, not Emma. Canute chose you to accompany him to his homeland." Abandoning her chair, Bri kneeled before her niece. "All know you're his favourite. Including Emma."

Aelfgifu looked up. "How do you know this?"

"She tells all who will listen how inspired she is by the excellence of her husband and that Canute rejoices in their union, he is so pleased with her compared to other women of his acquaintance."

Aelfgifu stood suddenly and began pacing. "How dare she speak these words?"

Bri rose, struggling. "By repeating these lies she tries to convince all, including herself." Aelfgifu felt her aunt's hands on her shoulders and was soon facing the woman. "No one believes her except the bishops, who are easily convinced in this matter."

She allowed herself to be led back to the chair by her aunt but sat stiffly, still furious. "It was probably their idea, these holy men! They hate me!" She turned to Bri. "Did you know they even added a new law while in Oxford? That a man may not marry if he already has a wife. The law states that he must formally cast the first wife aside before being allowed to join with another."

Bri had known this. "Canute signed the law but so far has shown no sign of abiding by it. It's a clear sign of his preference for you. And also a clear sign to the bishops of his intention to continue loving you."

The flame that was Aelfgifu's anger was now replaced by one of hope. She nodded and began to believe again.

Chapter Eleven

Denmark

It was a relief to Aelfgifu, and the court, that Canute was easily able to defeat those who opposed him. He returned in triumph, his mud-splattered men following and grinning as the court came out to greet them. As they entered the great hall, Aelfgifu was there to receive the king.

"My lord, welcome back." She curtsied deeply and felt his hands on her shoulders, pulling her back up. She smiled; after all their years together she found it amusing that Canute was still uncomfortable when she was formal with him.

"My lady, I thank you for your greeting."

She wasn't surprised by his brevity; he wasn't one for long flowery speeches. Stepping forward, she addressed the hall. "There will be a banquet this evening, to celebrate our king's victory and the peace that continues to reign in Denmark!"

The hall erupted into cheers and people started streaming out of the room. Canute's men remained, waiting by the king. "You're dismissed. Go," he waved a hand at them, "clean yourselves up, bed your wives and prepare for tonight!" The men grinned and, shoving each other in jest, left the hall. Canute motioned one to stay behind.

"Aelfgifu, I wish you to meet someone." He looked over at the young man who stepped forward. "This is Godwin. He has proved himself most valuable in battle and I've made him one of my housecarls."

Aelfgifu smiled at the man and offered her hand. "You're welcome, Godwin of . . . ?" she looked at Canute.

She felt the roughness of his skin as he took her hand and kissed it, his eyes looking directly into hers. "Just Godwin, my lady." She turned to the man and, frowning, snatched her hand back. She was not used to being so directly addressed by a stranger. Looking him up and down, she could see that his clothing and armour, though well cared for, were not well made. Added to this, his forward behaviour and lack of name, and she knew immediately that his background was of a working family, one of the many men whose ancestors had helped shape the country.

Stepping back, he bowed, the hint of a grin on his face. When he straightened his expression was smooth but there was a light in his eyes, as though he found something amusing.

"We must get ready for the feast!" Canute nodded at Aelfgifu and left the hall, Godwin laughing and joking beside him.

The banquet was spoken of for days afterwards and Aelfgifu was glad, as it took her mind off the seemingly constant presence of her husband's new carl, Godwin. Not that there was anything wrong with the man, quite the opposite. After his initial blunder when they'd first met, the young man had been polite and respectful every time she'd encountered him. But he was always with Canute, even when her husband came to meet with her. She was looking forward to dining alone with Canute that night; it had been a long while since they'd had any privacy.

She arrived at her husband's room expecting to see an intimate table set for two with perhaps a few servants to aid them should it be needed. Instead she found her husband already engaged in an animated conversation with one of his carls. As she approached the table she recognised Godwin. She controlled her disappointment but couldn't keep the bitterness from her voice. "Husband, I thought we were dining alone this evening."

Canute looked up, startled. Rising quickly he went to her side. "My lady, I didn't hear you enter. I'm glad you're here at last." He guided her to a chair across from the young man and sat back at the head of the table.

Aelfgifu smoothed her dress and made herself comfortable before pouring some wine. She sipped, relishing the tangy taste. "What were you both so excited about that you didn't even notice a woman had arrived?" She tried to lighten her voice but couldn't disguise her disappointment.

Canute noticed her tone and reached over to take her hand, squeezing hard. It was his way of apologising and she showed her acceptance by bringing his hand to her mouth and kissing it. He squeezed again briefly before letting go. "I apologise, my lady, we were talking of the recent battle." He held up his cup. "And of Godwin's deeds." Nodding at the man, he drank his toast.

Addressing Godwin she smiled politely. "Your feats must indeed be great, to occupy the king's attention so."

The young man smiled and almost looked embarrassed. "It was nothing, my lady, I was better placed than others at that moment."

Aelfgifu leaned forward. "I'm intrigued! Tell me, what moment was that?" She knew Canute would recognise the teasing quality in her voice and knew that he shared in her sense of fun and would say nothing.

Godwin, emboldened by the wine and his attentive audience, threw himself into the story. "My lady, let me tell you of savage lands and dangerous men. We spent days traversing through dense forest, our goal a group of men in the south who stood against the king." He took another long drink from his cup before continuing. "We discovered where these men were camping and hid in the forest not far from them. We settled ourselves for the night but I was restless and decided to sneak away with a few men, to scout the enemy camp, perhaps discover something we could use to our advantage." Despite her earlier mood Aelfgifu found herself interested in the man's story. His plate was empty and she signalled for a servant to bring over a platter of beef. Once he'd taken a few bites of the meat he continued. "We expected them to be asleep and hoped to probe the outer limits of their camp, but when we arrived we found them fully awake and preparing to attack the king as he slept."

Without thinking her hand flew to her mouth. "What did you do?"

"I gathered those I had brought with me and explained the significance of our discovery, for many of them didn't realise what was happening. Then I placed them around the enemy camp, bidding them hide until I gave the call. Once we were ready, I signalled to them by banging my sword on my shield, hoping the noise would also startle the enemy and give us an advantage. As it was we attacked with such speed and force, and were so unexpected, that the camp fell without the loss of any of my men. We took a good many men prisoner that night."

Aelfgifu noticed that he started referring to the other warriors as 'his' men but kept her comments to herself. "You tell a good story of a daring deed. I understand why my husband is so grateful to you."

Godwin bowed his head at her compliment. "Any one of the king's men would have acted so, my lady."

She waved the modesty away with her hand. "Still, you've shown your bravery and loyalty, these are qualities much admired by my husband. And myself." He bowed his head again. He had a pleasing appearance, was young and there was a light of intelligence in his eyes. This was a dangerous combination, for those looking for a leader, someone to follow, would easily submit to Godwin's charms. She wondered where he'd come from. She changed the topic. "Who are your parents?"

Godwin shook his head. "No one of consequence, my lady. My father was called Wulfnoth, he was a minor thegn in Sussex, my home. My mother died when I was young, I didn't know her." Aelfgifu sensed he didn't wish to tell her more and couldn't blame the man; she herself had suffered the same loss and understood the pain speaking of it caused. "My father is descended from the first Aethelred, King of Wessex."

She smiled; it was a claim made by many, for who wouldn't want to believe their family came from the great rulers of Wessex? "And have you a wife?"

Godwin looked over to Canute, remaining silent. "Godwin will marry my sister-in-law Gytha." She'd heard nothing of this; Canute must have made this decision recently. She had to think for a moment to remember the woman. Canute's sister was married to a man named Ulf, a Dane who Canute intended to leave in charge when they returned to England. Ulf's sister was Gytha, the woman who was to marry Godwin. "I've never met her."

"It's an honour for me, my lady. I don't know how to thank the king for the great generosity and favour he shows me."

It was an honour, perhaps more than the young man realised. But she knew what this man wanted. She didn't trust anyone who rose to power and wealth quickly; they never seemed to be satisfied with their lot; she had learned this well enough from Eadric. Perhaps Godwin would change her mind.

Chapter Twelve
England

Early in 1019, Aelfgifu and Canute returned to England. Ulf, Canute's brother-in-law, was left in charge of Denmark and had provided them with an enormous feast and expensive gifts to see them on their way. It was a smooth crossing with favourable winds, and Aelfgifu had been able to spend the time admiring the presents Ulf had given them, especially the bolts of silk from lands far to the east. Even Canute had been impressed with these, if a little suspicious of how his brother-in-law could afford material of such expense, usually reserved for royalty.

The sailing might have been calm, but Aelfgifu was still glad when they reached land, for Bri had not had such an easy time. She'd never quite recovered from the previous crossing, and this trip home had made her illness worse. But any attempts at aiding her were met with scorn; Brihtwyn would accept no help, vigorously insisting she was well. There was nothing for Aelfgifu to do but keep a close eye on her aunt.

Thankfully much of her time was spent administering Canute's affairs in the north of England. He returned to court in London, as was expected of the king. She couldn't help but feel proud that Canute trusted her, while Emma was left with a minder in the shape of Thorkell the Tall.

Aelfgifu remained in the north when the marriage ceremony between Godwin and Gytha, took place. She'd been invited, indeed even encouraged to attend by Canute, but she just couldn't bear to be in the same room as Emma, whom she knew would also be present. She received a report that described the occasion as lavish and expensive, beyond the means of one such as Godwin and suspected her husband had a hand in paying for the celebration.

"It was a Christian ceremony." She was sitting on a bench in the garden with Brihtwyn, watching the servants tend the garden. Summer in the north of England was a magical time, Aelfgifu's favourite, and she enjoyed the hot sun and smell of fresh earth. She gently swatted a bee away, guiding it back in the direction of the hives behind the manor.

Her aunt had been dozing on the bench and started at her niece's voice. "Aye, so I heard."

"They're all Christian marriages, these days." Aelfgifu reached down and plucked a dandelion from the grass.

"Most follow the Christian faith."

"But what of the old gods?" There was a church in her village, and a priest, but she didn't attend and wasn't thought poorly of for it. There was still an accepted mix of old and new faith in the north and no one was looked down on for their beliefs. But in the south, where politics were more important than faith, Christianity had taken a firm hold long ago. Deep down she knew it was a good thing for her country, for most of Europe was now Christian and would prefer to trade with other Christian nations. What she couldn't understand were the strong feelings and hurtful comments made about her own faith.

Bri turned toward her, fatigue in her eyes. She seemed smaller, frailer these past few weeks. But her voice still held authority and wisdom. "The old makes way for the new, it's the way of the world."

She took her aunt's hand, shivering at the words. They sat in silence, enjoying the quiet of the garden. But even the warmth of a summer sun couldn't rid her of the coldness that now spread through her body as she felt Bri's grip on her hand weaken.

It was late in the harvest season and Aelfgifu had been up since dawn, supervising the activities. The remainder of the crops had to be brought in from the fields, pigs had to be slaughtered and salted for the coming winter, feathers from the geese collected to stuff pillows – there was much to do and the day was a long one. She'd just collapsed into bed when a maid came to summon her.

"It can wait, I'll take care of whatever it is in the morning." She waved her hand at the short woman in dismissal.

"You must come, my lady! It's your aunt."

Aelfgifu was immediately awake, exhaustion forgotten. Jumping from the bed, she grabbed her robe and hurried from the room, the small maid trying to help her dress as they walked. Bri's chamber was only a short distance from her own and she was still barely dressed when she arrived in her aunt's room. The windows were all open, allowing the cool autumn breeze into the room. A few candles were lit and she grabbed one as she approached the older woman's bed.

"Niece." A thin hand lifted itself from the covers.

"Bri, I'm here." Her aunt struggled to raise herself into a sitting position. "Lie still. Is there anything you need?"

Heavy breathing accompanied the reply. "No, there's nothing."

She looked around the room at the servants who had gathered. "Has the healer been summoned?" She directed the question at the room.

"No." Her aunt's hoarse voice drew her attention back. "There's nothing that can be done for me."

"But Bri . . ."

"I'm old." Bri relaxed back into the bed, the effort of speaking having exhausted her. Her aunt had spoken of this only a few months ago, about the old being replaced by the new. Aelfgifu had known then that Brihtwyn was not much longer for this world, although she fought to ignore her feelings. But the thought of not having her aunt was too painful; the ache that pierced her chest was almost unbearable. "I'm sorry I've not spent more time with you, I've been so busy with the harvest . . ." Even as she spoke the words, she felt ashamed.

"You're a strong woman and a good wife," Bri said, struggling for breath. "Your husband . . . is proud of you. And the work you do for him." She paused, gathering her strength. "I see it in his eyes when he looks at you."

"Is there nothing I can do?" Aelfgifu took her aunt's hands and was shocked at how thin and delicate they were. How had things gone so far without her noticing? Or had she merely been fooling herself?

"Stay with me, child. I'd sleep a while."

Aelfgifu waved away the servants until they were alone in the room. Lighting a candle infused with lavender, she placed it on the small table beside Brihtwyn's bed and blew the others out. Then she closed the shutters. Her aunt seemed to rest easier in the dark. She sat and watched the only mother she'd ever known, grateful that Bri was able to sleep but still regretful of the time she should have spent with her aunt over the last few months.

Aelfgifu wondered if she should get another blanket and looked around the room. Then, tucking the existing sheet tighter, decided it was warm enough, despite the sharpness that came with early Autumn. Was it too warm? She placed a hand on the side of her aunt's face. No, Bri was fine. She walked around the room, stretching her arms above her head, feeling the movement after sitting for so long. She only left the room to relieve herself, asking that all visitors be sent away and all her business be brought to her in Bri's room. But just as she couldn't work on the charters and letters that demanded her attention, nor could she eat the food that the servants brought her.

She lit another candle, ignoring the expense she knew her aunt would complain of had she been better. The thought of Bri complaining about the monks and what she claimed was their exorbitant pricing of candles made her smile. Aelfgifu continued her vigil at Bri's bedside, watching her chest rise and fall beneath the covers, soothed by the movement. Aelfgifu breathed deeply. She was tired, and the exhaustion caused her thoughts to wander to her childhood, and Bri's mothering. Happier, more carefree days.

Her throat tightened. "Please don't leave me," she whispered. "I still need you."

She leaned forward and laid her head on her arms, beside her aunt, careful not to disturb the sleeping woman. "I'm just going to close my eyes for a moment."

When Aelfgifu woke the sun was up and she could hear movement in other parts of the manor. Remembering where she was she sat up, feeling an ache throughout her body. Turning to her aunt, she placed her hand on Bri's. It was cold.

"Bri!"

She watched as her aunt's chest rose one last time before falling still, her last breath escaping to join the cool air that warned of winter.

It had been nearly a year since Aelfgifu had last seen her husband; the business of running two countries took him away from her for longer and longer periods of time. So when the opportunity to be with him presented itself she hurried to meet him.

"I am sorry. About Bri. I know how much she meant to you." Canute took her hand as they walked around the grounds.

Aelfgifu smiled grimly. Despite the time that had passed since Bri's death, she still missed her aunt terribly. She squeezed his forearm in thanks for his sympathy and they continued towards the door of the hunting lodge. She'd received a message a few days earlier that she was to join her husband there. "She was a good woman." Aelfgifu had lost count of the number of times she'd used that expression to describe her aunt, so many that it now came automatically. It had just been too painful to speak of her, and the short summary, used as acknowledgement whenever any expressed their sympathy, seemed to suffice. She lived among practical people and thoughts or discussions about death were not expected or encouraged.

They entered the building and were helped with their cloaks and boots by silent servants. The hunting lodge was one of the only places Canute could meet with her in complete privacy; even the number of servants with them was minimal. There was no court here, no prying eyes or disapproving looks, only Aelfgifu and her husband. And while most of his visits, infrequent as they were, were used to complain about court, she was happy to provide a safe haven for the king. She was the only one who could. They went to the small hall where a simple lunch of bread, cheese, pork and ale had been laid out for them.

Aelfgifu wanted to avoid speaking further about her aunt and tried to lighten the mood. "How is Thorkell? Does he find it terrible living in London?"

Canute laughed. "He's well. Emma tries to befriend him at every turn and he tolerates her attempts. She finds it frustrating that he won't succumb to her charms, yet she keeps trying."

Aelfgifu smiled; it always made her happy, if slightly wicked, to hear of the woman's foolish antics.

"And Thorkell hasn't found a wife?"

Canute snorted. "Oh, he has a wife. A piece of work she is too." He shook his head. "No, he's better off as far away from her as possible."

"Too bad. Is there no one in London to keep him company?"

"No respectable woman will come near while Emma hovers so close." He waved a hand. "It's unfortunate, but I need him there, someone must keep that woman from trying to rule."

"Poor man."

"Hah! 'Poor man' nothing, he has female company when he needs it and is handsomely rewarded for his service. Did I not make him an earl?"

They discussed all manner of topics, Aelfgifu keeping the conversation light until she was sure Canute had relaxed.

"Tell me of your recent visit to Denmark."

Canute shook his head. "That brother-in-law of mine, Ulf, is just as incapable as I suspected." He took a drink of ale. "But what choice did I have? He was popular with the people, and he's a relative."

"What happened?"

"More trouble in the south, something that should have been quelled easily."

She nodded. "I saw a copy of the letter you sent, addressing the country." She speared a bit of pork with her knife. "There were many references to the Christian god in it."

He sighed. "I included them to satisfy the bishops."

She could see by his face that there was more, and that it bothered him. "And did it work?"

"No! These men and their religion, they only think in one way, no one dares to suggest otherwise." He slammed his cup down on the table.

Aelfgifu thought for a moment, an idea forming. "You should found a church."

He frowned. "Why would I do such a thing?"

"It would make the bishops happy, both to see evidence that their king follows the same path as they, but also for the revenue the new church will bring them."

He nodded, seeing the wisdom. "But isn't it surrender? Am I not giving in to them?"

She smiled. "No. You'll build this new church at Assandun."

He laughed and banged his hand on the table. It was an ingenious idea. A new church would satisfy the bishops but the location would remind all that Canute had gained his crown on that very spot. "You're more clever than any of the men in my council, I'm glad you fight for me and not for my enemies!"

She kissed his hand before reaching for her own cup. Canute leaned back, a smile playing on the edges of his mouth. He nodded, the small move more telling than any praise. Aelfgifu sipped her own ale, a smile hidden behind her goblet. She sat straighter in her chair and regarded the man she adored, feeling the pride and pleasure of knowing that only she could help him so.

In the summer of 1020, news arrived that Emma had given birth to a baby girl, named Gunhild. Saddened by the news, Aelfgifu spent the day with her own sons. She'd always wanted a girl of her own but despite the intensity of their marriage and their lovemaking, she'd not been with child since Harold was born. Instead of letting it wear her down, she accepted it as her wyrd, the path that fate had set for her.

Through the next year, Canute remained in the country and Aelfgifu was able to see him more often, as he made frequent visits to her and their sons. He began to take an interest in the boys' education and hired a tutor for them, as well as a sword master to teach them the art of war. Aelfgifu argued that they were too young at five and four, but Canute insisted that he was younger when he learned to hold his first weapon; besides, they were princes, and should be taught accordingly. She kept her other comments to herself;

one of her main worries was what would happen to her and her sons should any harm come to Canute, as she was still seen as the king's mistress by most at court, instead of his true wife. She'd even heard a rumour, difficult to ignore, that Emma had threatened to withhold gifts to the church unless Canute abandoned Aelfgifu. But her husband had explained that Emma was jealous of their relationship, one that Canute would never abandon, and when this ploy failed her, Emma would turn her attention to something else.

She was watching Sweyn and Harold practising with their teacher when a messenger arrived from London. Taking the letter, she dismissed the man, sending him to the kitchen for a meal, before sitting in the main hall with her new maid, a young woman named Lufu. Canute had brought her with him at his last visit, the daughter of some nobleman trying to ingratiate himself at court. Despite her age (she'd been told Lufu was seventeen) the girl surprised Aelfgifu; she was a hard worker and an intelligent companion.

"Come. Pour me wine and sit while I read." She pointed at a jug that sat on a side table, not caring what it contained. Lufu rushed to do her mistress' bidding and Aelfgifu was barely aware when the girl sat across from her at the table. It was a brief letter, written by Canute, but the words held tremendous import. "Thorkell and my husband have had a fight." All of the important people, both at Reodfeld and at court, had been explained and described to Lufu, who asked a few reasonable questions before showing she remembered all she'd been told.

"What about, my lady?"

Aelfgifu read the letter again, slower this time. "Thorkell's eldest son has been murdered, apparently at the hands of his wife. She has been accused of being a witch by the authorities in Denmark, but Thorkell denies it, saying his enemies are to blame. My husband has never liked Thorkell's wife, he believes she is grasping and greedy.

Canute and Thorkell were having dinner in private and my husband tried to persuade his friend to abandon his wife, who he believes killed the son, telling him it was the right decision." She took a drink before continuing.

"Thorkell became upset and rather than listen to his liege lord, argued back. The situation escalated and Thorkell accused Canute of abandoning his true religion, of being too keen to accept Christianity." Aelfgifu knew that Thorkell hid his beliefs while in the company of the court, but in private he spoke freely of his faith in the old gods.

"My husband says Thorkell didn't believe that the new churches and land granted to the bishops were to merely placate them, and that Thorkell said they were an affront to the All Father."

"What did the king do?"

She pursed her lips. "He says he tried to explain to Thorkell but the man wouldn't listen. He accused Canute of betraying his ancestry and his past and told the king that he may as well have been born in England."

Lufu gasped. "My lady . . ."

They were both aware of how proud Canute was of his Danish ancestry, and to even hint of anything contrary to that was the gravest of insults.

"The letter continues. Thorkell told Canute that he'd become soft, that his honour and his family were forgotten while his efforts to please the Christians took over everything he did."

Lufu's eyes widened, a single word escaping her. "Oh."

"It was too much. Thorkell, once my husband's good friend and teacher, has been made outlaw, and is now banished from England."

Chapter Thirteen
England

The news of Thorkell's banishment was met with mixed reactions. In the north, where many knew of the friendship between the huge Dane and the king, there was sorrow that such a partnership had been broken. But in the south, where Thorkell had been an object of mistrust, the announcement that he'd fled the country left many overjoyed, none more so than Emma. Aelfgifu received stories of a grand feast that Emma had arranged to celebrate what she saw as her freedom, for no more would she be watched and guided like a child. It amused Aelfgifu that in a few weeks, unbeknownst to Emma, Godwin would arrive to take Thorkell's place as her minder.

A year came and went, accompanied by all of the duties and responsibilities Canute had entrusted to her in managing the north. There were regular meetings between lords and thegns, as per Canute's new laws, and these gatherings alone added additional items to the already large list of things that needed to be done. Taxes had to be calculated, collected and tallied, farms needed to be tended, harvests brought in and tithes paid to local churches. Meetings needed to be held to hear the law spoken and witness the guilty receive their due for crimes both large and small – it seemed the list grew longer each year. There were also guests to see to, sometimes from the court in London, but often a guest from Europe would visit. On these occasions Aelfgifu would host a lavish banquet, in the large hall that Reodfeld boasted. She was certain that, for many of the European guests, meeting her would be distasteful; the churchmen had labelled her Canute's mistress, but never within the king's hearing. So it was always a surprise to have

Canute send these men to her, and even more pleasant when they accepted her; she was grateful for the support, even if ultimately these visitors always wanted something from her husband. Soon the days were once more at their shortest and the wind at its sharpest. Aelfgifu and Lufu sat beside a large fire in her chambers, embroidering a new tapestry. It was to be a gift for Canute, and depicted the story of his conquest of England.

"Where is your husband at present, my lady?"

Aelfgifu frowned as she concentrated on the miniscule stitching. "He travels to the Isle of Wight with his men." Her face relaxed as she looked up. Examining Lufu's work, she was impressed yet again with the girl's skills. "He's gone to meet with Thorkell."

Lufu's eyes widened. "Why?" The girl immediately looked down, her cheeks colouring.

Aelfgifu had grown fond of the young woman and formalities were dropped when they were alone. She shook her head. "I don't know, perhaps to offer Thorkell payment." At Lufu's raised eyebrow she continued.

"Thorkell is a decent man, and not likely to attack England. However even decent men need to eat and clothe themselves and to do this they need gold." She stopped, focussing on another stitch. A moment later she continued.

"Or maybe they'll meet to reconcile." She waved a hand, her movement restricted by the needle she held, still attached to the tapestry by a deep blue thread. "He didn't say when he left, I think perhaps he'd not come to a decision yet." She pulled the needle through the heavy material and leaned forward, biting through the thread. Putting the needle in its case, she saw that Lufu still looked concerned. The young woman was clever but she had little experience of the ways of men and the court, despite her privileged upbringing.

"You needn't worry yourself. Canute will do what is best

for his realm, both for Denmark and England." Aelfgifu spoke these words with utter conviction, knowing them to be true.

The ground was still frozen when Aelfgifu travelled north to attend a scheduled meeting with Canute's thegns a few months later. As the king's representative in the north, she had full authority to act on his behalf. Canute was still on the Isle of Wight, but she'd received word that he would be returning soon and she was eager to hear how his meeting with Thorkell had gone.

Her own meeting had been announced well in advance and the hall was filled with men of all states and statures. There were the usual issues to resolve: money, land and crimes, but Aelfgifu was relieved there was nothing major to concern her; everything could be dealt with from here, on this visit. Her thoughts wandered back to her own manor and the many tasks that awaited her return. There were still repairs to make around the property, work best done during the winter months when crops didn't need attention. Fences, troughs, even some of the houses needed work.

"My lady?"

Her attention was drawn to the floor in front of her where a middle-aged man, slight of build but with a strong jaw and vivid hazel eyes, was twisting his leather cap tightly in his hands. "Yes . . ." She didn't know his name.

"Hoffsson, my lady. I'm known as 'Hof' and I'm a tenant. Our thegn wasn't able to attend the meeting and sent me in his place."

Aelfgifu made a mental note to find out who the absent thegn was, for all were required to attend these meetings. Should they have a legitimate reason for missing a meeting, they were to send a messenger or letter to Aelfgifu, not send another in their place with no warning. She frowned. She wanted to ask Hof why his thegn couldn't come to the meeting, but it was growing late and people needed to get back to their homes. Irritated, she forced a smile. "What can the crown do for you?"

The man dipped his head before speaking, his grasp on his hat betraying his nerves. "My lady, I've come to discuss the matter of taxes with you."

Even the whispered conversations in the room stopped when the man spoke. No one but nobles spoke of taxes in the presence of the king or his representative; it was the way of things.

"State your case." Aelfgifu knew she could probably do nothing for the man, but it was her duty to listen to all who came here to seek her counsel or justice.

Hof stood quietly for a moment. As if coming to a decision, he stood straighter and Aelfgifu could see that he was taller than he'd first appeared.

"My lady, I understand that taxes must be paid, but we don't understand why we must pay twice."

Aelfgifu frowned. "I don't know what you mean. You don't pay twice."

Hof shook his head. "My lady, I don't wish to be disrespectful or to contradict you but those of us living along the border between the north and south of the country are often forced to pay twice: once to the men you send, and again to the men Queen Emma sends."

The hall erupted in noise, as if a sudden thunderstorm had started. Aelfgifu winced at the mention of the name, and glanced over at Lufu, who stood silently at the side of the dais. Taking a breath she raised a hand and waited until the hall was quiet once more.

"If what you say is true, this is a gross misuse of power and authority. Have you any proof?" She already believed what the man said, it was just the sort of thing Emma would do, but there was a protocol to follow.

"Yes, my lady." He waved to another man, motioning him forward. "This is my friend Egil, he also lives along the border but in the next village over."

Aelfgifu was surprised to find that this second man, Egil, looked remarkably like the first, so much so they could be brothers. It must be their clothing, she thought. Most men in this area dress alike: woollen tunics and trousers with a wool cloak to keep out the cold. She caught a flash from one of the men's cloaks and nodded slightly. Even their plain silver cloak pins are alike in design.

"He's here as witness to these additional taxes." Hof stood aside, bowing and interrupting her thoughts.

"Speak your piece."

"Lady, it's as Hof said. We're paying your men as required but also men that . . ." he stopped. She saw his face wrinkle in concentration before relaxing again. "Men that are sent from the south."

Aelfgifu nodded at the man and watched him sink back into the crowd at the edges of the hall. This was hardly proof. Barely more than hearsay, she thought. But something in the men's demeanour, the way they behaved, convinced her that they were not lying. Hof stepped forward again, watching her. It wasn't possible that villagers such as these could fight off trained men at arms, but she'd have to find out more.

"Did any refuse to pay them?"

Hof shook his head. "No, lady. What choice did we have? They insisted the tax they collected was authorised, and the money paid to your men was false. They threatened our lives before we even had the chance to speak our minds. The lives of our children and livestock too."

Once more the hall exploded with noise. Aelfgifu felt herself grow hot; it was just like Emma to be so heavy-handed when she wanted something. She rose from her chair; all conversation stopped as soon as she moved.

"Thank you for bringing this to my attention. I'll see that it stops." She bowed at everyone before sweeping out of the hall, her housecarls and Lufu following close behind.

"How are you enjoying court, my lady?" Godwin said with a glance to Aelfgifu as he leaned over the table and took a piece of pork with his knife. His wife, Gytha, frowned at his use of the formal title.

"I'm afraid I've never grown used to the number of people here, 'though my visits are infrequent."

Godwin laughed. "Yes, all men seek out favour and a royal court is like nectar to a bee." Aelfgifu fought the urge to shake her head in bewilderment. Was it possible this man had forgotten all that the court had given him?

"Try as I might, I'm unable to see why anyone who didn't have to be here would choose to remain." Seeing Gytha's frown deepen, she added, "I prefer a simpler life."

"But London is the centre of power," said Gytha.

Aelfgifu looked at Godwin's wife, surprised by the interruption. She was dressed as though she'd been born to a royal life: a yellow silk gown, despite the cold season, with light green threads weaving a delicate pattern across the bodice, and her hair was held by a gold circlet dotted with rubies. But the lines on her face suggested a life more roughly led than one accustomed to courtly riches. Aelfgifu had learned that Gytha, before being married to Godwin and placed within the queen's household, had been involved in the trading of slaves. That her own people had been forced from their homes and transported to Denmark to work for strangers was horrifying enough, but the added fact that this woman had made profit from the practice was sickening. She realised the woman was waiting for a response.

"Power is wherever the king is." She turned her attention back to Godwin, about to speak when she was interrupted.

"But what of the power of the queen?"

Aelfgifu's anger flared and she took a long draught of her wine, letting the liquid numb her feelings, before speaking.

"It's the king who rules the country. To say otherwise is treason."

She was gratified to see Gytha's eyes widen in panic. Taking another drink, she relaxed into her chair. She was about to speak when, incredibly, Gytha interrupted again.

"She's very good to *me*." The voice was barely above a whisper but Aelfgifu could hear the sneer within, the petulant tone of a child proven wrong.

A look from Godwin silenced Gytha, and was quickly followed by one of apology to herself. Aelfgifu nodded her acknowledgement, seeing something else there, behind his eyes and in the shape of his mouth. Then a thought occurred to her: Godwin had already tired of his tedious wife. She supressed the urge to smile.

"So what will you do about the problem?" She'd written to Godwin before her visit, warning him of her arrival and of the twice-taxed border towns.

He shook his head. "I'll speak with her, what else can I do?"

"You'll do what is necessary to keep the peace. That's why you're regent."

Godwin's shoulders slumped and she remembered just how young he really was, barely out of his teens.

"But the nobles only pay lip service to my decisions. They feared Thorkell but not me."

"Then you must make them fear you. Be bold. Stand by your decisions, never allow these men to see you waver."

"There's also Emma. She has many supporters at court."

Aelfgifu reached for her cup and brought it slowly to her lips, sneaking a glance at Gytha. The woman had remained silent since the look from her husband but Aelfgifu could tell she was listening intently, despite the pretence of fussing

Kelly Evans

with the sleeves of her dress. Any words spoken here would be repeated directly to Emma, of this she was certain. And there were more than enough issues to address without the worry of a stupid woman misrepresenting what she'd overheard at this dinner. In future, she would have to be more careful and ensure when she and Godwin met, it was alone.

"Perhaps we could move our chairs nearer to the fire and discuss this further?"

Godwin smiled to her in relief, understanding. "Gytha, we need to talk of matters that don't concern you."

Gytha stood, unsure. Godwin took her by the arm and led her towards the door. Gytha turned back, insisting that her presence was necessary, but Godwin pushed her toward the door again before returning to his seat by the fire. With a final look that displayed her displeasure, Gytha was gone. When they were settled and warm, and had been served fresh wine, Aelfgifu spoke.

"Emma is married to one of the most powerful men in Europe, of course she has supporters. And before that she was married to another king. But many, if not all, of these people will abandon her in a moment once they get what they seek. If they saw no gain under Aethelred, they'll fawn and flutter around her to access Canute." She shrugged. "It's how the court works, and Emma has had much practice."

"But the woman is impossible!" He threw his hands up. "She does what she will at all times, without thought. She pronounces based on whims, then acts immediately, with no planning or advice from any who would speak reason to her." He took a drink, wiping his mouth with his sleeve, a singularly un-courtly habit. "Or else she acts in secret then grandly announces her endeavour, seeking praise."

Aelfgifu shook her head. "You must learn to deal with these things. Do all in your power to gain the trust of men who'll support you. If those men currently champion Emma and you're able to claim their loyalty instead, so much the better, for they are a valuable resource."

Godwin thought about this for a moment. "You're a wise woman, my lady. For one who spends so little time at court, how is it you come to such knowledge of the minds of these men?"

She smiled grimly. "You forget. I'm also the wife of the king."

Chapter Fourteen
England

Aelfgifu found reason to be grateful for Lufu's presence yet again the following summer. The girl's father was a prolific letter writer and had included many amusing details and stories about life at court in his missives. The letter, carried by a merchant travelling north, relayed details about a significant event in London: the moving of the body of Aelfheah, former Archbishop of Canterbury, from London to the town of Canterbury. Aelfgifu had discussed this event with Canute earlier in the year.

"The current tomb is the focus of anti-Danish sentiment in London." Canute had been thinking what to do about the archbishop for a while now, but was at the point where he needed advice and reassurance that his instincts were accurate.

"Where is he buried now?" She'd bent to inspect a seedling, breathing in the smell of new life spring always brought.

"St Paul's." They'd walked in silence, each enjoying the first warm breeze of the year. The year 1023 had so far been a fair one and the signs were good that it would continue.

"And there's been trouble?"

"Yes, reports of fights between Englishmen and Danes. Insults thrown, and sharper things." He shook his head, disgusted, incredulous. "If I could, I would just ignore them, but a few weeks ago there was a death."

She'd been shocked. "A death? How?"

"A stabbing. It started with insults and ended in the death of a young man, born in England, but with a Danish father."

The wind had grown colder again, a reminder that there was a while to go before they could walk the grounds without a heavy cloak. She'd rubbed her arms and he'd guided her into the hall, next to the fire that was always kept stoked. When they were settled, she continued the conversation. "And this is the archbishop whose death was used by your father as a ploy to send Thorkell over to Aethelred's side?"

"The same, yes. Although the ploy was false, the story of the man's death was true. A small group of my father's men, tired of waiting for plunder, kidnapped the archbishop and held him for ransom." He rubbed his hands in front of the fire. "Aelfheah refused to allow this, sending word to the king that no money was to be offered for his freedom. The men, made violent by their impatience and drink, were angry about the lack of ransom and killed him." Her husband had shuddered and she knew that, even after all these years, he still felt the distastefulness of the situation. He'd been eighteen and in charge of his own men. "I wouldn't have wished the manner of his death on anyone."

Aelfgifu knew enough not to ask for details, besides, she had her own sources of information. It had been a horrible death: Sweyn's men began by throwing small bones at the man while he knelt in prayer before a makeshift altar. When this elicited no reaction, the men grew bolder and started throwing larger, sharper bones, some of which had been deliberately whittled to a point. Blood was soon flowing from the numerous wounds on the archbishop but still the man knelt, unmoved, before his god. Until that point, they'd been avoiding his head but with the further lack of reaction from Aelfheah they began in earnest, throwing larger objects at him. She'd been told that one particularly drunken man had poured wine over the man's wounds, hoping to get him to cry out in pain. She shuddered, feeling a sudden chill. The mood had become morose and Aelfgifu nudged the conversation away from the dark. "And you believe moving the body to Canterbury will dampen these feelings?"

"Not entirely, no. I know men, this resentment will exist

for many generations, of that I'm certain. But it'll disperse this new group of dissenters. Canterbury suffered much under my father's attacks. This'll be seen as an act of benevolence by the scurrying monks at their cathedral." He'd wrung his hands and sighed, taken her own hands in his, kissed them and risen. "I've much to do," he said.

A gentle cough brought Aelfgifu's mind back to the present. "I'm sorry, Lufu, my mind was wandering. What does your father say?"

They were sitting outside, enjoying the summer sun.

"He writes that the event was very solemn, with all at court dressing in simple clothing, mostly in black." Lufu screwed up her eyes as she examined the small parchment; Lufu's father had appalling handwriting. "He says except for Godwin's wife, who wore bright red." She looked up at Aelfgifu, the puzzlement clear.

"Your father provides these details for me, he knows you read your letters aloud." She smiled at the thought of Gytha appearing in so bold a dress, and then laughed aloud at the look that must have been on Godwin's face. "It's a wonder he didn't order his wife back to their rooms so she could change! What a sight she must have been!"

Lufu smiled, though still unsure whether to laugh. "He says there was a procession, with the king at its head, and his housecarls. Then the queen and her retinue, one of whom . . ." she stopped.

Aelfgifu looked across at the young woman. "What? Why have you stopped?"

"I'm sorry, I'm only reading what my father writes." She raised the letter, a worried look on her face. Aelfgifu waved at her to continue. "Next came the queen and her women, one of whom carried the king's son, Harthacanute."

She absorbed the words, staring at the blades of grass that her bare foot was fidgeting with. If this had been some sort of personal attack, something that woman had done to deliberately spite her, then she'd feel differently. Uncertain of her place in Canute's life, fearful, a young girl again. But this was different. This time Emma was using her child, showing everyone that HER son was the rightful heir and as such was taking his rightful place in the ceremony. But where her sons and their rights were concerned, Aelfgifu was no longer a fearful young woman. She knew where she stood and what she wanted for them. She was certain that Canute wouldn't have allowed Harthacanute to participate in such an important occasion, and guessed that Emma had, yet again, found a method of getting her own way. Her anger rose. Curse that *bikkja*! Taking a deep breath she calmed herself. "Carry on . . ."

Lufu was watching her carefully, but to her credit the girl said nothing and continued. "Next in the procession came Godwin, and his wife Gytha."

She nodded; it made sense to have Canute's next in command close to the front. "Did your father write anything of the casket itself?"

Lufu flipped quickly through the pages, skimming her father's spindly handwriting. She stopped and began to read from part way down the third page. "He does. He says it was a large casket, specially made for Canterbury, and that it was covered in gold leaf and many jewels." She read in silence a moment before continuing. "He also says that when the tomb of the archbishop was opened, it was found that the body was intact, no corruption had occurred. He confesses he never saw this for himself but that it was generally agreed to be true among all the court."

Aelfgifu laughed, unable to contain her cynicism. "Ah yes, the faith of courtiers." She wondered if Canute would follow through with her suggestion on quelling the ridiculous rumours that Emma was spreading.

Canute looked out over the waters from the shores of Thorney Island, a short distance from the palace walls that he had built. Godwin had been sent to summon Emma, who was told only that her husband requested her presence. He met her on the beach, his throne already placed near the water's edge.

"My lord." She barely moved her lips and Canute saw the muscles twitch in her jaw. "What are we doing?" She smiled and nodded at the onlookers.

Pulling her beside him, the king addressed the growing crowd. For not only were the most important men in the country there, Godwin had sent his men to the townspeople to deliver news that their king was about to perform a miracle. Canute had informed his guards beforehand to allow any and all to pass.

"People! You have no doubt heard of my many and great deeds! Of my mastery with a sword and my skill on the battlefield!" He paused and, glancing sideways at Emma, was satisfied that she looked panicked. Canute continued.

"For these wondrous stories that so entertain you, you must thank my wife, the queen." He took a step away from Emma and held out his arm to ensure all eyes were upon her. With a smirk he continued.

"My wife is a wonder, is she not?" Taking her hand, Canute led her to the throne. "Stand with me, my queen, and today we will see first-hand evidence of one of your many tales." Sitting, he faced the waves, holding tightly to Emma's struggling arm.

"What are you doing?" she hissed.

"Proving a point." He pointed to the water, its edge closer now than it had been only moments ago. The tide of the Thames was fast and unpredictable, taking numerous lives each year. Canute saw the apprehension in Emma's eyes, and her struggle to maintain her composure. Standing once more, he called to the waves.

"Great tide of this mighty river! I, Canute, command you to stop your pace, halt your flow and be calm!" He held out his hand at the last minute, enjoying the role he was playing. He felt the collective breath being held by those watching.

The tide poured in as it always did and as it always would. Canute sat and waited, still holding Emma's arm, the struggling more and more frantic as the water rose. Soon it was to their knees.

"How long shall we wait? Until we are both drowned? You've proved your point. I wish to leave, I'm cold."

Canute pulled her in close and whispered roughly, "You'll wait as long as I say you'll wait." He shoved her back in disgust, watching her fall to her knees in the water.

Enough. He addressed the shocked crowd; they had expected a wonder.

"Now you see, that only the Lord God has the power to control nature! It is vanity . . ." he glared at Emma, who was shivering from the water and covered in sand, "to believe otherwise."

He nodded to his men and they started back towards the palace, leaving Emma. He soon heard her coming up behind him and turned to face the queen. She stopped before him, her eyes blazing and her voice low.

"You've made a fool of me in front of everyone. I'll not forget it." Backing away she had hurried to the palace, reaching the main gate before him.

A barking dog from the stables brought Aelfgifu back to the present. Lufu was looking at her expectantly.

"As you know most of my husband's advisors are of the new faith, so he took advantage of the opportunity. It was an astute move and did much to further seal the loyalty of the bishops."

By now the sun was getting high in the sky and Aelfgifu

could feel her face growing hot. Putting on her shoes, she rose and they walked slowly towards the main building to shelter from the sun. Lufu kept reading.

"My father writes that Aelfheah's body was carried to the bridge in Southwark, where it was loaded onto a ship." Lufu looked up from the letter as Aelfgifu guided her around a small bush.

"Canute accompanied the casket onto the ship, and steered it to Rochester himself. Once there, they continued overland to Canterbury, where the archbishop's body was received by the monks with great solemnity."

"And what charters were granted I wonder."

Lufu looked up at her mistress and Aelfgifu could see the surprise in her eyes. "How did you know?" At her mistress' wave, she continued. "You're right, my father says that Canute has given part of Sandwich to the church, along with the customs, dues and trading taxes."

She nodded. It was a good gift, worth much. They'd reached the door. "Anything else?"

The girl nodded. "Something odd, my lady. It says here that the king also took the crown from his own head and offered it to the church." The girl frowned. "Why would he do that?"

Aelfgifu smiled. Her husband was indeed clever. "The people of Canterbury are no supporters of my husband. It's true that they were treated badly by Canute's father, and they have long memories. In returning the body of their beloved archbishop to them, the king has publicly acknowledged the respect he feels for Canterbury. But in giving them his crown, he also shows them his love."

"Why are you here? Didn't you get my message?" Canute's worried face looked up at her as she sat on her horse, which stamped impatiently, waiting to be rubbed down.

"I received no message." She shielded her eyes against the late autumn sun.

"Damn." Canute had started using English words more and more, including when he swore. He helped her from the horse. "Emma is here."

Aelfgifu nearly twisted her ankle in the stirrup, she turned to face Canute so violently. "What?"

"I didn't know, I swear. She surprised me, arrived this morning. I sent messengers to meet you but . . ." He shrugged.

She began to pace before him. "Do you want me to leave?" She understood immediately the embarrassment and discomfort having both her and Emma there would cause, not only to her and Canute but to everyone that had accompanied them.

"No. It's you I invited. And Thorkell asked for you."

She paced again for a moment before stopping before him. "Then you have to ask her to leave."

"I have, at first politely, but she said no, so I demanded! She relented, but is taking a lot of time readying herself, and now it's too late. She'll have to leave in the morning."

Aelfgifu sighed. Damn that infernal woman! Emma didn't even like Thorkell and had no reason to be here celebrating the renewal of trust and friendship between Canute and his old teacher.

"Where are my chambers? I'm tired and dirty." She signalled for her belongings when she saw a quick look flash across Canute's face. "What else?" Anger replaced whatever she'd seen a moment ago.

"Emma has taken your rooms."

"Of course she has! She's Emma, queen of us all, what Emma wants, Emma gets!" Looking around, she saw that her horse was still nearby. Without another word, she stormed over and mounted it, pulling the reins and swinging the horse around in a single practised movement.

Alarmed, Canute rushed after her, just catching the reins as she was urging the horse to a canter. He held fast until Aelfgifu finally gave in, sagging in her saddle. She allowed herself to be helped from the horse and Canute handed the reins to a servant. She let him take her face in his rough hands and look directly into her eyes.

"You're the one I want here, not her. I didn't invite her, nor is she welcomed by anyone." As before she felt the same doubts that, no matter how hard she tried, she couldn't conquer.

"It's Thorkell's wish that you be here." He placed a gentle kiss on her lips. "*And* my wish."

There was nothing she could do. She could ride away into the night and risk injuring herself, or stay and force herself to smile in the presence of the one person she hated most in the world. A glimmer of a thought began to glow in the back of her mind. Perhaps she could use this situation to her advantage somehow. She was closer to the people in this area than Emma was, surely the queen's already deteriorating reputation could be further eroded while she was here? And there was Thorkell to think of, he'd asked for her specifically. She would show everyone that she was the mature one, the one Canute had chosen, loved and trusted first for good reason.

"Where am I to sleep, my lord?"

"With me, of course."

She looked at him, one eyebrow raised. "Emma will be furious."

Canute winked and led her toward the house, where people were already coming out to greet her. Their friendliness and warmth added to her triumph and she returned their feelings in kind, unable to keep the wide grin from her face.

The manor, the very same from which Canute had managed his conquest of England, was crowded with people, all rushing around with errands or tasks to perform. She settled into Canute's rooms with Lufu's and her other maids' help, occasionally sending one of her women to obtain an item she'd forgotten to pack. There was no sign of the queen herself, but anyone could see that she was near, from the number of well-dressed men and women who hurried about on her business.

"They look down on us," Lufu said as she folded the linen.

Aelfgifu was nearby, unpacking her dresses. "Why do you say that? We've only been here a few hours." She had asked Lufu to keep her eyes and ears open, and to report back. She always encouraged honesty between them, it was one of the reasons the girl had become a cherished friend.

Lufu shrugged. "It's the way they look at us, and you, my lady." Aelfgifu looked up, surprised. "They show a disgust on their faces when we pass, they don't try to disguise it. And when you walk by . . ."

"Yes. When I walk by?"

"They show their revulsion, as with us, but something else also. Pity perhaps? I was never very good at reading these court people." She went back to smoothing a blanket.

All eyes in the room were on her, waiting for her reaction. She waved a hand dismissively in the air.

"Ignore the supposed looks, it's silly to try and interpret every look or glance one gets. I'm certain these southerners are just unused to seeing such beauty from the north!" She smiled and went back to her unpacking, grateful no one could tell that her stomach had knotted and that her hands shook with rage.

Later that night, as the torches grew dim, Aelfgifu had finally had enough wine to relax. So far only Canute, Thorkell and their closest men had been in the hall, enjoying the food, drink and music. And stories! These men could talk the horns off a goat, telling and retelling their tales of battle and bloodshed and glory. And in the privacy of the hall, with his closest friends around, Canute was relaxed and himself.

"By the All Father, Thorkell, didn't we have some great times?"

"That we did. But it wasn't always so."

Aelfgifu was enjoying the men's joking; she was as comfortable as they were, and felt accepted by them. Thorkell's bushy eyebrows, now completely white, raised up on his forehead and his mouth, nearly hidden by a snowy white beard, curled up at the corners.

Canute had been taking a drink from his drinking horn when Thorkell delivered his last comment. Sputtering, he raised a hand in protest. "Nay, don't even think to speak of those times!"

Thorkell smiled and winked at Aelfgifu. "Oh, I think your good lady wife deserves to hear a more humbling tale of her husband." The men in the hall roared with laughter and Canute looked sheepish, feebly trying to persuade his old teacher to stay his tongue. To no avail.

"I remember a long time ago, when Canute was barely a man . . ."

"I was a man!"

Thorkell ignored Canute's interruption. "Canute was barely a man," a glare at Canute ensured no further outbursts would be forthcoming, "and he decided that he was ready to take on his teacher in a real fight." Thorkell drank and continued. "He would hear no protest so I arranged a battle between us, in the yard behind his father's palace." Knowing that those present may not have a sense of the layout of the kingdom in Denmark, the older man used his arms to mark out places in the air in front of him.

"It was spring and the ground was muddy and slippery,

but my student was too stubborn to admit it was not a good day to fight. We agreed to meet in the morning, just after sunrise, and to both use the training swords we usually practised with."

Lufu leaned forward, listening intently to the man's story. Aelfgifu herself was fascinated, for it was a rare occurrence to learn details of her husband's childhood. She noticed Thorkell's cup was empty and signalled for a servant to refill it. He nodded his thanks at her.

"True to his word, Canute was waiting for me when I arrived. I'd arranged for the sword rack to be brought out. We both took a sword and shield and, putting on our helmets, circled each other. Canute attacked first, a blow which I easily side-stepped. He attacked again, and again. I blocked each blow without much effort and after a while Canute's attacks became even sloppier and less accurate. He looked exhausted and was practically dragging his sword around after him as he struggled to hold up his shield. But still he fought, he wouldn't give up. I stepped forward and raised my arm high, intending to bring it down close to his side to frighten him. But he held up his shield to block. Then I saw the look in his eyes, as the shield overbalanced him and he fell over into a patch of mud and dung so deep he was covered entirely!" Thorkell took another drink. "I laughed my arse off!"

The room burst into laughter and Canute looked embarrassed, trying to shield himself from the friendly arm punches that suddenly rained on him. Laughing, he looked up at Thorkell. "You cheated!"

Thorkell put on an offended look. "Cheat? Me? No, not cheating. Teaching. And a valuable lesson at that."

Lufu leaned over and whispered to Aelfgifu. "I don't understand."

Canute overheard. "Unbeknownst to me, my teacher had gone to the training room the night before our battle. He added weights to both the sword and the shield."

"But how did you know which sword he would take?" Aelfgifu couldn't help it, she was intrigued by the mystery.

Thorkell laughed. "Your husband was a very predictable young man. He always chose the same shield and same sword every time we practised."

Canute's face turned red and as he mumbled something about a comfortable grip.

"And did he learn his lesson?"

"He learned many that day, my lady. First and foremost, never let your weapon out of your sight. Second, when you can avoid a fight, avoid a fight. And third, never challenge Thorkell the Tall!" He stood and raised his drinking horn before downing the contents in their entirety. The room erupted again, this time in shouts and cheers. It took everyone a few moments to realise that someone new had entered the room.

"Husband, I'm retiring for the evening, I came to wish you a good night."

Canute's face reddened, but not from embarrassment. "You were told to stay in your rooms," he growled.

Emma curtsied to Canute. "It was my duty as your wife, my lord." The room was completely silent, the echoes of the recent shouts still ringing in Aelfgifu's ears. She had stood with the others when Thorkell raised his drink. But despite the company of the men in the room, she felt exposed. Emma looked directly at her, eyeing her up and down. The *bikkja* was taking in every detail: her hair, her clothes, the way she held herself, the shape of her body, how tightly she clasped her hands together, everything. With the tiniest of smirks, Emma nodded, an almost imperceptible movement. Aelfgifu returned the gesture.

After Emma had left, they tried to recreate the earlier carefree atmosphere but it was too late, the mood was broken. Aelfgifu guessed that this was Emma's intent. And, as it always seemed, Emma got what Emma wanted. But there was another element to the forgiveness ceremony. Canute made Thorkell co-regent of Denmark, to rule with Ulf on Canute's behalf. It was a great honour for Thorkell who understood that it would be he, and not Ulf, who would hold most of the power. Emma was not there to witness this new arrangement: Emma's son with Canute, Harthacanute, would now be under the guardianship of Thorkell, and would move to Denmark with the older man. It was a move Aelfgifu was sure would break Emma's heart, and one that Canute hoped would break her spirit.

Aelfgifu spent nearly a month at Gainsborough with Canute, delighting in having her husband to herself for such a length of time. Canute was able to run his kingdom well enough from the hall; Gainsborough had always been a favourite residence. But Aelfgifu suspected that Canute had other reasons for wanting to stay away from London, as evidenced by his refusal to read any letters or messages delivered to him from the queen. In fact, any and all who came on her behalf were immediately turned away. She also suspected that he would've stayed longer had news not arrived from Normandy: Emma's brother, the duke, was dead, poisoned by his own son.

Chapter Fifteen
England

"What does this mean for England?" Aelfgifu was helping fold a pair of Canute's breeches.

"Nothing, really." He rummaged through his worn leather saddlebag, a gift from Aelfgifu from before they were joined. "Now that Denmark and England are under a single ruler the previous treaty signed by Emma's brother is no longer needed."

Emma had come as part of an agreement between King Aethelred and Duke Richard of Normandy, Emma's brother, in the year 1002. The contract stipulated that, in exchange for England taking Emma, the Normans must close their ports to the Danish fleet, particularly in the winter where it was more convenient for the then-enemies of England to repair their raiding ships. Duke Richard also promised that the selling of English plunder would be outlawed. Now that Denmark was no longer a danger to England, the selling of English goods to the continent via Norman ports was openly encouraged, and any country that welcomed English or Danish ships was an ally.

Canute closed the flap of the bag. "But for Emma it means a great deal."

She stopped her work for a moment. "How?"

"She can no longer use her homeland as a threat to get what she wants in England."

Aelfgifu nodded. Emma had used the Norman threat for a multitude of reasons, many of which she claimed were spiritual. She was known for her donations of land, altar crosses made of silver and gold and tapestries to churches and monasteries. "Will her nephew not still support her?"

"No, he has no liking for her, or her sons." Canute

snorted. "Edward and Alfred have been forced to live on the charity of their uncle. Her daughter is there too, Goda. From what I hear Emma's nephew, Richard, is resentful of the fact that these abandoned relatives are treated as his equals."

"And they'll have to flee Normandy now that their uncle is dead?"

"Yes, if they wish to live out their lives in peace. Emma has been away from home so long she no longer has much support in that quarter."

"So she's no longer a worry?" Aelfgifu couldn't help the hopeful tone that crept into her voice.

He shook his head. "She still has many supporters and has her own sources of power both at court and in the counties she owns. And she has given so much to these cursed churches and their greedy clergy that she has the good will of all the bishops. But she still needs leverage."

Aelfgifu was going to ask him about divorcing Emma but she now understood that, even with Normandy no longer a threat, the English churchmen were. "What will she do?"

Canute climbed into his saddle and took the reins from a servant. "She's very resourceful. We'll find out soon enough."

Aelfgifu, back at Reodfeld, heard of no scandal or intrigue at court, at least none involving Emma. The usual rumours of who was fighting with whom and which earl stole land from which other made their way to Reodfeld, but in these the queen played no part. Had she learned her place? Had she really stopped her constant scheming? And was Aelfgifu and her family finally safe? It became easier to believe this was true as time passed and all remained calm. The activities of not only running Reodfeld but of running the north for Canute took all her time, time she did not have to give.

The seasons passed, as did the activities of the manor.

Fields ploughed, crops planted and harvested. Births, marriages and deaths of friends and strangers. The north echoed the activities of Reodfeld – seeds strewn across fields, shoots pushing through earth, eventually being torn from that very soil in an endless cycle of death and rebirth. As the Christians said, 'to everything a season.' Very apt, Aelfgifu thought.

Canute was in the south and he wrote as regularly as he could, sending messengers with gifts when he couldn't pen a letter. He was one of the few men she knew who could write. Canute had been educated by the Jomsvikings, a group of mighty and elite warriors, and a part of his training included time with the monks who had come to spread their faith to the heathen wild men in the north. While their preaching was largely ignored, Canute's father Sweyn understood that a ruler needed to be able to fight with words as well as a sword and ensured that Canute learned his letters. When he was able to write, his words spoke of his frustration, and he would often use the opportunity to voice his concerns and fears to Aelfgifu.

"I sometimes wonder if her plan is to drive me mad with waiting for something that may or may not happen; the anticipation of disruption distracts me and keeps me from applying my full concentration on matters more deserving than the queen's petty behaviour."

Towards the end of the year, Godwin arrived at Reodfeld, his face more heavily lined since he had taken up residence at court; she'd seen the same effect on Canute.

"My lady, how are you?"

"Godwin." She smiled as she curtseyed. "What brings you here?" Canute usually sent his most trusted carls with messages for her, but never someone as senior as Godwin.

"My lady, I'm sorry to be the one to report, but Thorkell the Tall is dead." The news was so bluntly delivered that she gasped, dropping the cup she had been holding. She waved

Godwin away as he rushed to her side.

"No, I'm fine. It was just a shock." She took a deep breath. "You really need to learn the art of tact, Godwin. Especially if you have the ear of the king."

Godwin nodded, frowning all the while. "I am a warrior, my lady. First and last."

She looked at him steadily. "Yes, you are. I forgive you. Come, tell me everything."

"The king thought you should hear the news from someone you trust."

She nodded. Canute was still thinking of her, even in this time of sorrow. It helped ease the pain in her chest at the news.

"I'm very sad. He was a good man and my husband's oldest friend. He'll be sorely missed." They walked to the main hall together. "What happened?"

"He was hosting a feast to thank the gods for an end to winter. Much food and drink was served. One man, a distant relative of a guest, had too much mead and began to insult Canute." Aelfgifu's eyes widened but she let him continue. "He was warned a number of times but would not be stilled, his insults growing ever worse. Finally, Thorkell, patient until now, challenged the man to a fight. A holmgang."

"I thought they were outlawed?"

Godwin nodded his head. "Yes, but only recently and most turn a blind eye when the cause is just."

They had arrived at the hall and sat, a servant sent to bring drink. "They arranged to meet a week later. Thorkell broke the man's first shield easily. He then had his own shield broken. They each went through three shields before reaching each other." Godwin took a long draught of the mead that had arrived before continuing. "They fought fiercely and it was difficult to know who was winning. But then Thorkell gathered his strength and with a mighty heave of his axe hewed the man's head in two, from the top of his skull to his neck.

Aelfgifu felt ill but recovered quickly. "And Thorkell?"

"He returned home and had his injuries treated. But they were too severe and they festered." Godwin's voice trailed off. "He died with his armour on and his sword in his hand, his brother's sons with him."

She nodded. "Good. So he wasn't alone."

"No, lady. And he is now with the gods."

They sat in the hall, the room where most of her guests were entertained. Servants came and went. A meal was being coordinated by Lufu. "How's my husband?"

"He took the death hard. It has made the atmosphere at court . . . difficult."

She understood his meaning. It was common knowledge through the land that Canute and the queen argued, and that Emma spent much of her time at her house in Exeter. Aelfgifu could only imagine how Thorkell's death would affect her husband. Her heart ached for Canute and she wished she could go to him.

"There's more, my lady." She nodded at him to continue. "Canute has given full control of Denmark to Ulf.

Aelfgifu nodded again. "Yes, it's as I'd expect."

"But the king has also given the guardianship of Harthacanute over to Ulf as well."

Her hand flew to her mouth before she could stop it. Despite her hatred for the queen, as a mother she could sympathise: Emma's seven-year old child had been passed to someone else to raise, someone she'd never even met. It was common practise and helped to forge valuable alliances but this fact did little to help a mother's grief. Aelfgifu shivered, pulling her cloak more tightly. Emma would be more dangerous now than ever before, for what wouldn't a mother do for her child?

As winter passed Aelfgifu felt as though she lived in

expectation of an event, and whether real or imagined it affected her physically. Some days she caught herself carrying her shoulders more tightly than before, or holding her neck more stiffly, causing her headaches at night. Canute's visits were, as always, welcome, and in his presence she could forget the events at court and believe there were only the two of them.

"How has this happened? Why has she been allowed to do this?" Aelfgifu had already inflicted her anger on a table, two chairs and numerous goblets, all of which lay scattered on the floor around her. The scene was in stark contrast to the summer activities taking place around the manor.

"She's not been 'allowed' to do anything. She did it without my knowledge." Canute had had weeks to quell his rage and his calmness only made Aelfgifu angrier. Though perhaps the calm was actually resignation, and that he was just as heated as she was.

Aelfgifu paced the room, stopping to call for wine. "How did she think she would ever get away with this?"

Canute righted the table and chairs that she'd upended then collapsed into a chair. "That's her problem, she doesn't think. She acts and then charms to gain forgiveness."

Dropping wearily into the chair across from her husband, Aelfgifu worked through the details in her mind. Emma, upon hearing that her son Harthacanute was to be raised by Ulf in Denmark, had embarked on an audacious plan that had only been discovered a few weeks ago. She'd stolen the king's seal, the one Canute used personally to authorise charters and letters of importance. There was no other in the land; anyone receiving a document with the wax imprint of that seal would know immediately that the message came directly from the King of England. And Emma had somehow managed not only to steal the seal without being discovered, but had also written to Ulf, claiming to be Canute, and demanded that Harthacanute be made king of Denmark.

She'd then validated the command through the use of Canute's seal.

Ulf, upon receiving the letter, believed it to be from Canute and immediately had the seven-year old boy crowned king. Aelfgifu almost laughed, imagining how Emma must have felt when she had made her son king. There were few emotions stronger than that of a mother's pride.

"And now because of that stupid woman's actions, you have to go to war." The wine had been served and she brought the cup to her mouth. The sour smell of the drink made her feel ill and she put the cup back on the table.

Canute sighed, his body sagging deeper into the chair. She watched her husband, only vaguely aware of the sounds of Reodfeld and its workers floating in through the unshuttered windows. The faint lines she'd noticed only a few years ago were now deeply etched into Canute's forehead and around his eyes. She was sure she would find these same lines as deeply grooved into the areas his moustache and beard covered.

"Yes, I must return to Denmark. No one will accept a child ruler and I've already had reports that the kings of Norway and Sweden have allied and are planning to attack my country."

"All because of Emma?" She shook her head at the carelessness of the queen, not looking or caring about the consequences of her rash actions.

"If it weren't for her, Denmark would be secure. By putting Harthacanute on the throne we're seen as weak, ineffectual. Poor decision-makers."

She nodded, understanding. Weak countries with inadequate leadership would also have poor armies. It made sense that Denmark's enemies would chose now to attack. "Do you know how long you'll be away?" She regretted the question as soon as the words left her mouth, for what warrior could predict the future?

Canute shook his head. "I can't answer that. But I must leave tomorrow; Godwin is seeing that the fleet is assembled and ready."

"Will he sail with you?"

"No, I need him here."

Aelfgifu was relieved. England needed someone strong to watch over it while Canute was away. And Godwin had grown into his role and responsibilities; it was no wonder Canute had granted him the earldoms of both Wessex and Kent. He'd shown himself to be a capable leader.

"His wife will be pleased, I hear she has been delivered of a girl and has not yet risen from her birth bed. No woman wants her husband away during such a time." The thought of Godwin's new child reminded her of something. "What of Emma's other children, those by Aethelred?" Would the queen attempt to have her other offspring crowned as well?

"The eldest, Edward, hates his mother. Alfred is indifferent, from what I hear. And Goda no longer resides at the Norman court but is married and living elsewhere." He waved his hand dismissively.

She thought of her own sons. Sweyn was now ten but was still small for his size, taking after his Saxon descendants more than his Norse. But he was clever, had been taught to read and devoured any material he could find, mainly from the monks at Gainsborough. While Aelfgifu encouraged his education, she wasn't sure she agreed with everything he was taught, for the monks would include a sermon with every tome they lent. Harold was a year younger but was already larger and heavier than his older brother. He'd also taken the measure of his sibling and knew how to get a rise from him. She was often called to break up an argument that ended as more than an exchange of words. But Harold had a way of smiling and cocking his head to the side, making them all believe he'd only been in jest.

And now, because of that damn woman's reckless actions, their father must sail to war.

Three months later, Aelfgifu was in her chambers having a private dinner with her sons. She hadn't seen Canute since he'd left, and she constantly listened for messengers or visitors, no matter what she was doing. Even in her sleep she dreamed of news. But it was nearly the end of the year and there were the seasonal festivities to arrange, something that always lifted her spirits. Her thoughts of how to decorate the main hall were interrupted by Sweyn.

"Mother, when will father be back?"

"He's fighting across the sea, you know that." She could see by the look on his face that this wasn't enough. "The kings of Sweden and Norway decided to take advantage of your father being away from Denmark so often. They thought it would be easy to conquer when he was away."

She wasn't going to mention Emma's theft of the Canute's seal, nor the fact that the queen's actions had endangered thousands of lives; she wanted to shield her children from the machinations of the royal court for as long as possible.

"The enemy launched attacks and your father sailed to fight them."

Their meal was over and Aelfgifu motioned for a servant to clear the table. Settling herself next to the fire, she decided to share the story of their father's fight with the boys. It was a good tale, one that she would have enjoyed much more had the main character not been her own husband. She waved Sweyn and Harold over and waited until they'd gathered cushions and placed themselves comfortably at her feet.

"The King of Sweden is a man called Anund, and he decided that if he joined with the King of Norway, then together they might conquer your father's homeland." She saw the light of the fire dancing in her sons' eyes, their faces gazing up at her. Smiling, she continued. "The King of Norway is named Olaf, and he agreed to join with Anund to attack the Danes."

"Keep watch! The river narrows." Canute stood at the prow of his longship, the largest in his fleet, his men rowing slowly through the mouth of the Helgea River.

"Not long before we can see them." Osgar, a stout Saxon, stood beside Canute.

Canute nodded, warily watching his surroundings for any archers Olaf may have hidden in the brush-heavy shoreline.

The ship glided through the water, the silence disturbed only by the splash of a jumping fish. Then, something. A noise they could feel in their bones. A low roaring that was at once familiar and strange.

"What's that sound?" Canute frowned. "Thunder? I see no clouds." He stopped, staring down river, his eyes widening at the sight of a wall of water racing towards them.

The wave hit them hard, nearly forcing the boat under. Screams filled the air as Canute's men were thrown overboard by the force. But their vessel remained afloat, a fate not reserved for others.

"Shit, what the hell was that?" Osgar was scrambling to stand.

A jolt sent him to the deck again; a large log had hit the ship. "Help the others!" Canute shouted to those still aboard. Amidst the chaos men rushed to the sides, reaching out to those in the water, shouting to be heard over the sound of creaking and splintering wood.

"Here, give me your hand!" Canute reached for a drowning man but snatched his arm back as another log came crashing through the water, taking the flailing warrior with it.

The longships at the front fared the worst. The wave, at full force, had surged over the prows, pushing ships beneath the water. Those that turned to flee were easily overturned by the wave. The shields of lost warriors rushed by with logs and timber. And peat.

"They dammed the river!" Canute pointed to the water, now calming as the waves emptied into the mouth of the river. "That's peat. And the logs," he pointed again. "Used to block the river." He turned back toward Osgar. "Those *rassragr*, they meant to drown us all."

The noise of drowning men was fading and Canute looked around at his tattered fleet. "Back to the mouth. Now." At his order the men sat and rowed, silent once more, eyes wary for further danger.

Once the entire fleet had arrived at the river entrance Canute assessed the damage. "The ships at the back were undamaged, my lord." Osgar stood, steady again. "The first ships to enter the river were hardest hit."

"How many lost?" Canute's voice did not hide his irritation when Osgar hesitated. "How many!?"

"Ten ships, my lord."

Canute's tightening jaw cracked. "And the men?"

"Some were rescued, my lord, but not many."

Canute thought for a moment. "Distribute the men among the ships. We're not done yet."

The order was spread and the ships began to lash themselves together so men could move between them. Soon they were ready and rowing forward again.

"Careful, there are still logs in the water." Navigating the timber and peat, they eventually arrived at a bend in the river and found Olaf and Anund's combined fleet waiting in the distance.

"That is all they have?" Osgar snorted. Soon most of the men were laughing and jeering. Despite their losses, Canute's fleet far outnumbered the enemy.

Canute smirked. "They used their only trick, it didn't work and now there is nothing they can do. They'd be mad to fight."

The two sides remained facing each other at a distance, each waiting for a sign from the other. "Osgar, do you see that shield? Front ship, on the right."

The Saxon squinted. "By the gods, isn't that . . . "

Canute held up his hand. "Wait. There's movement." A smaller longship was approaching; a karve.

The karve arrived alongside Canute's great longship and a young man came aboard, his eyes wide, glancing quickly from side to side as the men surrounded him.

"I serve King Olaf, my lord."

Canute raised his eyebrows. "And? What does your master want?"

The man hesitated then spoke, his voice wavering. "The king wishes to come to an arrangement, my lord."

Canute glared at the man, enjoying his discomfort. "Wise. Very wise."

"And did father kill his enemies?" Harold's hands were clasped together, a large smile upon his face.

"Father wouldn't do that, it would only cause more trouble." Sweyn, ever the pragmatist, added his opinion.

Harold turned to his brother and pointed at him. Sweyn knew Harold's sore points as well as Harold knew his. "It's not true! Father is a warrior; he would never allow his enemies to live!"

Sweyn was about to reply when Aelfgifu leaned forward and put her arm between them. Harold would be disappointed, but Sweyn was right.

"Your father is a warrior, it's true," she nodded to Harold, "but he's also a wise ruler. He allowed Olaf and Anund to return to their own countries. But he made them sign a declaration stating they would never attack Denmark again, and took members of their families to the Danish court as insurance."

There was no point in pretending these people were anything other than hostages. The boys were getting older and could understand this practice and its value.

"Your father will be home soon, I'm sure." She held up her hand at the interruption about to come from Sweyn. "I don't know when. Soon."

The candles were burning low and she made a mental note to retrieve more from the storage cupboard. Gathering her children to her, Aelfgifu hugged them hard before sending them to their beds. She saw the frustration in Sweyn's face, and his need for exact time and places, the security of knowing. But her reply to Sweyn's unasked question would have to do. There were other issues for Canute to deal with, the most important of which was his brother-in-law Ulf. Aelfgifu hadn't told the entire story to her boys, and had deliberately left out the most shocking detail: that the shields their father had recognised with the enemy belonged to Ulf. Canute had been betrayed. It hadn't seemed to matter to Ulf that he was married to a powerful man's sister. For reasons she couldn't fathom, Ulf had joined with Anund of Sweden and Olaf of Norway against Canute. From the position of trust in which he was placed by Canute himself, Ulf had used his power to aid Denmark's enemies: he'd helped them to build the dam that had nearly destroyed Canute's fleet.

But when the strategy failed, he'd fled, returning later to the court to beg Canute's forgiveness. She wished she'd been there with her husband to witness that scene! He claimed he'd had no choice, that his life and that of his family had been threatened and would've been in grave danger if he hadn't agreed to help. Canute had explained all of this in his latest letter to her. He'd also written that he'd some matters that needed attention in Denmark but he would, indeed, be shortly returning to England.

True to his word, Canute arrived back at England six weeks later. It came as no surprise to Aelfgifu to learn that Canute's sister Estrith, who had been married to Ulf, had returned home with the king. Canute had decided not to accept Ulf's apology and the man had paid for his cowardice with his life.

Aelfgifu lingered by the manor gates; lately she'd been finding excuses to be in the courtyard. She wanted to be the first to know when her husband arrived home. She'd sent the boys to stay with their sword master, using the excuse that he would be able to teach them more with his own weapons to hand. The man only lived a short distance away but she wanted at least one night alone with Canute before calling the boys back to pester their father with questions about his battles. And after he'd spent so much time with her sons, she trusted the sword master like a member of her own family. She had to admit that the manor was much more peaceful when her sons weren't in it.

She took another look down the lane and, seeing nothing, went inside. The sun was warm for February but winter still held its grip on the land, and Aelfgifu was grateful for the fire. She rubbed her hands, feeling the warmth start to come back into them. Lufu joined her, bringing her a cup of watered ale. As she drank she kept looking towards the courtyard, wishing she could see through the building walls.

"You'll be told as soon as he arrives."

She smiled at Lufu, embarrassed her feelings were so transparent. She supposed that to many of the men and women who'd served her faithfully for so many years, her thoughts and emotions must be obvious, for they'd grown with her and knew her so well. "I know, it's just . . ." Her words were interrupted by the clatter of a horse's hooves outside. "He's here!" She stood, practically throwing the cup at Lufu as she ran out. Her heart fell when she saw it wasn't her husband, rather, a nervous-looking young man.

"Who are you?" She hadn't meant her tone to be so harsh but her disappointment at the visitor not being her husband was fresh.

He stumbled forward, kneeling before her. "My lady . . ." he stuttered, unable to say the words.

Aelfgifu felt sorry for him, and, looking more closely, saw that it wasn't a man at all, merely a boy. He couldn't be more than fifteen.

"I ask again, who are you?" She softened her tone, hoping the messenger would calm a little.

It worked. "My lady." Silence, then he took a deep breath. "I work for Grim, the sword master."

She frowned. He looked familiar, she'd seen him before, of that she was sure. Was it with Grim? When he was teaching her boys, there had been an assistant. She nodded. "Continue. Why are you here? Where is your master?" After the let-down of not finding her husband, then the puzzlement of who this boy was, came a small creeping tendril of panic. It started in her stomach and slowly wove its way through her chest and throat.

"My lady, that's why I'm here. I deliver grave news. There was an attack, an attempt on the lives of your sons."

Aelfgifu felt dizzy. She was shaking as she felt panic rising, but she quelled it, fighting her emotions. Her voice was tight with controlled rage. "My sons! Are they hurt?"

When the boy remained silent, the look on his face showing the shock of his ordeal, she spoke again. "Are my sons hurt?"

Finally, whatever had been staying the boy's tongue released its grip. She could barely hear his whispered words. "My lady, I don't know if your sons are alive or dead."

Chapter Sixteen
England

Aelfgifu sank to the ground, a cry escaping her lips. It was a howl of pure instinct, of a mother being torn apart. She didn't know how long she stayed like that, but the first thing she became conscious of was utter silence, then of arms around her, lifting her.

"My lady."

Oswulf, once her husband's messenger and now a trusted advisor, helped her to stand. "I'll ride immediately." Aelfgifu wasn't sure where the words had come from, but she knew the moment they left her lips that this was her intention. But first she needed more information.

"Boy, what's your name?"

The young messenger looked miserable. "Egil, my lady."

"Egil, tell us what happened."

The boy took a few breaths before speaking, his chest rising and falling in quick uneven movements.

"We were riding. There's a copse my master favours for training and we were heading there when two men attacked us."

"Only two men? Are you positive?" Oswulf's voice was calm but carried authority.

"Yes, I think so but I can't be sure. As soon as we were attacked my master ordered me to take the boys and flee."

"But they're not with you!" Aelfgifu cried out in desperation. She felt Oswulf's hand on her shoulder, a secure, steadying influence.

"I don't know how to tell you this, my lady, but the boys left me. Harold told me he would return and fight and turned his horse back to where we were attacked. Sweyn remained with me for a few moments more but then followed his brother." He lowered his head. "I'm ashamed that I alone fled. I should've gone back and helped my master."

Anger flared and Aelfgifu shrugged Oswulf's hand from her shoulder. "You let my sons—my children!—go back to a fight on their own?"

Before the boy could answer Oswulf spoke.

"You obeyed your master, as you were taught to do."

Aelfgifu couldn't believe her housecarl would dismiss Egil's actions so lightly. But as she opened her mouth to argue further, Oswulf stayed her words with a whisper.

"This isn't the time."

She nodded her agreement. "Let's ready ourselves."

"My lady, no . . ."

She looked into Oswulf's stern face. He was a few years younger than her husband but sported the same deep wrinkles the king showed.

"You may ride with me or not, it's your choice." She started across the courtyard toward the stable. And her sword! She must retrieve her sword. She'd need help preparing.

"Lufu!"

Aelfgifu turned, uncertain what to do first. She saw Oswulf approaching.

"My lady, you can't go. You must remain here."

"You believe because I'm a woman I can't fight? I was taught by my father, and am joined to the best swordsman in the country!" She felt the anger mingling with her panic, each vying for her attention.

Oswulf held up a hand. "I'm certain you're as skilled as any shield maiden, and as fierce, but it would be more appropriate for you to stay at Reodfeld, should any news arrive."

Aelfgifu was about to respond, her raw emotions taking over her reason, but the look on her housecarl's face made her pause. It took only moments to realise he was right. It made more sense for her to stay. He bowed quickly before rushing off, barking orders as he went.

The next few hours were the worst of Aelfgifu's life. As soon as Oswulf left, she went to her chamber and took her sword from the carved whale-bone casket where she kept her most treasured possessions. She tested her arm, swinging the weapon a few times before replacing it in the casket. Not knowing what to do with herself, she wandered from room to room, moving objects she found on tables from one spot to another, straightening tapestries and smoothing bed sheets. She declined offers of food, but found herself carrying a goblet of wine with her, the cup never empty.

Finally she decided she had to act. She rushed to her bed chamber and pulled out an old chest from beneath her bed. Lufu silently followed, keeping a wary distance.

"I must do something to aid my sons. I'll make a sacrifice to Odin and beg him to return them to me."

Lufu nodded. "A goat?"

Aelfgifu turned with a knife in her hand, old as time and passed down from her father. "No." She thought for a moment. What would please the All Father? "A horse." She heard Lufu gasp but thankfully the girl kept her thoughts to herself. A horse would make a fine sacrifice. "Gather the household in the back, at the oak."

Lufu nodded and hurried out. Aelfgifu held the knife in front of her, the flames of her small fire dancing in the worn steel. Running her thumb along the blade she winced and licked the blood that was now welling from the cut. Gazing at the blade, spellbound by the reflected ghostly images, she whispered. "Please."

Aelfgifu was the last to arrive at the ancient tree and was gratified to see that nearly all of her household had joined her. She took her place at the base of the tree and nodded at the carl who maintained her stables. Those assembled stepped aside as a horse was led over to Aelfgifu and the reigns handed over.

"Odin, look favourably upon this sacrifice, a gift to you, the mightiest of all the gods!" Despite her worry over her sons her voice was calm and steady. Raising the knife to the nervous animal's throat, she raised her head to look skyward.

"All Father, if you are satisfied with my gift, please bring my sons home to me." As she spoke she reached under the horse's neck with the hand gripping the knife.

"Odin, I beg you, bring my sons home." Before the last word had left her mouth she brought the knife swiftly back toward her, cutting through the beast's great neck. Blood flowed as the animal's front legs buckled and it fell to the ground, its panicked whinnying growing less and less frantic. Those at the front of the crowd reached for the blood and began to smear it on themselves, each offering their own silent prayer to the All Father. Aelfgifu also reached over, one hand cupped for the blood, the other covering the now-still animal's eyes.

"Thank you, my friend." Smearing the warm blood on her face and neck, she led the household back into the manor.

They went back inside and continued with their chores as best they could. Hours passed and Aelfgifu was on the verge of calling for her horse when there was a commotion from outside. She rushed from the building and saw her sons, along with their sword master Grim and her carl Oswulf. Oswulf acknowledged her still bloody face with a raised eyebrow, knowing what she had done. Throwing herself at her boys she gathered them both in her arms, holding them tightly. Even when they began to squirm she held on. She finally released them and looked them up and down, glancing from Sweyn's leg to Harold's arm and back to

Sweyn again.

"Are you injured?" She ran her hands up and down them, desperately hoping she would find no wound. "Are you hurt?!"

Harold spoke, his young face displaying his irritation. "No mother, we're fine." He shrugged out of her reach and stepped back.

"Sweyn?"

Her eldest son spoke so quietly she'd to lean close to hear him. "I'm unhurt."

"Thank the All Father." After a last embrace of Sweyn and an attempted one of Harold, Aelfgifu ordered baths be drawn for the boys. It was only when they followed Lufu into the manor that she noticed Grim was still standing by his horse, his hand grasping the saddlebow tightly. Before she'd taken three steps towards him the sword master lost his grip on the saddle and sank to the ground, his cloak opening to reveal the dark stain on his side.

Both Aelfgifu and Oswulf rushed to his side. Grim was barely conscious but winced when she examined his wound. A sword slash, raw and bleeding, ran across his left side and there was blood on the side of his head, perhaps from a knock with a sword hilt? Running her fingers on the area she felt swelling around the wound. She ordered Grim to be placed on the table in the main hall and gathered her healing supplies.

When she had all she needed Aelfgifu approached the table. Already the blood from both wounds was dripping onto the reeds on the floor. She would have to act quickly. Handing two lengths of rolled cloth to Oswulf, she told him to press them tightly to both wounds. This would help to staunch the bleeding and allow her a better look at the actual injuries. While Oswulf did this she prepared a poultice over the fire, mixing herbs she had picked with some more exotic ones Canute had procured for her. When she was satisfied with the poultice's progress she left the bowl near the fire and went to check on the sword master's injuries.

She was pleased to see that the cloth had worked and that the extent of the damage was now visible. Focussing on the side wound first, she felt Oswulf standing so closely to her, peering over her shoulder as she examined Grim, that she could feel his breath on her neck. As a soldier the older man knew sword wounds and could tell minor ones from those more life-threatening, so it didn't surprise her when she felt him take a deep breath and blow it out in relief. He'd seen the same thing she had: the wound, although bloody, wasn't deep. Next she looked at the head injury. There was a horrifying amount of blood but Aelfgifu knew not to panic; head wounds were often bloody, even minor ones. It was difficult to see the damage through the man's hair but using her hands she could tell that the actual cut wasn't serious. The swelling, however, gave her more worry. A wound such as this shouldn't be so distended; there was an opening through which the fluid could drain. There wasn't much she could do to help except treat the wound and hope the swelling would go down.

Aelfgifu had Oswulf apply the swabbing back on the wounds while she made final preparations to the poultice. She'd warmed water on the fire and had torn linen sheets to make suitably-sized bandages. With Oswulf's help she cleaned the wound on Grim's side, applied the poultice and wrapped the sword master's body with the bandages. She then did the same for the head wound. Grim drifted in and out of consciousness as they saw to him, and even when Aelfgifu knew she must be causing him pain, not a single cry escaped his lips. He became more aware as they were bandaging him but was still unable to answer any of their questions; his words were slurred and slow. This worried Aelfgifu but she prayed that when his body had rested his speech would return to normal. When they were finished, the sword master tried to rise from the table and if Oswulf hadn't held him down he might've made it a few steps, such was the determination in his face.

"Nay, sword master. Lie still, we're preparing a bed for you. You must rest."

He struggled to rise and speak once more, and a rictus of pain flashed across his face. Leaving Oswulf to keep watch, she prepared a drink for her patient, warmed wine with ground valerian root to aid sleep, and willow bark to dull the pain and fight infection. Grim drank the mixture and she waited until his eyes dulled before having the servants carry him to the guest chamber. By the time they had folded the blankets around him he was asleep. She would have to wait for her answers.

While Grim slept, Aelfgifu went to be with the boys, both of whom were taking their baths. She got a sense of their anxiety by the atmosphere in the room and could see immediately how excited Harold still was. He was talking animatedly with Lufu and the other servants, emphasizing his words with his hands, resulting in water splashing everywhere. Lufu insisted on helping the boys wash despite Harold's protestations, and by the looks of her she had been in the way of Harold's animated story-telling more than once. Sweyn, on the other hand, sat virtually unmoving in his tub, allowing a servant to wash him without protest.

Harold was the first to see her. "Mother! Finally! Where have you been?"

Aelfgifu wasn't sure if the boys knew that Grim had been injured and was grateful to discover the man had kept his injuries hidden from them. "I had things to attend to." She dismissed Harold's question, knowing that normally her youngest wouldn't be satisfied with this answer, but she could tell today he was more interested in his own tale than any of her activities.

"We were attacked by bandits! In the forest! Two men attacked us!"

"I know, and you were told to run, were you not?" He shrugged a shoulder dismissively. "But you didn't do as you were told, did you?"

"Fleeing is for cowards." She could hear the disgust in his young voice.

Before she could reply Sweyn spoke. "We should've listened."

Aelfgifu saw the sullen look on her eldest son. Harold was about to retort, his disagreement plain on his face, and she decided to stop the potential argument right there. All of their emotions were frayed, making it easy for immature words to explode into something more the moment her back was turned.

"Enough! We'll talk later."

Harold backed down but insisted on being heard. "Where's Master Grim?"

"Resting, which is what you should be doing."

"But it's still daylight!" He had a whining tone to his voice.

Aelfgifu could see easily enough that they wouldn't sleep, even for a short while, in their present state, so she allowed them a small cup of wine each, warmed and with added spices. Soon both boys were falling asleep in front of her, and this time didn't resist when they were led to their beds.

She left Lufu to watch over the boys as they slept and went to sit in the main hall. Oswulf was still there and looked up at her expectantly as she entered. Shaking her head, for there was nothing to tell him, she saw that Oswulf had had the room cleared of all evidence of her work on the sword master.

The manor was silent as they sat waiting for Grim to waken, and Aelfgifu felt like the building itself was shocked by the day's events. She tried discussing the attack with Oswulf but as neither of them had any information it was pointless to speculate, at least until they'd heard from Grim. So here she was, waiting again. It was also pointless her trying to perform her usual daily activities; she'd tried earlier but had got nothing accomplished. It was still early enough in the year that the days were short and soon the light was fading. Aelfgifu was about to go to the guest room to check on Grim when the man's servant entered the hall, his face full of relief.

"My master's awake! He's asking for you my lady!" As she hurried to the man's room, Oswulf followed.

She was pleased to see his colour was much better; instead of the pale grey he'd been when he arrived his complexion was pinker. He winced in pain when he tried to move, however.

"My lady."

Aelfgifu clapped her hands together in delight as she approached the bed. "You can speak!"

"Yes, my lady. My mind was confused before but I'm able to think more clearly now."

She dragged a chair from its place beside a table in the middle of the room and put it beside the bed. Sitting quietly, she waited for the sword master to tell his story.

"We were riding from my home, Sweyn, Harold, myself and my servant," he waved a weak arm at Egil, who'd followed Aelfgifu back into the room. She saw the boy nod his agreement. "We were travelling to a practice spot I know and were perhaps halfway there when two men came out of hiding and attacked us. I drew my sword and fought the men, while watching the area around us for further attackers. When I was certain there were only the two I ordered my servant to take the boys and flee."

Aelfgifu could see the man was tiring, even with this small amount of talking. But she saw the determination on his face and said nothing. Instead she let the sword master continue his tale, holding her questions until he was finished.

"I continued fighting, wounding both men but, alas, not mortally for they both fled." He shook his head and Aelfgifu could see the movement made him feel ill for he suddenly paled. She held a goblet of wine for him, helping the man as he sipped the liquid before lying back.

"You acted bravely. My sons are alive because of you."

"Nay, my lady, there was minimal effort on my part for the attackers were poor swordsmen." He smiled wearily. "But that didn't prevent one of them from getting to me." He glanced down at the bandage wrapping his side and Aelfgifu saw the embarrassment on his face. "I followed them a short distance but they escaped. When I returned to where we were first attacked, and where I'd left my horse, I found Harold riding back, followed by his older brother."

It was obvious to Aelfgifu, a practised healer, that the man was suffering. His face showed his pain and he had wrapped his arms around his body as if to protect it. He held himself stiffly and she suspected that he wanted to avoid any more movement that would cause him further discomfort. But she had to know more.

"Did you recognise these men?"

The sword master's attitude changed; she could no longer see pain on his face, although she was sure it must still be there. She frowned, not recognising the new look. Was it fear?

"I'd speak to you alone, my lady."

Aelfgifu looked around the room. There were only a few servants, including Egil, who hadn't left his master's bedside since arriving at Reodfeld, herself and Oswulf. She ordered the servants out. At a nod from Grim, Egil left the room as well, stopping at the door to glance back at his master. Grim waved weakly at the boy as he left, closing the large wooden door behind him.

"What would you say to me?" Aelfgifu saw Grim look nervously at the large Dane standing just behind her. "You may speak freely in front of Oswulf."

She saw the sword master nod, accepting her carl instantly. "My lady, I didn't recognise the men who attacked us, but I did recognise the emblem on the shoulder of one of the men." He took a breath, grimacing as he did. Aelfgifu let him catch his breath, feeling helpless that there wasn't more she could do for him. "Lady, the emblem was Norman."

Aelfgifu rose from her chair, her rage causing the contents of her stomach to rise to her throat. "You're sure of this?" She resisted the urge to grab the injured man. Emblems were rarely worn in England; they were mainly used to show loyalty to a particular family in Europe, where fighting between families was common.

"Aye, madam, I'm sure. I've travelled much, I know a Norman badge when I see one."

She thanked the man for his help and ensured he was comfortable before leaving the room with Oswulf. Egil ran back to his master's side once the door had been opened, narrowly missing Aelfgifu. She barely noticed the boy.

Only when they were back in the hall did she speak. "You know what this means," she asked rhetorically.

"Yes, lady."

She stared at him and saw he spoke the truth. He knew what she knew, that only one person could be responsible for this attack on her children: Emma of Normandy.

Canute arrived three days later, direct from the port of Yarmouth where his fleet had landed, back finally from Denmark. Without a word Aelfgifu rushed over to him as soon as he'd dismounted and held him, needing to feel his arms around her, protecting her. She remained that way for as long as she could, ignoring the noise and bustle of arriving soldiers and carls until too many calls for her and for Canute disrupted her peace. She released him and stepped back.

"Where are the boys? Are they well?"

She took his hand in her own and led him into the building. There, she stopped and pointed to the hearth.

"Boys!" Canute's face lit up, his relief evident.

"Father!" Sweyn and Harold rushed toward their father, throwing themselves at him. He leaned down hugging them and Aelfgifu felt such pride at seeing her family, safe and together. Harold threw questions at Canute, one after another with little chance of hearing a reply to any single query.

"Harold, Sweyn, back to your work. I'd like to speak to your father before you tire him out." She winked at them, letting them see she was in jest, but they obeyed and returned to their places.

Lufu had announced Canute's arrival, and had stayed behind in the hall to arrange the food and drink. It was late at night and despite the food being cold, it still smelled appetising. Her cook knew as much about cooking with herbs and plants as Aelfgifu did about healing with them. And here was the proof: tender seasoned pork that fell off the bone with a minor flick of a knife. Canute piled the meat atop the bread that had been made that morning and made light work of the meal, talking to Aelfgifu as he ate.

"What happened? I received word as soon as we reached the *hithe* that there was trouble." He wiped crumbs from his beard which, Aelfgifu noticed, was shorn much shorter than the last time she'd seen him. He noticed her gaze and waved a hand, dismissing it.

"A new fashion in my homeland. Sometimes I must look like a noble, even when in the mud with my soldiers."

She nodded. "What have you been told?"

"Only that my sons were attacked while away from the

manor, and that someone had been mortally injured."

Aelfgifu shook her head, frowning. This was why she rarely relied on rumours or stories if she could help it; at best they were incomplete, at worst completely inaccurate.

"Two men attacked Sweyn and Harold as they travelled with their sword master. He fought the men off and ordered the boys to flee. The attackers escaped but not before the sword master was rewarded with a wound for his efforts." She stopped to drink, wondering what else she could tell him to delay revealing the end of her tale.

"The boys were unhurt. Harold was disappointed he took no part in the fight, but for that I'm grateful." She paused again. "The sword master is upstairs recovering."

"So not mortal then? No one was seriously hurt?" Canute relaxed further into his chair. She shook her head, no. "Then he's able to speak! Did he say who these attackers were?"

This was the part she'd been dreading. Delaying again, she spoke. "He managed to injure both of the men, he acted very bravely."

Canute nodded. "Yes, but did he recognise the men?"

She sighed. Normally news of Emma's indiscretions could be shared freely between them, in fact they were something that had brought them closer in the past few years, something she didn't think was possible. But this news was different. Serious, and deadly. "The sword master recognised a Norman emblem on one of the men."

This time it was Canute who flew from his chair, causing the boys to look up from their studies. "Emma did this? She tried to have my children killed? My own sons?"

His voice grew louder with each word and Aelfgifu could see the fury in him rising too. The stance he took, his physical presence changed the tone of the room instantly. He was a man used to fighting and who was prepared to fight again.

"Why? Why would she do this? A warning?"

Aelfgifu shook her head. "No, I believe she truly meant our sons harm. If it weren't for Grim . . ." she shuddered.

Canute began pacing the hall, ignoring the alarmed look from Sweyn. Harold's face showed his curiosity and Aelfgifu saw that although he pretended to focus on his work, his attention was on the room and those in it.

"She allowed Grim to see the emblem, that was clever."

Tired of hearing how about how 'clever' Emma was, Aelfgifu's nerves stretched even further. But she kept her comments to herself, for what use would railing and ranting be now? "I don't understand."

Canute was at the far end of the hall but his long legs closed the distance in a few strides.

"She has left herself blameless. There's no proof she had any part in this."

"But what of the emblem?"

Canute snorted. "What noble would believe the word of a servant?" He held up his hand to stop her interrupting. "No, even a high-placed servant such as the sword master is still a servant, or seems so to the men who would need to be convinced of Emma's complicity. She knew he would know enough to recognise the badge, but low enough that none but us would trust him. And even more, who would believe she would be so stupid as to let them wear her badge?"

"She's been watching us?" The horror she felt at such an invasion frightened her.

"Having you watched, yes, so it would seem. How else would she know when to have her men attack?"

The feeling came over her so suddenly she'd not the time to rush outside. She took a few steps, then, leaning over, Aelfgifu's body spasmed until everything she'd eaten that day came back up onto the rushes. Even when her stomach was empty her body shook, uncontrollable tears flowing from her eyes, blurring her vision until everything was a tapestry of muted colours and shapes, all running together.

She felt Canute's arm around her waist, holding her through each shudder until finally her body was done and allowed her to stand once more. Canute guided her back to the chair and only then did she notice Sweyn and Harold, standing still, their eyes wide in alarm. She waved at them and smiled but there was still anxiety in Sweyn's eyes as she sat down. Canute went to a side table and brought back watered-down ale and bread.

"Eat, it'll settle your stomach." He tore a piece and urged it on her, almost forcing the food into her mouth. It only took a few morsels and a small cup of ale before she started to feel better.

But while her body felt better her mind didn't. She was more frightened and disturbed and angry and alarmed than she'd ever been in her life. And suddenly tired, very tired. With so little energy left for that day, she didn't care about her words. "You can't divorce her. You can't send her home. You can't kill her."

"I'm stuck with her, and you see now how she is."

She saw much more than Canute realised. This hadn't been a warning or rash act aimed at Canute. This was a message for her, Aelfgifu, one wife to the other. And the message was clear: stay away from the king and our children.

Chapter Seventeen
England

Canute had been in Northampton with her for nearly two weeks when the messenger arrived. Aelfgifu used to wonder how Emma may have felt during these times, knowing that her husband would rather be with her. But now she cared so little about Emma's feelings that the thought hardly crossed her mind. Except when the messenger arrived. It reminded her that the threat was still there and here could be news of yet another of Emma's intrigues. The messenger, an expensively-dressed young man from London, judging by his accent, insisted that he deliver the message to none but the king himself. He was clearly determined, and though feeling mildly slighted, but nevertheless intrigued, she showed the messenger to the stable where Canute was speaking with the farrier, Arvid.

The messenger rushed over to Canute and fell at his feet, interrupting the conversation. Aelfgifu, watching from the doorway, smiled at Arvid's confusion. Canute looked at the farrier and frowning, shook his head slightly. The movement said wait, there may be some amusement here.

"Stand up, boy."

The messenger rose clumsily, slipping once in the mud before righting himself. "My lord, I deliver a most important letter that has come from overseas." He bowed and presented a sealed parchment.

Canute, still amused by the young man, donned a serious look as he took the document. "And how, may I ask, do you know of its importance OR of its origin? Did you read it?"

The messenger turned pale and Aelfgifu had to cover her mouth and turn away to avoid laughing. Canute's humour always improved, the longer he stayed with her.

"My lord, no, I don't, that is I mean . . . "

He was interrupted by the king's laughter. "I speak in jest. Go, find the kitchen, you'll be served there. You can stay the night if you wish and take any provisions you need for your return journey."

She watched the relieved messenger almost run to the manor as she joined Canute. He dismissed the farrier and tore open the seal, reading quickly while she waited. His eyes scanned back and forth over the words and widened as he read. Finally he folded the letter and frowned.

"What? What does it say?" She couldn't bear to wait any longer, the look on his face obviously indicating that the letter contained news of importance. He shook his head, unable to speak. Aelfgifu grew impatient. "Tell me! What news?"

He cleared his throat before speaking. "I've been invited to Rome for the coronation of Conrad."

"The Holy Roman Emperor!" Eyebrows raised, she took the letter and read. It was true. Looking up at him from the parchment, she said. "Will you go?"

He began to pace the stables, stopping every so often to straighten a hanging bridle or stroke one of his horses. Finally he spoke. "I haven't decided. It'll be a costly venture and there's much to do, both here and in Denmark."

She knew these were excuses. The money could be found, indeed would be offered by the Bishops for a journey of such momentous importance. As for England and Denmark, England had been calm for years, save for the usual land disagreements and petty squabbles between nobles. And Canute had left a worthy and respected regent to watch over and protect Denmark. There was no real reason for not going, but when she pointed this out to him, Canute remained unsure.

"You've even started ensuring allies amongst the Swedes and Norwegians." Canute had told Aelfgifu of his plan to win over the nobles of these two countries, starting with gifts of gold and silver.

He waved her words aside. Then he stopped and turned to her. "I'll go if you come with me."

For a moment she allowed herself to believe that his suggestion could work, that she could indeed accompany him on this wondrous journey. But sadly it couldn't be. And she was positive he knew it.

"I'd dearly love, above all things, to make this voyage with you but you know as well as I that my presence would be an affront to all the kings in Christendom."

She could feel the bile rising in her throat, as always happened when she spoke of this matter.

"These men, religious leaders and shining examples of the new religion, who worship a forgiving and humble man, yet who won't forgive anything themselves and who only seek to grow their own fortunes." She stopped herself before her anger got the better of her. While Aelfgifu had often advised Canute to give money to religious houses for political reasons, she hated that he had to do so, that the bishops had so much power that the only way to keep them loyal was to offer bribes. She herself gave money to worthy groups, those who went out into the world and helped heal people, who supplied clothing and food to the poor and those in need. These people needed her donations and she didn't care what god they worshipped.

He came towards her, both hands raised. "You mistake my meaning. I don't mean to take you to Rome, but to travel part way with me and live elsewhere with our sons."

The impact of what he was saying hit her immediately, like a physical blow to the stomach. "You'd abandon me and your sons this way? Move us out of the country so we're no longer a nuisance? So that you're no longer reminded of us? You'd deny our sons their rightful inheritance?" Her tears were flowing, the hurt so deep she couldn't breathe.

Grabbing her and pulling her towards him, he held her tight, kissing the top of her head. "No! I only want to protect you!"

She struggled to make her words heard; anger had made her voice hoarse and she was pressed tightly against her husband's chest. "So it's come to this. She's become so dangerous that the only way forward is for me to leave my homeland."

"Aelf . . . "

"No!" She struggled free from his arms. "I know what must be done. I won't be driven from my home, nor will my sons!" Calming herself she took both of Canute's hands in hers, forcing herself to remember the details, the roughness of the skin, the scars from battle, the still-soft area on his wrist just beneath his palm. "I won't leave England. But you and I must never see each other again." She felt him begin to pull away but held fast. "You must no longer visit Reodfeld, nor arrange to see me."

He jerked his hands away from hers. "No, I won't do it. Never. I'll be more discreet, less obvious in my planning and travel."

Aelfgifu sighed, frustrated. "You think she hasn't got spies? We know she does and she watches me. How else could her men have gotten so close to our boys?" She saw that he recognised the wisdom in her words and softened her voice. "You must write less, use fewer messengers, and hide your affection." He still looked doubtful. "Can't you see it has to be this way?" Finally there was resignation.

"I'll still write. I won't stop contact with you, not ever! But I'll be careful."

That night they made love with a passion neither had felt since their younger years when they were newly joined and the woes of the world hadn't discovered them yet. But there was also sadness and desperation. Afterwards Aelfgifu listened to the muffled snores of her husband. She'd had to be strong, but now, lying in the dark, the tears came.

Canute left the next morning and headed back to London to prepare for his journey. Months later, Aelfgifu learned of the fight between Canute and Emma when the queen found out she was not to attend the coronation ceremony with him. Fleeing from court, Emma had locked herself into her manor at Exeter and would see no one. But this was small comfort for Aelfgifu, as she still grieved at the necessity of what she had done.

Chapter Eighteen
England

"Why wasn't it done when I asked? Go, you stupid woman, do your job!"

The young maid ran from the room, her hand raised to unsuccessfully hide her crumpled features. No doubt to the kitchen to complain about her, Aelfgifu guessed. She sighed. She hadn't meant to shout at the poor girl, but her anger had been coming to the surface more and more lately, and her manor staff and carls had been suffering the worst of it. She wasn't angry at them, not really. She was angry at Canute, at herself, at the whole situation.

"My lady?"

Lufu stood before her, eyebrows knit together. Her closest friend and confidant, and even she'd been stung by Aelfgifu recently. "Lufu."

"It may not be my place to say this, but . . . " She did not need to finish the sentence.

Aelfgifu picked up the thought. "You're worried? About me?" Lufu blushed and lowered her head. Aelfgifu stood and began to walk the room. Although it was only early afternoon, the fire was burning brightly; the summer had been cold and the fall was the coldest any could remember. It didn't bode well for the winter ahead and Aelfgifu had ordered that supplies be gathered and stored early, in case the season should suddenly turn.

"My lady, what can I do to help you?"

She waved a hand in the air as she walked, needing to move to keep her nerves occupied or she felt she'd explode.

"Nothing. There's nothing you, nor anyone, can do." She felt her emotions wearing thin.

"Aelfgifu . . . " Lufu was close enough, had spent enough

time with her mistress to be allowed to use her first name when they were alone.

"Why? Why didn't he fight me? Why did he just accept what I proposed?" Lufu would know what she was speaking of; they'd discussed it over and over in the past few weeks.

"He had no choice, it was a wise decision. You're safer for it."

"But if he loved me so much, he would've protested!"

"I'm sure he did, my lady. Your emotions are clouding your memory."

Aelfgifu stopped mid stride and thought back to that day, remembered Canute's face as she told him they could no longer see each other, for the sake of their sons. And for her own safety. She moved back to her chair and sat across from Lufu. "You're right of course. But it's not fair! Why should that *bikkja* care so much about me? I only wish to be left alone!"

"She cares because she wishes to remain queen when Canute is . . . gone. And for her son to be king. You're a threat to her, whether you think so or not."

Aelfgifu nodded. She'd heard the same words so many times they'd almost become meaningless. She marvelled that Lufu hadn't given up on her, that she had the patience to explain the same things over again. Something else to add to the growing list of things she felt guilty about. She rubbed her hands, leaning back in the chair; they pained her lately, more so in the colder weather. Her knee also bothered her at times. She made a mental note to make a poultice to help with the stiffness. "I know. I do know. Canute also said the same. I just can't seem to accept it, despite all that's happened."

"Your head may not believe it, but your heart certainly does."

Aelfgifu looked up sharply. "What do you mean?"

Lufu's face took on a look of pity. "You walk Reodfeld as

if being followed, always looking over your shoulder and into the shadows. You suspect any who comes to visit. And your bed is still . . . " Again she left her sentence unfinished.

It was true, all of it. As soon as her friend spoke the words she knew it was so. How could this have got so bad without her even realising it? Or had she known and somehow managed to convince herself it wasn't true? And her bed. Sweyn and Harold had no qualms about bringing up that sore subject. The previous night, they had objected strenuously.

"Mother, why must you sleep in the same room as ours?" After the attack on her sons she'd moved her bed into the room adjoining the boy's chamber, to better keep them safe. Or so she told herself, and them.

"To watch over you." She was readying them for the night, straightening the sheets and replied without looking up.

Harold took up the cause. "But we're no longer babies! We're men and men don't have their mothers with them when they sleep."

It was very nearly true; Sweyn was twelve, his brother a year younger, both on the cusp of adulthood. "You're not men yet." She knew this response would infuriate Harold but what else could she say? That the real reason she'd moved her bed was more for her own peace of mind than theirs? Of course they didn't need their mother so close, they made it clear enough when they were awake. Lately they had been shrugging off her attentions, dressing themselves and they no longer allowed her to smooth their hair or straighten their jerkins. And she'd had to solemnly swear not to go near their room when they bathed. Her sons were indeed becoming men.

Sweyn, ever the sensible one, joined back in. "It's embarrassing. All in the manor know and no doubt half of Northampton knows by now. It's unseemly for the sons of the king to have their mother sleeping in the same chamber."

She looked up at this comment, startled by the adult reasoning. Her son spoke the truth; she hadn't thought about how it would look to outsiders.

Her thoughts returned to the present. "You're right Lufu. See that my bed is returned to my own chamber." She waved at the empty space where the bed had been originally. "But ensure that there are guards posted around the manor. And I wish to know at all times where the boys are."

A few weeks after Aelfgifu had moved back to her own chamber a messenger arrived at Reodfeld.

"Who are you?"

"My lady, my name is Higa."

"And who do you serve?"

"Earl Godwin, my lady."

She looked him up and down, seeing no evidence of his loyalties from his clothing. "Why have you come here? Why are you not with your master, if you are his loyal servant?" Her eyes narrowed.

"My lady . . . I . . . he, that is my lord Godwin . . ." He stopped and took a deep breath, stretching out a hand to steady himself. "My lady, lord Godwin has sent me here with a letter."

Aelfgifu paused, staring at the man. She so wanted to believe it was true, that here was perhaps news from her husband. But experienced caution took over. "From whom did you get this letter?"

"The earl himself gave it to me. He told me to let no one see it save for the lady Aelfgifu."

This was still no proof that she could trust the contents of the letter. She was about to ask another question when the man spoke. "My lady, the earl told me to remind you of a conversation, about a certain lady you both know and of an inappropriate red dress?"

Aelfgifu sighed. This was certainly a message from Godwin, for there was no one else in the room when they had laughed at his wife, Gytha, and the dress she had chosen for Canute's coronation. Godwin had been so angry! She smiled. "Hand me the letter and go find the kitchen." She pointed to the kitchen. With an awkward bow and grateful smile he was gone.

She hurried to the hall, calling for Lufu to bring wine and to join her. They sat by the main hearth while Aelfgifu carefully opened the letter. "It's from Godwin. He travels with my husband to Rome." She shook her head; of course Lufu knew who and where Godwin was.

"To the most gracious Lady Aelfgifu, in King Canute's name I greet you and your children, may the gods watch over and keep you safe. I write to tell you of our journey and news of our voyage so far."

She smiled; Godwin knew of her recent brush with Emma and her men and started the letter by telling her that there was to be no bad news contained within.

"As you know the king departed your manor and returned to London, there to be met by the queen with much respect. So agreeable was she that all wondered at the change. Her true purpose became more clear in the days leading up to our departure: the queen would travel with us to Rome and only waited for the king to respond positively to her ploys."

Aelfgifu stopped to take a drink and saw the look of disgust on Lufu's face that, she was certain, mirrored her own.

"For nearly a week she behaved thus, finally erupting at him over dinner one night, demanding to know when they were to depart and what she should take with her. I was in the room and made to leave, but was ordered to remain by

the king's command. When the king told her she was not to go, she stood from her chair, took her plate and threw it at Canute. The king was not hurt and had the queen led by force to her chamber. The next morning the queen fled the palace for her property in Exeter.

We sailed and were fortunate to get fine weather, despite the lateness of the year. We arrived in Denmark in good time and were greeted by the king's son, Harthacanute. We tarried a little at the Danish court, ensuring our supplies were sufficient for our journey before continuing. Canute has continued with the business of ruling his realm, despite leaving Leofric, the Earl of Mercia, to act as regent in England."

Aelfgifu knew Leofric was another of Canute's most trusted men and would do a good job of watching both the country and the queen while the king was away. She looked over the paper at Lufu and saw the other woman's rapt attention focussed on her.

"The king also made a plan to sow discontent among the Norwegian nobles, to further punish King Olaf for attacking Denmark, so we paused on our way to Rome to travel briefly to Norway. As we passed on our way, Canute offered gifts to these nobles, gold and silver plate, coin and jewels. There are many who are unhappy with their king, those who follow the old ways, because he wishes to turn the entire country Christian. We continued our travel south and followed a path that took us through the land of Flanders as well as France. Our pace was slow for we had many animals and wagons with us and the snow and hills hindered our movement but we now approach the north of Italy and soon will be within sight of Rome."

Aelfgifu sighed. While Godwin was a decent reporter she wished his writing included more about the sights he witnessed, the sounds about him and the people he encountered. The writing was stiff and formal, written with a heavy hand but still she was grateful for any news at all of her husband.

"I am forever at your service."

The letter finished with an illegible scrawl that Aelfgifu assumed was Godwin's signature. She wondered if he'd practised this or if he even cared that no one could read it. She folded the letter and looked at Lufu.

"My lady, the journey goes well it seems."

She nodded her head, yes, it all sounded good. "It's a well-written letter; the earl is very gracious to have written to us with these details. I'm grateful to him." A small, barely acknowledged part of her wondered if her husband missed her, and was grieved by the lack of her presence, but she dare not speak the thought aloud.

As Aelfgifu had expected, the weather turned suddenly; the winds blew harsh and cold and the skies became a dark grey, noise booming all around them as if the gods were doing battle in some unseen place.

"I need to go into town." She was donning a warm cloak as she spoke, her stiff fingers struggling with the cloak-pin. It was her favourite, a silver brooch with a dragon design; one of the first gifts Canute had given her. Lufu approached and she reluctantly let her friend help.

"Why? It's a day to stay inside." Lufu spoke as she tucked the pin inside the clasp and stood back, checking to see the brooch was straight. A clap of thunder from outside emphasized her words.

"The weather will get worse and I need a few things before I'm unable to travel at all. I'll not be long. Oswulf will accompany me to town, so I need you to watch over the boys."

"But they don't listen to me."

"You'll be fine, there are many carls in Reodfeld and Canute has sent more men to watch over us."

"And what of you, my lady?"

She stared at the girl. "Just watch my sons, I'll return shortly."

It took her longer than she thought to collect what she needed, and there were those who would, despite her impatient stance or look, stop her to speak of town matters. As the owner of the land where these people lived and worked, she had a responsibility to them and couldn't turn down a request or question. But today she didn't have the patience for it; she wanted nothing more than to get home, especially after she heard rumours of two men-at-arms being sighted in town. Some said they acted naturally but others swore the men hid weapons beneath their cloaks. She had to get back to Reodfeld. Besides, did they think nothing of being out in this weather? Stopping her to talk, their words whipped away by the wind, she strained to hear over the thunder. She shook her head in wonderment. Northerners were a hardy people and proud of their toughness, sometimes to foolishness.

She finally managed to escape the townspeople and hurry back home. The skies opened as she approached the manor and, while it might be unseemly, she ran as fast as she could, surprising her guards. Shaking the rain from her cloak, she called to the boys from the entrance way.

"Take these to my room, please." A maid took the packages from her mistress. Lufu appeared, bringing spiced hot wine to take the chill from Aelfgifu and Oswulf. "Sweyn! Harold!" Aelfgifu called to her sons.

Sweyn appeared first and came over to Aelfgifu. She kissed the top of his head. "Where's your brother?"

"I don't know." Sweyn shrugged.

A small tendril of worry began to wind its way up her spine. She called for her youngest son again, remaining silent afterward to better hear him. Still there was no sound. Worry turned to fear. "Oswulf, please find my son." She kept her voice calm but saw that Oswulf's eyes were wide and alert. She heard Oswulf whisper to someone outside in the corridor and soon the entire manor was alive with movement, every member of staff looking for her son. During all of this activity Sweyn sat by the fire, his eyes cast down.

"Where is he? Why can't they find him?"

She felt Lufu's hand on hers. "He'll be found my lady, and everything will be well again."

"I told you to look after them, both of them." She struggled to keep her voice even.

"My lady, I did as you asked! I only left them for a moment, to relieve myself, but I left a guard at their door."

"What guard? Whom did you leave with my sons?" She could feel the hysteria rising inside.

"Lady, I don't know his name." The other woman's arms flailed, as if trying to grasp the words from the air.

Aelfgifu stood, willing her body not to strike Lufu. Oswulf arrived at just that moment, his face dark. "My lady, we've searched the manor and grounds and couldn't find your son."

She felt herself about to collapse and grabbed the back of the chair to steady herself. Seeing movement from the corner of her eye, she turned to see her eldest son squirming uncomfortably on his chair. She rushed over. "Sweyn, where's your brother?"

The boy avoided her gaze. "I don't know." His voice was a whisper and she leaned forward to better hear.

"You're not in trouble, we just want to find your brother."

He avoided her gaze a moment longer before turning his eyes toward her. "I told him not to go, that you'd be angry!"

Aelfgifu turned her son so that he faced her. Kneeling before him she took his hands into hers. "I'm not angry, I only wish to see Harold."

Instead of answers all she received were more deflections.

"It's not my fault! I told him not to go outside, he knew we weren't allowed." His eyes widened, knowing he'd given something away.

"So he went outside? Do you know where he went?" Aelfgifu still held Sweyn's hands, hers icy cold and his hot and moist with sweat. She looked into his face and saw his eyes glance toward the back wall. "The stalls? Has he gone to the stalls?"

At the smallest of nods, Oswulf shouted to a guard standing in the doorway. "You, did you check the stalls?" The man nodded.

"Yes, they were searched."

Oswulf looked back to Aelfgifu. She leaned toward Sweyn again. "Why did Harold go to the stalls?" When he began to look away again she shook his hands. "Why, Sweyn?!"

"To see the new puppies! There, now you know! I've broken my promise! Are you happy?"

Oswulf had already run from the room and they felt the outside chill enter the manor as he opened the main door. It thudded closed again a moment later. They waited in silence; Aelfgifu pacing, Lufu nearby and Sweyn scowling in a chair across the room. The waiting was interminable. Where were they? Why was it taking Oswulf so long? She heard the sounds of other staff bustling around Reodfeld, still looking everywhere for Harold. Aelfgifu had just decided to get her cloak and go out herself when the door opened and once more the front entrance was flooded with cold air and blowing leaves. She rushed to the door as Oswulf entered, carrying a bundle.

Before Aelfgifu could speak Oswulf's deep voice reached

her. "He's fine, my lady." She nearly fell to the ground with relief but managed to follow Oswulf into the hall. He laid the boy on a table before the fire. "He sleeps, that's all."

She saw her son, face pale, his cloak wrapped closely around him. Reaching forward to stroke his face, she drew her hand back in horror. "He's freezing! Quickly, get blankets! And furs, off the beds, as many as you can find!" She sent the order to the room, not addressing anyone in particular but knowing her command would be obeyed. Soon Lufu returned and handed Aelfgifu a grey wolf fur. She threw it on top of her son as Oswulf arrived with more furs. Together they placed them on and around Harold, who remained unaware of their ministrations.

"I'll see that broth is prepared." Lufu didn't wait for Aelfgifu's reply but turned and left the hall. Her friend's relief, just as great as her own, made Aelfgifu feel even more guilty for her earlier harshness.

There was nothing to do now but wait, the very thing Aelfgifu always found most difficult. She'd spent most of her life waiting, for news, for visits, for sons, for her husband. But she'd never found a way to cope with the frustration waiting always brought with it. Fortunately her son was not insensible for long.

"Mother?" The small voice reached her ears from deep within the pile of furs on the table. Rushing over she saw Harold looking up at her, a confused look on his face.

"Harold! How do you feel?"

She watched him struggle to sit up, not sure if the cold had hampered his movement or the furs under which he slept. "What happened?"

Aelfgifu tried to keep her son from rising but was unsuccessful. Giving in to his wishes, she removed some of the furs. "You were found in the stalls, half frozen."

A spark of recognition appeared in Harold's eyes and she hoped he would be more willing to speak than his brother had been. "I remember. I went to see the new litter. I must've fallen asleep." He shrugged as if all of this was perfectly reasonable.

"You fell asleep? Outside? Didn't you think it was too cold? Didn't you fear the weather, as others do?" She saw no apology on his face. "If it'd not been for Oswulf you might've died out there, do you understand?" She watched as his face transformed itself into that smile, the one he used to melt her heart and gain her forgiveness. It usually worked. Not today. "You disobeyed me, Harold. I told you to stay indoors and you ignored my command and went outside anyway."

"But I wanted to see the dogs." Aelfgifu could see that her son finally realised that he couldn't escape her displeasure this time.

"I don't care what you wanted to do, this isn't about what you want." She caught herself; her voice was sharper, her frustration growing. She had to make him understand. Harold began to climb from the table and Aelfgifu helped him, sitting him on the bench alongside the table. She sat beside him as Lufu brought in broth and placed it in front of the boy, talking as he ate. "Listen to what I've got to say. I don't make these demands because I don't love you nor because I want to keep you from having fun. I make them for the opposite reason." She watched Harold's eyebrows raise; good, it meant he was listening. "You remember those men who attacked you in the woods?" He nodded. "You were brave but wouldn't it be best to live without the worry of such attacks?" She was gratified to see that Harold was considering her words.

His spoon hung halfway between his bowl and his mouth, his frown creased. "I like to fight."

"I know you do, and being a good fighter is necessary, a commendable talent. But there is a time and a place for fighting. Even great warriors must return home and rest, run their manors and take care of their families. Do you think these men want to be constantly worried about attacks? How would they ever get anything done? How would they raise crops and animals to sell for money to buy weapons and armour?"

Harold's face changed once more; this time she saw understanding. She pressed her point. "I ask that you respect my wishes when I ask you to remain indoors. There are men who don't see the wisdom of a peaceable living and who would do you and your brother harm. If I'm strict it's because I've more knowledge than you of these things and am better equipped to protect you while your father is away."

Finally she saw acceptance on Harold's face. "I understand. I'll obey your wishes." He turned back to his broth, thinking the conversation over. "There's one other thing I wish to discuss with you."

A frown appeared on Harold's face. "You made your brother promise to keep your whereabouts a secret, did you not?" A noise from across the hall caught her attention: the scraping of Sweyn's chair as he straightened, now paying attention. At Harold's silence she continued. "Well, did you or didn't you?"

"I did."

"You shouldn't have done that. It's wicked to force another to lie. Imagine yourself in the same position." She waved Sweyn over and when he was standing across from Harold spoke again. "You're always telling me what men you've become, very well, you'll deal with this as men do." She turned to Sweyn to address him. "You're the injured party. You deserve payment for your injuries." Returning her attention to Harold, she continued. "You're the guilty party. You'll pay wergeld to your brother. Agree an amount between you."

Before Harold could speak, she asked Oswulf to see both boys to their chamber. It was late and the last few hours had made them all tired. As they left both of her sons turned to look back at her. Sweyn's look was one of gratitude, Harold's angry. Odd, she thought, it was usually the other way around.

It was early in the year 1028 when another letter arrived at Reodfeld. This one had come far and was worn from the travel. The trader who delivered it said he had been given it in Canterbury before coming north for wool. He was told that it had been carried from Rome by a mendicant monk returning to England. This letter was from Lufu's father, who had been selected to be part of the retinue accompanying Canute to Rome. Aelfgifu was disappointed that the letter wasn't from her husband but she enjoyed Lufu's father's lively voice, so different from other officials at court.

"Will you share my father's words with me, my lady?" Lufu asked.

Aelfgifu was grateful for the invitation. They ended up sitting in the exact same places as the last time they read news from Rome: in the main hall in chairs pushed close to the hearth with heated spiced wine nearby.

"My darling daughter, I greet you from the great city of Rome and hope and pray that you, the Lady Aelfgifu and her sons are well."

Lufu stopped, looking at the letter through narrowed eyes.

"We've finally arrived in Rome and my daughter, what a city is this! I dearly wish I could have brought you with me, such sights and sounds, you would be amazed."

This was more like it, so unlike Godwin's tone. Even when he spoke of gossip his writing was stiff and factual. Aelfgifu smiled, grabbed a cup of wine and leaned back in her chair.

"The journey was difficult and many times we were forced to stop and help our horses pull the wagons out of the mud or snow. In some places we found the way treacherous; ice and snow at higher elevations slowed our progress. But in the lower places, where the melting ice runs, we encountered much mud. For a good part of our travel we were either sliding or sticking! Once we descended the hills our way grew easier and even the horses displayed their pleasure by trotting proudly, legs held high."

Lufu stopped once more and Aelfgifu saw her peering over the letter, as if to gauge her mistress's reaction. It was this more than the fanciful descriptions of happy horses that made Aelfgifu laugh; that the woman should be so embarrassed by her father, a studious man, devoted parent and wonderful storyteller, amused her. She saw Lufu's face turning more and more red. "My dear, I laugh with your father, not at him. His words are delightful! Please continue."

A smile appeared on Lufu's face before it disappeared back behind the letter.

"Wherever we went people came to see, lining the roads to watch us pass. I'm certain many of these villagers had never seen a sight such as we presented! The king was generous, throwing coins to the people. And he stopped along the way to give to abbeys and other religious houses, impressing those who had joined us on our journey."

Aelfgifu smiled; it had been her idea to contribute to these places, for in England Canute could be forgiven for following the old ways but in Rome the idea was unthinkable. No, he must present himself as the most devout man in Christendom.

"We finally arrived at the great city itself and my dear, you cannot imagine the sights and sounds of so large a place! And so many people, I've never in my life seen such!

As we travelled further into the centre, to buildings that had been assigned to us, I took in more of our surroundings. The city smelled of those who lived there, the familiar scent of living as it is in England, but here there is something different in the air, something exotic and strange. Incense from the many chapels mingles with smoke from hearths and cooking food. You should be here, my daughter, to help me identify the many and various plants that are sold at the market. We passed through the main walls of the city and could see signs of the sack of Rome by the barbarians still visible. Inside the walls the crowds grew less but still the colours and sights remained. The men of Rome are more conservative in their dress but the women wear finery such as I've never seen. They think themselves very beautiful, preening and flaunting, I think the queen would be very comfortable here! But there are none as beautiful as you, my daughter."

Lufu stopped and Aelfgifu saw her once again peering over the top of the letter, as if expecting a comment. "Your father is very proud of you." She nodded for the other woman to continue.

"We passed by the place where, it's said, the bones of St Peter are buried. Even the outside of the building is solemn and there is an air of some mystery surrounding the place. The songs the monks sing came drifting out of the building and in that moment I realised how far from home I really am.

"We've arrived at our lodgings and are preparing for the coronation, which takes place in three days' time. I'll end my letter here for there is yet much to do. I send my love to you, my beloved daughter, may the gods watch over you."

Lufu showed the letter to Aelfgifu. There was further writing after the signature, small letters meant only for Lufu. She stood and, walking out of the hall, a nod indicating her thanks, left her friend to read her letter again.

It was the middle of spring before Aelfgifu received more news from Rome. She was in her garden, pruning herbs and picking weeds when Oswulf appeared. With a smile he wordlessly handed a letter to her and left. She looked down and saw the seal. Her heart leaped; it was Canute's personal seal. She brushed the dirt from her skirt and forced herself to walk to a bench, feeling her body trying to run, to rush forward and tear open the letter. She chose a bench that sat out of the direct sunlight and, looking around to make sure she was alone, carefully broke the seal and opened the letter.

"To she who is most precious to me in the world, my wife Aelfgifu."

She felt her stomach tighten; part of her was angry that Canute had broken his promise to not write, but another, larger, part of her was overjoyed that he had.

"I can imagine your face as you read this, for had we not agreed that there should be no contact? But I couldn't help myself, I cannot and won't abide by our contract for I must and will continue to see you and write to you."

She sighed, relief and happiness flooding her. It had pained her to cut off contact with Canute, more than anything she'd ever felt. But it'd seemed the most prudent thing to do, given the threat posed by Emma. Instead of going over the arguments for and against contact in her head, she simply allowed herself to trust her husband.

"We're soon to depart Rome, it has been a worthwhile visit but I'm anxious to return home and to all that is familiar to me.

"The coronation of the Holy Roman Emperor Conrad was the most lavish and expensive ceremony I've ever witnessed or even heard of, and put my own coronation to shame. Every prince and noble from across Europe was in

attendance, all dressed in finery and all laden with lavish gifts for the emperor. The man himself is worthy, about my age. We have much in common, despite our different backgrounds and we spent enough time together to become solid friends. He's as skilled in the political arena as he is in the field, both are as a hunt to him and this too we had in common. It was through him that I was able to meet with the Holy Father."

Aelfgifu unconsciously raised an eyebrow, marvelling at this meeting. Only a well-respected prince would be allowed into the presence of the man responsible for all Christians. All of their efforts to placate the clergy, the donations to monasteries and the creation of religious houses and the compromises made to keep the archbishops content and supportive, it'd all paid off, for here was proof of her husband's credibility, his trustworthiness.

"Papa Ioannes is what the Christians call him; he's of very small stature but carries himself with great authority. We met in his private chambers and I was able to convince him to lower the taxes paid by my people in England and Denmark who wish to travel to the Holy City. No longer will our pilgrims and traders be made to pay enormous fees when they journey across Europe, a victory."

She smiled once more, a wide, proud grin. Not only had Canute been permitted to meet with the pope himself, but he'd made demands of the man! She imagined the pope's face as the large Dane before him started delivering his mandates. Aelfgifu was positive the great man had never experienced such a thing, a meeting with a king who didn't fear him. Her grin remained as she continued reading.

"I've also gained something for the holy men in England and Denmark that will make them happy. When a bishop is consecrated, he must pay a fee and is then given a cloak to represent his position. I spoke plainly, telling the pope that these fees were too high for my people. He tried to

argue but I suggested that if the fees were not lowered, there would be fewer men from my realm sent to Rome to be consecrated. This gave him pause and he agreed to my petition, so afraid are these Christians that the spread of their faith be hindered."

Aelfgifu nodded her appreciation, for this move alone would ensure the Archbishops' support for a long while.

"We're to travel back using the same route that took us here; the mountains will be more easily crossed than when we came and our journey should be much shorter. There are also fewer wagons to pull as the gold and plate I brought as gifts have all found new owners.

"I've started work on a letter to the English people, telling them of my victories on their behalf here in Rome. I'm certain all will be pleased with these successes."

Aelfgifu could hear the pride her husband felt coming through in his words. And writing a missive to alert the country to his news was an astute move, for if all knew of these things at once, none could claim responsibility for them save the king.

"My most precious Aelfgifu, indeed a gift, I miss you and our sons. I'll be in Denmark by early summer but sadly must cross direct to London. It breaks my heart that I don't know when I'll see you next but be assured I carry you with me always. Your faithful husband, Canute."

She sighed and put the letter in her lap, gazing out across her lands. It would have to do, just knowing Canute was back again. She would make it do.

Chapter Nineteen
England

Aelfgifu heard whispers and before she could react, the doors burst open and a man charged in. Lufu yelped, leaping to her feet as her sewing fell to the floor. By the time Aelfgifu stood, the man was beside her. He grabbed her, knocking her embroidery from her hands. Then he lowered his hood and laughed.

She stared, speechless. Finally she found her words. "Canute?"

He laughed again and drew her into his arms, his chest heaving with mirth. "Are you surprised? You thought I'd land at one of the southern ports, yet here I am!"

Aelfgifu untangled herself from his arms and stared up at him. She glanced at Lufu who, picking up the hint, quickly left the room, bowing her head to Canute as she closed the door behind her.

"What are you doing here?"

She saw the disappointed look on her husband's face and took his hand, leading him to the chair Lufu had just vacated.

"I had to see you. I won't obey you, will never agree to a separation between us, to never see you again! How could I submit to such an idea? To keep me from my wife and sons is unfair, an act of cruelty."

Sitting down and drawing her chair near, she took his hand once more. "But you know my reasons, you understand the danger that exists."

Canute leaned back in his chair and raised a boot to his knee. Seeing him struggle with it, she knelt before him and pulled it off. Frustrated by his silence but wary of saying anything, she waited for him to speak. When he'd cast off his travelling clothes and was comfortable, ale in hand, he smiled, finally taking pity on her. "I know the danger, yes. But I learned a few things on my travels that may prove useful."

Aelfgifu frowned. "You have ideas?" She saw a wide grin take over her husband's face. He started to laugh until she couldn't help herself. Swatting his leg in frustration, she ordered, "Tell me!"

He patted her hand, laughter dying away. "All right, all right, I was only teasing. And you should be told, for it was you that gave me the idea, something you said in passing months ago." Leaning forward, his face close to hers. When he spoke it was as if they were sharing a great secret. "I've arranged for Gunhilda, to be married to the son of the Holy Roman Emperor." He sat back, a smug look of triumph on his face.

"But she's only a child!" Aelfgifu counted silently. "She counts only eight summers."

"Aye, but she'll go to live at the German court." He laughed again, this time the sound was heavier, less joyous. "That'll take the wind out of Emma's sails."

Aelfgifu felt the cruelty in her stomach, as any mother would. She'd heard that Gunhilda was the most cherished, always with the queen. But it was necessary, for how else could they hope to protect their sons and still be together?

"So you're bartering with the girl?".

"Yes. She'll still go to Germany but perhaps not for another year or two." He took a drink of his ale before continuing. "Depending on Emma's behaviour."

Aelfgifu thought about this for a while, mulling over the details of what could go wrong. "Do you think it'll work?" All she got in reply was the raising of an eyebrow from Canute. With so much at stake, she had to believe it would.

Dozing in the early morning light, her legs intertwined with Canute's, Aelfgifu was nearly asleep when a voice brought her back to the room.

"I must go to Norway."

Fully awake she scrambled to sit, pulling the covers around her. It was nearing the end of summer and they'd spent nearly a month together. She knew the visit must end but never could she have guessed it would be in such a manner. "Norway? Why? Is there danger to Denmark?"

Canute pulled himself up beside her. "There's always danger. But this time I intend to solve the problem once and for all." He climbed out of bed and pulled on his leggings.

She climbed out of the opposite side, hurrying around the bed to grab her shift from a nearby chair. Standing before him as he shrugged on his jerkin, she stared. Fearing his reply, she asked anyway. "What will you do?"

"I'll invade." She knew her face showed alarm for he put his hands up as if to stop the protestations that were about to explode from her. "I've already received word from significant families that I'll be supported." Aelfgifu backed away and slipped down to sit on the edge of the bed. Words escaped her once more. Canute came and sat beside her.

"The people of Norway are unhappy with their king, Olaf. He's too austere, his taxes too high and his rewards for service too low." She saw him shake his head and knew there was more to come. "And Olaf is a devout Christian, with no patience or tolerance for the old faith. Many of the Norwegian nobles have converted but a great many still follow the old ways, powerful clans who are tired of Olaf's treatment. He burns down their temples and destroys any signs of the gods."

Her hand flew to her mouth by instinct, so horrific was this last news. Could a ruler really be so intolerant? Of his own people? "Is this true?"

Canute nodded. "Yes. And there's more. The clans are

tired of Olaf trying to unite them into a single group, with him at its head. The current balance of power between the families is fragile but it has worked for many generations."

She believed this, for it was known through Denmark, and thus also England, that Olaf was a poor ruler; until now Aelfgifu hadn't known exactly how he'd earned this reputation. "When do you leave?"

His voice grew softer. "I must travel to London, to gather men and supplies, and then I'll sail to the port of Nidaros. The nobles have agreed to meet me there with their men. Together we'll march on Olaf and take the country."

He'd not answered her question, but she chose to ignore it and ask another. "And you'll also take men of your own?"

"Fifty of my best longships."

She nodded, thinking. It sounded as though her husband had planned this invasion well and if the support promised came through, it should be an easy task to take the country.

"Who will you leave to watch England?"

"The Earl of Mercia, Leofric, as before. Leofric will care for the south, and I'd ask you to again care for the north."

It wasn't an unusual request, for hadn't she done the same on Canute's behalf every time he'd gone abroad? Her thoughts were interrupted when Canute continued.

"I've asked Oswulf to stay here, to protect my family." Knowing by the tone in his voice that he would broach no argument, she resigned herself and smiled.

"My lord, I trust Oswulf with my life." She dared not mention how tiresome it was to be watched every moment of the day, to be followed everywhere she went, to have virtually no privacy at all while he was away. But in her heart she knew he did it out of love for her and their sons. Turning to him she asked once more. "Husband, when do you leave?"

She saw the look of pain in his eyes and instinctively prepared herself for the worst.

"Tomorrow."

The temperature the next morning was already high, and in the courtyard the grooms and carls who were to travel with Canute were damp with sweat, despite the early hour. Even the horses were impatient, stamping their hooves and pulling at their bridles. Aelfgifu stood by and watched as her husband said goodbye to Sweyn and Harold.

"You obey your mother, do all she says, you hear me?" This was mainly directed at Harold, who bowed his head as his cheeks reddened. Canute put his hand under the boy's chin and lifted it.

"You're both nearly men. You must also protect your mother and this manor." He looked from one to the other. Then he straightened and came toward Aelfgifu.

"I'll be fine my love, don't despair!" He put his arms around her and held her tight. His cloak pin pressed into her temple but instead of shrinking away, she accepted the pain, for it stopped her from crying. When he finally released her she looked up into his eyes, hoping to see the same emotions she felt. But while he was here physically, she could tell that already his mind was far away, thinking of the conquest of another country.

By fall of that year it was over, just as Canute had predicted. Aelfgifu was in the manor house kitchen, discussing herbs with the cook, when a messenger arrived.

"Wulfred! You're a welcome sight." Aelfgifu brushed the residue of crushed herbs from her hands and led the man to a sitting area just outside the main door leading to the courtyard.

"My lady, I've come with news from your husband." He walked over to his horse and searched through his saddle bag. The first item out of his bag was his drinking horn. Aelfgifu smiled and ordered ale for the man.

"Sit with me, enjoy your drink. The weather won't be this

mild for much longer."

They sat side-by-side on the bench and Aelfgifu waited until Wulfred had had a long draught of his ale. Wiping his beard and sighing, the large man began.

"The king regrets that he didn't come to you in person. There was a lot of business to attend to in London and he couldn't spare the time."

The way the carl delivered this news it sounded as if Canute didn't care enough to visit her. But she knew Wulfred and knew it was just the man's way of speaking.

"He asks that you be content with his lowly messenger." He smiled and half bowed.

She nodded as she smiled. "I'm more than content; as usual my husband's choice is unsurprising. Now tell me of the campaign!"

Taking another drink, he looked directly at her before speaking, taking his time. He was a natural story-teller and she suppressed her impatience.

"We sailed from London with fifty longships, the finest in the fleet. The waters were calm and the gods blessed us with an easy passage. We landed in Norway at the town of Nidaros, one of the country's busiest ports. Haakon Eiriksson was there, waiting to greet us." He took another drink.

Aelfgifu thought for a moment, searching her memory. "Haakon fought with my husband in the past, did he not?"

Wulfred shook his head, the ties in his now-grey beard swaying with the movement. "No, my lady, you're thinking of his father, Eirik." She saw him look around and realised his drinking horn was empty. She'd forgotten how much this man could drink! She picked up the jug of ale that had been left on the nearby flagstone path for them and filled the horn again, nodding at the carl to continue.

"King Olaf of Norway, being the coward he is, fled as soon as he heard of Canute's arrival." He laughed, a deep sound

Aelfgifu could feel in her own chest. "He ran away! From his own country! He hides in Sweden to this day." He laughed again and shook his head. Aelfgifu could well understand that a warrior would not be able to comprehend a ruler who would abandon his country.

"And what of the nobles? My husband told me they were tired of Olaf's rule and had pledged to support Canute."

Wulfred nodded. "He spoke truly, my lady. As we travelled along the Norwegian coast, many of the nobles came to meet us. They brought gifts and swore to honour Canute's rule."

She nodded. "And what manner of people are the Norwegians?"

Aelfgifu watched him thinking, the lines on his forehead standing out. Then he shrugged. "They're like us I think. Most just want to be left alone to farm or fish and raise their families. Their dress is similar to ours, even their language is comprehensible, so close is it to our own." He chuckled. "Of course we had trouble understanding their accents, and they sometimes used expressions that were meaningless to us, especially the fishermen." He leaned forward and whispered to Aelfgifu. "Or that might've just been me." Leaning back, he winked at her and she smiled wryly. She was a grown woman but Wulfred had a way of making her feel like a child at times. She wondered if he did it on purpose with her or if he treated everyone like that.

"So it's true, then, that there was no fighting? The country was taken without battle or bloodshed?" She'd heard rumours but needed to hear it from someone who was there.

The beard swayed again and she'd to force herself not to stare at it, so wild was the growth. "Yes, lady. With the king gone and the nobles on our side, there was no opposition."

"And who did my husband leave as regent?"

"Haakon."

She frowned. "Why? He's little known."

"Oh, he's very well known to the Norwegians, my lady. He comes from one of the oldest and most powerful families in all Norway. And one that has suffered directly under Olaf. Your husband made him regent to further ensure the support of this respected family but also to reward the son for the father's loyalty and service."

"It was a wise move. But then, when have my husband's moves NOT been astute?" She smiled, missing him, wishing he were here.

Wulfred reached over and patted her hand. "Norway will be glad of its new ruler; they only need see the prosperity of England and Denmark to know they're in hands blessed by the All Father himself."

And so it proved; for the next year Canute's growing realm lived in peace. And, as if approving of his reign, the goddess Frigga herself saw to a mild spring, warm summer and a bountiful fall. It was the most fruitful harvest that many could remember and the relief of being ruled by a competent and forceful king grew.

Even the winter was proving mild and Aelfgifu had no trouble walking to the village when she needed to wander and clear her head; when she needed solitude. The Christians and those who followed the old ways lived in peace at Reodfeld, each group respecting each other's ceremonies and customs. There was a chapel in town for the Christians, and the ancient oak behind the manor served as the place of worship for the older religion.

Aelfgifu would brook no fighting at the manor, or on any of her properties, especially on matters of belief. Each man and woman would be allowed to follow their own path; what right did anyone have to deny that?

Still she had her housecarls keep vigil; Canute had used his daughter as a threat against Emma, but she knew what the woman was capable of. Her guards grew bored, so she allowed them to instruct the boys in some of the more practical ways of fighting. Their sword master, Grim, had recovered fully from his injuries and she could sometimes see the indignant look on his face as one of the guards showed Sweyn or Harold an effective but less elegant sword trick.

Today she travelled with the boys, plus two guards. She left Wulfred at the manor to watch over things there, promising him she wouldn't tarry in the village. It was only after she'd allowed him to choose the guards who accompanied her, and she'd shown him the dagger she now kept with her at all times, that he'd relented and agreed to her leaving. Not that he could've stopped her but she knew he took his role of protector very seriously and she was grateful for it.

"Mother, did the Norwegians really hate their king?"

She looked up at Harold, already taller than her, and sensed there was more to his question. There usually was; lately he took a more roundabout way of getting information, instead of blundering in directly. She'd indulge him this time for she knew what he was fishing for; he'd been bothering her for weeks. Besides, she was enjoying the exercise, her knees feeling better with the movement and the wind holding the hint of an early spring.

"They weren't happy with him, no."

There was a look between her sons, then she saw Harold grin and Sweyn roll his eyes. "Why weren't they happy?"

She turned to him, an eyebrow raised. "Why do you ask so many questions?"

His face grew solemn, but there was a glint of mischief in his eyes. "How am I to learn the art of politics if I don't ask these questions, Mother?"

With a derisive snort she quickened her pace and threw her reply over her shoulder. "And how are you to learn the unseemly details of Olaf's rule, am I right?" She turned and grinned at him, enjoying the embarrassed look on his face and the sniggering that Sweyn was trying to hide.

"Mother, just tell us! Are the rumours true?"

The weather and the peace had lifted her mood. Why not? she thought.

"As you already know, King Olaf was a very devout man, he adopted the new religion and wished for his country to follow in his footsteps." She took a breath before continuing, slowing her pace. "Many in Norway still follow the old ways and didn't wish to change their beliefs. At first Olaf left them in peace, offering gifts to persuade them. But when this didn't work he grew more aggressive."

Even Sweyn, who had rolled his eyes at the idea of hearing this story, was engrossed by her words.

"He began to burn temples and destroy all signs of the gods. The nobles grew angry but no one expected the king to go as far as he did."

They were approaching the town now and many people had had the same idea as her, the mild weather calling them from their homes. The spirit of the season had infected everyone and as they passed they were greeted with smiles and nods. As they headed to the outdoor stalls, Aelfgifu continued her story, the boys weaving in and out of the crowd to keep up and listen.

"One of the nobles had a wife. Nay, I won't tell you who. She was proficient with herbs and roots and made medicine for any who had need. Many people owed their good health to this woman. But when Olaf heard of her, and her cures, he accused her of being an evil spirit, come to earth to harm them. He would listen to no argument nor listen to any around him. He declared that the evil must be purged and ordered the woman hanged."

Aelfgifu was relieved to see the looks of horror on her sons' faces.

"But I don't understand." Harold's attitude displayed his honesty; he no longer sought details of the despicable crime but rather strove to understand it.

"She wasn't only the wife of a noble, Harold, but also a wise woman. She used plants to heal people, instead of prayers to Olaf's god. The king was offended by this and sought to remedy what he saw as the result of evil instead of a simple understanding of plants."

She shrugged, grateful for not having to live under such circumstances. Aelfgifu herself was no wise woman but she did know the uses of many plants. She wondered if this would be enough to condemn her, under different circumstances. Shaking the thought from her head she realised both of her sons were silent, each lost in his own thoughts.

Harold was the first to speak. "If I ever ruled, I'd be a much fairer king than Olaf. All would be safe under my protection."

"It's fine to think that now, but a situation may arise where you're forced to make a difficult choice, what would you do?"

The question returned him to silence. Looking ahead, she gave her last piece of advice on the subject.

"You'd do well to follow your father's example. It's no easy feat to keep an entire country happy, never mind three. A strong presence is needed. And when unable to be present, a strong regent."

Three weeks later Aelfgifu received a message with alarming news: Haakon Eiriksson, regent of Norway, had died. Now no one ruled in Canute's name.

Chapter Twenty
England, Norway

"How did it happen?" Aelfgifu rolled over in the bed to face Canute.

"He was taken by the sea."

She frowned. "He was swimming? At this time of year?"

Canute shook his head. "He was sailing."

Shivering, she rolled back, moving closer to her husband. She felt Canute's arms around her. "What a horrible way to die."

"Aye, but it's part of being a Norseman, it's in our blood to sail."

Aelfgifu had to strain to hear him, his face was buried in her hair. "Is there any suspicion that it wasn't a mishap?"

She felt the shake of his head. "No, just an unfortunate accident."

They lay together, listening to the silence of Reodfeld around them. Since Canute's journey to Rome, and the promise of Gunhilda in marriage to Conrad's son, the queen had been virtually absent from their lives. It was nearly a year since Canute announced his news to Emma and, after what was apparently the worst fight the couple had ever had, she had moved to her manor in Exeter, taking her daughter with her. When required, she would appear to sign charters or officiate over some ceremony, but afterwards she quickly and quietly returned home.

It'd taken all of this time for Aelfgifu to feel as though she could breathe again, to finally stop looking over her shoulder wherever she was, and to lessen her worry for her sons. All this, combined with Canute's more frequent visits, allowed her to hope life was finally on the path it was meant to take. She had her sons, her husband and her lands, and all were safe. She sighed happily and moved closer to Canute. Gathering the sheets around her she turned to face him again.

"What'll you do?"

He shrugged. "I don't know."

Looking at him closely by the moonlight that shone through the window, she saw how age and rule had begun to overtake him. He was still a large and powerful man who carried himself with great authority but there were signs that, perhaps, only she noticed. The grey in his hair and beard made him look more distinguished and regal, but the fine lines beneath his eyes showed how tired he was. He often winced when he stood, only enough for her to catch a glimpse of it, and heaved a sigh of relief when he sat or lay down and thought that no one else was aware. She saw the wrinkles around his eyes but when he caught her staring at him, the eyes themselves lit up, as if he were still a young man.

She began to doze off again when Canute sat up with a suddenness that startled her.

"You'll go!"

She shook herself awake. "What?"

Canute looked at her. "You. And Sweyn. You'll both go to Norway, to rule on my behalf."

"Me? Leave?" She began to panic, her mind scrambling to make sense of what her husband was saying.

He was nodding at her, grinning. "I trust you. You've helped me to rule all these years."

Fully awake now, she stared at her husband. "But leave England? My home? And what of Harold?"

Canute waved his hand. "The boy is twelve, nearly a man. He'll remain here; I'll see that he's well-protected."

Aelfgifu was thinking more clearly now, the shock of being woken so abruptly now gone. "What about Godwin?"

Canute shook his head. "He's needed here."

She looked away, into the darkened room. "And Leofric?"
"He's also needed in England." He lay back down in bed
and took her hand beneath the covers. "It's time for Sweyn
to take on some responsibility. He's fourteen and he's seen
nothing of the world. When I was his age I was already
bloodied by battle." His voice grew low as sleep began to
overtake him. "I've decided. You and Sweyn will be my
regents." She felt him squeeze her hand. "I love you, and I
trust you. You're my fiercest warrior and wisest counsellor."
Her hand was released and in a few moments she heard
gentle snoring.

Aelfgifu lay awake, thinking in the darkness, long after
Canute had fallen asleep. She would be leaving her home,
her son and her husband. All that was familiar to her. She
consoled herself that at least one son would be with her. And
she was positive Sweyn would take to the challenge as he'd
become more restless lately, more anxious to travel. She
only hoped she could become used to the idea and that she
could prove Canute's faith in her justified.

A few weeks later they were ready to leave England. Their
belongings had been sent on ahead, so there was little to
carry with them as they travelled, making it seem more like
they were going on a day trip rather than moving to a
different country. Sweyn, as Aelfgifu had expected, was
looking forward to the travel and adventure that awaited
him and was even now busying himself with the horses in
anticipation of their departure. Aelfgifu stood in the
courtyard, watching the activity around her but not feeling
a part of it. She'd been this way since Canute told her they
were going to Norway, aware of her surroundings and
performing her duties but all the while feeling as if she were
dreaming, as if perhaps she'd wake and find the whole thing
was an elaborate hoax perpetrated by her own imagination.

But no, the day had arrived for their departure and here they were, readying themselves to travel to Norway.

Harold's mood did nothing to help the already enormous sense of guilt she carried about leaving him behind. From the moment she told him that she and Sweyn were going, Harold had been petulant and jealous, showing his feelings by becoming increasingly argumentative with both her and his brother, mingled with silences that went on for hours, accompanied by baleful looks. Aelfgifu knew he was hurt by the decision to take Sweyn, rather than him, but he refused to listen to her explanations. Canute had finally had enough and ordered the boy to accept his path, but still Aelfgifu could see the anger that simmered just beneath the surface of her younger son's feigned acceptance. And, with Canute out of earshot, he brought up the argument she'd heard, and grown tired of, many times already.

"Why Sweyn and not me?"

She was packing her saddle bag and hadn't heard him approach. He already surpassed her in height and was showing every sign of taking after his father in stature. "Because Sweyn is the eldest." The same answer to the same question that had been posed before.

"It isn't fair. I'm the better swordsman."

"It's not always steel that makes a ruler." Aelfgifu finished packing and turned to Harold. "You'll be looked after by Oswulf." He was sullen and disappointed and she felt her heart breaking that this would be the way they parted. He looked over her shoulder and she sensed that Canute must have reappeared. It was time to leave. Taking her son's hands, she squeezed, then hugged him, unable to stop herself. She felt him tense then relax, her embrace returned. "Please don't let our goodbye be tarnished by ill will between us." Releasing him she now saw the same resignation in his posture that she herself had carried for these past few weeks. "I don't know how long we'll be away."

Sweyn had also returned and stood beside his brother. They were seldom so close these days and there were clear similarities and differences, both boys on the cusp of manhood. Sweyn, wiry and blond, took after his grandfather and his namesake, Canute's father. Harold however was more like Canute, wild red hair ineffectively tied with leather and clothing barely able to contain the man within.

Harold turned to Sweyn suddenly. "Brother, watch over our mother, and yourself. Be careful."

Aelfgifu smiled grimly. It was Harold's way of apologising, to both her and Sweyn. As those around her began to mount and move off, she glanced one last time at Harold and nodded her thanks. She was relieved to see him nod back.

Their travel was easy, despite the lateness of the year. It had been a mild winter so far and the sea was calm, the gods blessing their endeavour. As much as she tried, Aelfgifu couldn't pretend they were travelling for pleasure or that their reason for travel was anything other than it was. She'd had time to think and while it was sad to leave her home she had to admit that, now they were sailing and fully on their way, she felt a sense of adventure. Perhaps Sweyn's barely-contained excitement was contagious. She looked over at him, standing at the prow of the ship. He was a cautious, thoughtful boy who was turning into a serious man, yet there he was, grinning and facing his future head on.

Huddled in the mid-section of the ship was Lufu; the poor woman had admitted she was terrified of sailing and had spent the entire journey wrapped in a fur staring down at the bottom of the boat. Aelfgifu had released Lufu from her obligations to the family, knowing that her friend would enjoy seeing her elderly father in London once more. But Lufu had insisted on remaining with her mistress, despite the sea travel and move to another country. Lufu turned and looked at her, nodded a greeting before returning to her previous position. Both women were startled into looking toward the prow, for a shout from one of the men had announced that land was within sight. It was the last stage of their long journey, navigating the fiords, but soon they would be landing and Aelfgifu would be starting her new life. Silently thanking the gods, she took a deep breath of the cold sea air and readied herself for the challenge ahead.

They arrived in Nidaros in Norway, and were greeted with much more pomp and ceremony than Aelfgifu had expected. She guessed this was because Canute had travelled with them, in order to introduce his wife and son as regents. The nobles who had supported Canute in his bid to take over their country were there, wearing their finery and each pushing forward to greet their new ruler. The official ceremony of welcome would take place at the palace, and horses were waiting to transport them the rest of the way.

The palace was only a short distance from the sea and with Canute speaking to the men who had accompanied them, Aelfgifu had a chance to take in her surroundings. The land was beautiful, indeed as lovely as parts of her own home in Northampton. The smell of the sea was all around and Aelfgifu found it refreshing. The people they passed were dressed similarly to those she'd met in Denmark all those years ago, but with slight differences to cut and fit, giving them a subtle foreign feel. She noticed that there were fewer blond heads to be seen, instead the population appeared to be mainly red or reddish-brown. And the pins that held their cloaks were the same shape and style as those of England and Denmark but the carvings had a foreign look to them. Aelfgifu guessed these people had their own legends and stories of the gods, presented here, as they were at home, on their pins and brooches. They were showing their distinct personality, as did the people of England and Denmark, and by doing so Aelfgifu realised that perhaps they weren't so different after all.

Canute rode close and interrupted her thoughts. "What do you think?" he said, with a wave at their surroundings.

She smiled at him; she would never let him see anything but confidence while they were here. "It's a beautiful country. The people are similar to the Saxons, but there's something else . . . " She shook her head, unable to describe what she felt. "The accents are familiar yet not, and even the smells are the same but somehow different."

Canute laughed. "The Swedes have established trade with the regions to the east, the Norwegians trade with the Swedes. They have access to fabrics and designs unknown to England, as well as food and the salt which they use to season."

So that was it. If she was to rule effectively, she would have to work to understand these things, and quickly. Their conversation was cut short as they rounded a bend in the path and saw the great hall before them. It was a large wooden building, similar in design to the grand halls in England.

They were shown into the main hall where Canute took his place on the dais. Three heavily carved chairs had been placed there in advance and once Canute was seated, Aelfgifu and Sweyn joined him. Normally she would have no problem with sitting before a large group of people, for she did so often enough when meeting with the thegns in the course of managing the north of England. But this time she felt differently; these people were foreign and she couldn't read their feelings on their faces as easily as her fellow Englishmen. Her stomach clenched and it took all of her effort to keep a calm, composed look on her face.

Once they were all seated, a young man stepped forward.

"To our most noble lord, King Canute of England and Denmark, a most gracious and heartfelt welcome from your new subjects of Norway." He bowed at Canute and stood again, looking back at one of the men standing and waiting. "My lord, I present Earl Bernt, one of the greatest men in the country." A large man stepped forward, his bulk evident despite the heavy cloak he hid within. Her first impression was of a man who enjoyed a good meal, perhaps even going out of his way to procure one.

"My king." The earl bowed before the dais, huffed as he rose and stepped back into the crowd.

The young man announced another, this one tall and slight with thinning red-blonde hair. "I present Earl Einar, my lord. Another worthy noble of your court."

With two steps the man was before them, bowing. "My king." Two more steps and he was back in his original position.

"If your majesty prefers, I'll introduce you to the other members of your court in due course. You must be tired and hungry after your journey. A feast has been prepared to welcome you here, it's planned for tomorrow but there is food ready in your chamber, should you wish it." The young man bowed once more and stepped back.

Canute rose. It was evident he already knew the young man by the smile on his face. "Thank you Tallak, and to all here, you have the thanks of a grateful king." The hall filled with cheers as the men called and stomped their feet. Canute held up a hand and the room fell silent. "I wish to introduce my wife, the Lady Aelfgifu," he nodded to her, "and my son Sweyn." Aelfgifu looked across at her son and saw that his expression probably mirrored her own; his eyes were wide and the way he held himself, sitting on the edge of his chair, suggested he might bolt from the room at any moment. She caught his eye and smiled at him, nodding, willing him to calm himself. Canute continued. "It is my wish that Norway be ruled by my wife and son, together as co-regents, when I'm away."

Canute had warned her earlier that he would be making this announcement as soon as possible, for he wanted the Norwegians to have no doubt as to who was in charge when he left. At the news, Aelfgifu was alarmed to hear murmurings and whispers, so different from the earlier cheers that filled the room. She glanced at her husband and saw that he, too, was frowning. "My son and wife act for me, in all things."

There were further whispers, this time louder, enough for the words to reach Aelfgifu's ears, and surely Canute's too. She looked around the hall, barely noticing the decorations and furnishings so similar to those in England. Aelfgifu couldn't decide if she was grateful their language was close enough to the Danish for her to understand the noise that surrounded her or saddened. She saw the glares being passed between the men; expressions that she suspected were meant to be secret yet revealed much.

Earl Bernt stepped forward. His eyes darted right and left, as if seeking support. He stopped in front of the dais and cleared his throat. The room was silent, eerily so after the earlier noise. Aelfgifu shivered. "You're leaving a woman to rule? Is that wise, my lord?"

Anger gathered as a storm behind Canute's eyes and in the sudden tension of his jaw, but these men didn't know their king yet and saw only a composed face. Ignoring the comment he instead addressed the room. "You'll help keep this realm peaceful, all of you. It's what I expect of my nobles. But you'll always defer to my wife and son for decisions which affect the well-being of this country."

Again glances passed from man to man around the room. This time they were stared down by Canute, who'd risen to stand, and this time her husband chose to show anger. The sudden change in his mood startled Bernt, who quickly returned to his place. Through clenched teeth, his face red and his eyes narrowed, Canute's voice was low.

"This audience is at an end. I'll see you later at the feast." At a hand gesture to Tallak, the younger man nodded and began ushering people from the room.

The men continued to mutter as they left the hall, until finally she, Canute and Sweyn were alone. Even Tallak, who appeared eager to do the king's will, had departed.

"They're upset."

Canute nodded. He turned to face them and Aelfgifu saw Sweyn's face, his expression confirming he'd also heard the grumbling. "It's understandable." Canute took her hand in his right and Sweyn's in his left. "You must work hard, rule justly and they'll soon come to trust you."

Aelfgifu looked up into her husband's eyes, hoping what he said was true.

Chapter Twenty-One

Norway

Lufu had been busy exploring the palace, and was able to show Aelfgifu to her rooms. They were more lavish than she was used to and Aelfgifu didn't know what she would do with the extra space. There was an accompanying hall attached to her chambers, where Sweyn and she could meet with their advisors, and she was grateful for this as she still preferred smaller, more private meetings when the need arose. The main hall would be used for more formal occasions, as with her manor back in England, and for ceremonies that required a more regal setting.

"Sweyn's rooms are only a little smaller but just as impressive." Lufu unlatched one of the trunks that contained Aelfgifu's dresses.

"I don't understand these tapestries." There were the usual scenes of hunting and war, but also sections that displayed shield maidens in less than modest poses.

Lufu stood and gazed at the wall coverings. "I wondered too. I asked one of the maids, she told me they depict tales of Norse heroes."

"They're very . . . colourful."

Lufu giggled. "Yes, 'colourful'."

Aelfgifu smiled. She supervised the unpacking of the remaining trunks; there were many new gowns and cloaks, made at Canute's insistence, and she had been grateful, for looking at her old clothing, she realised now that they wouldn't be adequate for a co-regent. She must not only act, but also look the part. She wore the circlet given to her by Canute at their joining, refusing to give it up for something more lavish. There had also been new cloaks and tunics for Sweyn, and he'd been given his own arm band before they departed from England. She smiled at the memory: although Sweyn had remained serious when given the gift, she'd seen him try it on a few times during their crossing.

After her chamber was as organised as she and Lufu could make it, Aelfgifu dined alone with Canute in the adjoining room.

"Must you leave so soon? You see how strained things are here."

Her husband's head bowed sadly. "Yes. There's much I have to attend to. I need to go to Denmark to see Harthacanute." He stopped and she knew it was for her benefit that he did so. He knew she hated hearing anything of Emma, and that extended to her children. Was she being unreasonable? Perhaps. But she'd decided long ago that if these small things kept her happy, and her husband was willing to indulge her, what harm was there? Canute started again. "I don't like being away from Emma for so long."

Aelfgifu glared at him, unable to believe what she'd just heard, especially given his earlier consideration of her feelings.

He frowned at her. "You know what I mean." She saw his frown change to a hopeful look. "I don't like her out of my sight this long."

She nodded. She did know; she knew exactly what he meant, the thought gnawing at her as they ate in silence. They were so used to each other's presence that a long period of silence between them was comfortable, not a threat or warning that their partnership was troubled. But there was a great heaviness to this silence, one that Aelfgifu could finally no longer stand.

"Protect Harold. Let no one hurt him."

When Canute spoke, his voice was deep and even. "I swear on the All Father, no harm will come to the boy."

They stared at each other for a moment longer and Aelfgifu dearly hoped it was a promise that could be kept.

After a few months in Norway Aelfgifu had a more informed idea of how the country ran. She did her best to explain the various laws and treaties to Sweyn, and included him in her meetings but she found that she, herself, was often excluded from the everyday business of governing. The council frequently met to discuss matters involving the entire country but forgot to invite her. And when she was invited to their meetings the topics were meaningless, sometimes approaching the ridiculous. How many tapestries should hang in the new hall? What design of furniture would be placed in the banquet room? Obvious attempts to keep her from more serious matters. And Sweyn fared no better, for it became obvious enough to her that these men thought her son too young to be of any use. Aelfgifu was sitting in her rooms, reviewing charters when Sweyn burst in.

"They hate me!"

"You've only been here for a few months, they don't know you yet."

"They treat me as if I were a child." He stomped over to the table and sat heavily in one of the chairs.

"Is it any wonder, when you come to me like this at every imagined slight?" She could see the crushed look on her son's face and softened her voice. "We've only just arrived. You must prove yourself. You can do it. Show them and they'll love you as I do."

Sweyn heaved himself out of the chair, sighing as he left the room.

After six months Aelfgifu had finally had enough. She called a special meeting of the council and ensured watered-down ale was provided to keep them all cool as summer heat invaded the palace. Gratified to see that all of the council were present, she nodded quickly at Sweyn before addressing the table before her.

"I've asked you here to tell you of a decision I've made."
There were doubtful looks passed between the men.
Ignoring the reaction her announcement had elicited, she
continued. "I've decided to introduce a new form of taxation
to the country."

Every man stood suddenly, pounding the table with beefy
hands and exclaiming in deep voices. They openly displayed
their alarm, and this gave Aelfgifu a small sense of
satisfaction. Good! She had written to Canute to ask his
advice about this topic and his reply had been filled with the
usual confidence he had in her.

*"Do as you see fit, you rule on my behalf. My father went
through the same exercise, restructuring Denmark's tax
system, and look at the success he had! Is my country not
the most efficiently run of all my lands?"*

She saw the sense in mirroring Norway's tax system with
that of Denmark: more money collected meant more money
to create new buildings, fortify cities and support charities.
At present Norway's system only collected half the money
Aelfgifu estimated could be available, the majority lost
because of too many layers of officials and corrupt
collectors. A change would also mean easier trade with
Denmark, for the more similar the two countries were, the
more effectual would be the rules of commerce.

She waited until the men had quietened down. "The new
tax will replace the current system and will be based on that
used in Denmark."

There was more noise as the men stood again, almost as
one. Aelfgifu saw her housecarls move their hands to the
hilts of their swords and she waved them back. Finally Earl
Einar spoke, raising his voice over the remaining protests.

"Why? Why would you do this?"

"Because the current way is inefficient. The new way will
see taxes collected and tallied more quickly and with less
effort. It'll be of great benefit to the entire country."

She heard a voice from the end of the table, a lesser lord. "But our system has been in use for many years."

Standing to address the man, she saw that most of the men had re-seated themselves. "Just because something is old or common does not mean something new or better shouldn't replace it."

"You would say that." This time she couldn't tell where the comment came from.

The room became quiet and she felt a presence beside her. Canute had insisted that Wulfred accompany them and remain in Norway with her, and he stood close now, his hand on his sword hilt. Aelfgifu raised her hand to stay the man's actions; she wouldn't give them the satisfaction of showing emotion. They'd expect this, she was sure after hearing the last comment, for it showed they hated a woman ruling over them.

Earl Bernt, always seen with food in his hand, spoke.

"My lady, perhaps we could meet in private." He waved toward a room off the main chamber, smaller and more isolated. Bernt walked beside her, a sympathetic look on his face, almost fatherly. Earl Einar and a another man, a newly made earl of only a few months and also new to the council, Earl Sverre, joined them.

As she walked toward the room she addressed Wulfred.

"Wait here, I won't be long." Entering the chamber Bernt found the largest chair and struggled to squeeze his bulk into it. Once settled, he looked around, as if seeking something. Food or drink, she guessed. There'd be no time for drinking today. She took a seat in front of the three men.

"My lady, this new tax you propose . . . "

They hadn't even listened to her! She interrupted, her ire rising. "It's not a new tax, it's a new way of collecting existing taxes."

"But why? What need do we have for a new way? The old system works."

Earl Bernt spoke. "Many of our fathers and grandfathers helped to determine that system."

She nodded. "And at that time I'm sure it was the best they could do for the country. But there are always other ways of doing things." The men looked at each other; their faces they were still confused. "A similar process is in use in my homeland. The people there benefit greatly. Once implemented, the new way helped to lower their taxes."

"But the earls . . . "

"Earls and thegns perhaps had less money but were still able to maintain their lifestyles! However the people, farmers, millers, merchants, all gained."

The room was silent for a moment. Earl Sverre leaned forward. He was young, his features not yet hardened into a man's. In fact he was half the age of the other men, possibly more.

"My lady, let me explain the role of a leader to you."

Aelfgifu's anger exploded; she couldn't believe this man, this boy, who'd been an earl for less than three months, was speaking to her this way!

"You wish to explain the role of a ruler to me? I, who helped the king rule his country for nearly twenty years, am to be given a lesson in kingship?"

The young earl was taken aback; clearly he hadn't expected such a reaction. She saw him look to Einar and Bernt. The fat earl's face was red and his chest heaving with indignation.

"My lady, perhaps you don't understand many of the subtleties . . . "

He trailed off. She guessed her face betrayed her fury. Good, because she was afraid her emotions, running so highly and in a hundred different directions, would force unwanted tears to flow and she desperately wanted this meeting to be over. She breathed deeply. Through a clenched jaw, her neck aching with the effort, she spoke.

"Thank you for your help, my lords. I'll try to look carefully at these 'subtleties', as you call them, of my rule."

It was the hardest thing she'd done so far, feign agreement with these men. But it got her the desired result: the meeting was over.

She stood to go and walked toward the door before turning and speaking calmly. "My wishes will be carried out."

Wulfred had been standing just outside the door, close enough to have heard the entire conversation.

"See that it happens."

After a year, Aelfgifu's prediction had come true and the new system of taxation proved much more efficient than the old. More money was collected than ever before, to the astonishment of the men who monitored and protected the treasury. Still the council grumbled, not in her presence anymore but enough so that stories reached her from the few loyal friends she'd made.

Sweyn had finally proven himself adept at military matters, more from his study than any actual practise, and the council had begrudgingly begun to follow his edicts, understanding and accepting the soundness of his thoughts while still suspicious of his youth.

Aelfgifu had written to Canute, asking his advice on how the extra money now held in the treasury should be used. He'd written back in his usual manner, with much expression of love and trust but little said on the actual topic. "Spend it as you see fit, I trust that you'll use it wisely." That had been it, the only comment he'd made on the matter.

"What about our defences?" Lufu was tidying the room and helping Aelfgifu dress for the day.

She shook her head. "Nay, we're already well-defended." They'd already run through a list of possibilities, from new ships to larger walls to building projects. But none of these needed the extra funds. Then a thought occurred to her.

"What about a religious house? There're still a few around, more follow the old religion here than back home."

Lufu looked up from folding a blanket. "A temple?"

Aelfgifu nodded, satisfied. "Yes. Find me a deserving one."

A few days later, she was out walking in the garden, enjoying the warm air and the peace, as well as the exercise, when Aelfgifu realised she was no longer alone.

"My lady."

"Earl Einar. How can I help you?"

"I wished to ask about a rumour I've heard."

"You know my feelings about rumours, my lord, as does all of the council." She continued walking, facing straight ahead.

"Indeed, my lady. But perhaps you'd indulge me."

She rolled her eyes and nodded, impatient to get whatever purpose he had in seeking her out over. "Go on."

"I've heard you've given money to a few of the old temples."

"Yes, what of it?" Her patience was failing her.

"Do you think that was wise?"

Ignoring his question she asked her own. "How did you find this out?"

"Some of my servants were laughing when they should've been working. I asked them what had made them so happy that they'd shirked their chores."

"So you've come to thank me for making your servants happy?"

Aelfgifu saw his quick frown. "No my lady, I've come to

ask you why?"

She stopped walking and turned to face him. "One of the reasons you replaced your old king was because of his disrespect for the old religion, isn't that the case?"

"Yes but . . . "

"But what, my lord?"

She watched his face turn red. "We've decided that King Ulf was right. We should be a fully Christian nation and all pagan practises be wiped out."

Her eyebrows knit together. "You're here to chide me for giving money to temples, the exact opposite of that which caused you to depose the king?" She shook her head; there was just no winning.

"We feel the future of Norway would be better if the entire nation were Christian."

"We?"

"The council."

Of course. Another major decision made without her involvement. She'd been made to look foolish. "Is there a reason I wasn't told of this nor invited to any discussion on the subject?"

Einar looked embarrassed again. "We saw no reason. We never imagined you'd spend the money in," he hesitated, "such a manner."

She'd had enough and sighed. "Thank you my lord, I'll think about what you've said."

The man left, bowing and backing away quickly. He seemed satisfied, a feeling that eluded Aelfgifu all too often.

"Are you mad?" Sweyn had burst into her chamber, a habit from his childhood that he never grew out of, nor showed any inclination of stopping.

"What?" Aelfgifu was not in the mood for her son's rants today.

He crossed the room and took her chair, the one she used at the table during council meetings. He was adorned in finery, in the Norwegian style. He wore a gold circlet and his cloak pins were beautifully cast and obviously worth a great deal. It seemed her son was enjoying his role as co-regent. "You've given money to the temples?"

Joining him at the table she waited by her chair, glaring at her son until he looked embarrassed and moved. The frown on his face, however, told her he was in earnest.

"Yes. I've already been reminded of it today."

He leaned forward, his forearms on the table in front of him. "You've upset many on the council."

Aelfgifu threw her hands into the air, snorting as she did so. "My very presence upsets the council! They don't like a woman ruler."

"*Co*-ruler." Sweyn's voice had lowered to a whisper, but the words were clear enough.

She looked up at him sharply. And decided to let the comment pass. "They cannot abide the fact that a woman may know better than them." Hearing a high pitch of exasperation entering her voice, she cleared her throat.

"Is that what you truly believe, Mother? If so, then you're a fool." The words hit her like a physical blow and she sucked in her breath, staring at him. "They don't hate you because you're a woman, they hate you because you're from England!"

Once again, just as she was recovering from the shock the last words had elicited, here was more. She hadn't realised, she just assumed . . . What had she assumed? That England was well-respected everywhere. "But I thought . . . "

"You thought wrong. They think England is a land filled with savages and any wishing to visit are considered mad. They believe England is uncultured and uncivilised."

Aelfgifu could feel her face burning, the shame was overwhelming. The feeling was soon replaced by anger: at the council for their pettiness and hatred, at Canute for sending her here, and at Sweyn, who had told her the truth and who was standing, available, before her.

"How dare you speak to me like this? You forget, boy, you're also English."

His shrug only angered her further. "But I've made an effort to be more like those I rule."

"*We* rule." Her voice was as quiet and even as his had been when he'd reminded her of the same thing. She was prepared for her son's reaction; saw the anger and petulance on his face as clearly as it had shown when he was a child. As a man he'd still not learned to hide his feelings. He said no more and stormed from the room.

She eased back into her chair, leaning on the arms. It wasn't until nearly ten minutes later she noticed that she was gripping the edge of the chair arms, her hands white with the effort. Something would have to be done, and soon. Aelfgifu hoped the gods would help her find that something.

Chapter Twenty-Two
Norway

Two weeks after the solstice celebration and into the new year, Aelfgifu called another council meeting. The festivities had been designed to please followers of both the old religion as well as the Christians. Despite the fact that they acted superior, whispering that their faith was the true one (for had not the previous king been a Christian himself?) the days were mostly filled with peace and camaraderie, and everyone present shared in the spirit of the season. Aelfgifu even observed Lufu, who had resisted befriending the Norwegian maids and guards, laughing and drinking with them. The celebrations had left Aelfgifu feeling hopeful, and yet she was still filled with apprehension when she addressed the council.

She stood at the head of the table, chair behind her, her usual place at these meetings. The hall seemed bare and empty; all the decorations had been taken down only the week before and none of the usual household decor had been rehung. There still lingered in the air a faint reminder of the holiday: food, smoke from the torches and the herbs that had been used to bless the old year and welcome the new. Even with the council members all in attendance the room had a hollow sound to it when they spoke. The council members were all wearing new cloaks and pins, gifts Aelfgifu guessed, from family and friends. She had herself received a pendant from Canute, a silver Mjolnir hammer. It was a masculine symbol and traditionally worn by rulers. She appreciated both the craftsmanship and the sentiment, for it further expressed her husband's faith and trust in her abilities. Canute had also sent bolts of material and she puzzled at this until she recognised the cloth: it was woven in one of the villages she owned; a reminder of home. When she'd realised what it was Aelfgifu had to fight the tears and the swollen feeling in her throat.

Sweyn had received a shield from his father, a beautiful object made with great care. The arm strap was made of sturdy leather and the design on the front was of a stylised black raven on a red background. The boss was iron, plain but highly polished, showing the world around it in warped reflection. Even Lufu had received a gift from the king, more fine material from London. Although she'd also gotten gifts from her father and brother, it was Canute's gift that Lufu hadn't stopped talking about.

Aelfgifu held up a hand for silence, waiting until the room quieted down before speaking. "I've called you here to put before you a proposal."

The usual whispers, the usual looks, accompanied her words. Fortunately she'd grown used to it and was able to easily ignore the noise. Waiting again for the room to fall silent, she continued. "I wish to implement a system of public service."

As she'd expected, the men stood and voiced their opinions loudly. She sat down, exasperated. How could anyone deny a program of public service? Something that would be of benefit to all the people of Norway? She shook her head. No, they don't even listen to my words anymore; they're so used to arguing with me that they now do it by habit. Finally, Earl Einar spoke.

"What would this new way entail?"

There were nods around the room. At least they were allowing her to speak again. "The new system will ensure that the old and infirm are looked after, those who no longer have family. Widows of warriors who have fallen in battle or those injured while fighting with no one to aid them. There will also be a granary system, so that those without food in poor years will be fed." She heard the noise climbing again, the arguments from each man boiling over. Aelfgifu continued, raising her voice, almost yelling to be heard. "There will also be mandatory battle practise, for all men capable of fighting."

At this last news Aelfgifu could no longer be heard, so loud had the room become. But she'd learned the best way to deal with this situation was to sit back and let the men work all the words out of their systems. They would usually calm down, in time. She only had to wait. Aelfgifu picked up some papers she'd been reviewing earlier and continued to peruse them, ignoring the room around her. As she expected, one by one the men fell silent, astonished looks upon all of their faces. She nearly laughed; hadn't they ever seen someone actually getting work done before?

Earl Einar was the first to speak. "We already see to our own. We've no need for anything else."

Aelfgifu stood suddenly, enjoying the startled look on their faces. "Then why do I receive reports of old women and children begging in the streets?" This time no one spoke and most of the men had the decency to look ashamed. Softening her tone, Aelfgifu continued. "I know you do your best to look after the sick and elderly, and your war wounded, and I applaud these efforts. I only wish to help those who cannot help themselves."

She waited for her words to sink in and was grateful there was no further objection. But Earl Einar wasn't finished. "We also know how to protect our own realm."

"And again I approve of your efforts and methods. But is it not the duty of every ruler to ensure that their country is as protected as possible? To ensure the safety and security of every person?"

More noise as the counsellors debated with and against each other. Aelfgifu felt her head begin to ache, something she experienced often these days.

Earl Sverre stood, dressed in his usual expensive garb, a

look of entitlement on his face, and the room quietened. "I suppose this is another of your 'successful' ideas from England?"

Aelfgifu heard the mocking tone in his voice but tried to ignore it. She couldn't block out the laughing around the table that followed. It wasn't good-humoured, natural laughter but sly and hurtful. She let her emotions get the better of her. "No, it's not. It worked in Denmark." She felt ashamed of herself; as she said the words she could hear how weak they sounded.

Sverre turned to the other councillors. "You see? She's trying to 'fix' us! But do we need her help?"

The room erupted in shouts of 'No!' with hands banging on the table as accompaniment. Turning back to her, he smirked, his youth making him look like a spoiled child who'd just bullied a classmate. "We look after our own here."

There was agreement from the room and Aelfgifu had to shout to be heard. "But what of those who have no one?"

Sverre looked at her, his face wooden. "It's their wyrd." He said these words as if speaking to a child and as if the words explained everything.

She held up her hand, as she'd done to signal the start of this meeting. But this time the action signalled the end.

"These plans WILL go ahead. And I'll hear no dissent." Turning back to the papers she focussed on the words before her and not the nervous shuffling of the men around her. Finally they took her hint and exited the room. Only the carls remained. At a nod, they too left the room. Finally she was alone, the smells and memories of the peace and joy they'd shared only a few weeks ago swirling around her.

Aelfgifu tried reviewing the charters but her head wouldn't let her concentrate. These meetings always left her feeling this way: like she was a child and had done something wrong, like she had something to feel ashamed about. Finally she gave up and wandered the court grounds until the light began to dim, noticing Wulfred following her at a discreet distance. The shadows changed on the hills that surrounded the court and she felt a sense of awe at the beauty of this place, the ruggedness of the land and its people. Sighing, she returned to her room.

Changing out of her regal clothes, the Norwegian-style dress she wore when meeting with the council, Aelfgifu put on the plain clothing she preferred for day-to-day wear. She knew the court women looked down on her for this habit but she didn't care; as long as the work of the country was done, who should care what the regent wore? Sitting in her favourite chair she relaxed and breathed deeply for a few moments before retrieving the paper she'd left on the table. It was the latest letter from Canute and she re-read the last part.

"I understand your difficulties in dealing with the council but remember they're proud men, many whose families have served the king for generations. They're all from powerful clans who have long histories in Norway and you must do all you can to retain their favour.

I trust you and our son to do what is right, if I had any doubts I'd never have sent you. I need you there."

She'd cried when she first read his letter; these weren't the words she'd wanted to hear when she'd asked for his help in dealing with the council. Even now she felt the sting of tears as she re-folded the letter and placed it back on the table.

Something had to be done; she couldn't continue this way, having her words mocked and ideas ignored by men who thought they knew better. Aelfgifu made up her mind to take complete control, council acceptance or not. But, keeping Canute's words in mind, she would temper her anger at these men and their prejudices with understanding.

She would be like a mother, a loving parent to the entire country.

A few weeks later Aelfgifu had just had her last meeting of the day and, having dealt with more grievances from men and women from all levels of society than she could ever remember, returned to her chamber and allowed Lufu to help her change. She leaned back in her chair while her friend removed her circlet and brushed out her hair before braiding it loosely. Aelfgifu was exhausted, a permanent state these days, and there was never enough time to see to everything, even with Sweyn's help.

As if reading her thoughts, Lufu spoke. "I'm sorry my lady, I don't mean to be disrespectful but I don't like it here."

Aelfgifu had noticed that Lufu rarely smiled anymore, save when reading a letter from her father. But then her friend would grow sad and ask to be excused.

She turned to look at Lufu. "Sit and talk with me."

Lufu hesitated before nodding and joining Aelfgifu. "I'm sorry, my lady."

Reaching across, Aelfgifu patted her friend's hand. "You've nothing to be sorry for. Tell me, what's wrong?"

She watched Lufu look down before raising her head and speaking. "It's so different here. The people are strange! Their accents are coarse and their tales unknown to me." Lufu's voice grew soft. "They make fun of me for not knowing their stories." Aelfgifu saw her friend sigh, her shoulders rising and falling as she aired her frustrations. "The people are cruel. They don't like anything or anyone from England, even servants! And they say such things behind your back . . . "

Aelfgifu saw the alarmed look on Lufu's face, and watched her friend's arms wave in front of her, as if trying to take back her words. She grabbed Lufu's hands and gently placed them back on the maid's lap. "It's all right, I know these things already."

Lufu sprung forward in her chair. "But I defend you! No one listens, but I try. They call me a savage and laugh."

Leaning forward to meet her, Aelfgifu hugged Lufu tightly. She patted the woman on the back and tried to think of what she could say, because she knew exactly how Lufu felt. "We must make the best of it; we're needed here by the king." It was inadequate and she knew it. But she had to be strong, for both of them as well as Sweyn, Canute and the entire country. Besides, she was certain that Lufu must know that she felt the exact same way.

Lufu nodded and composed herself. After spending a few moments in silence, she finally spoke, changing the topic completely. "What will you take with you next month?"

Aelfgifu gestured vaguely. She'd had little time to think about clothing but she was relieved to be able to speak about something else. "The blue linen with the silver thread and the green and yellow dress. The rest can be simple."

There was more silence before Lufu spoke again. "Are you nervous?"

She thought. Was she nervous? Surprisingly, no. She was now resigned to her role. "No, I'm not." She was determined to strengthen her resolve with the council and act more like a parent-figure. This was an opportunity to do just that.

They arrived in Aker the following month. Aelfgifu had travelled south with her carls and council. They were here to observe the local town council pass judgement. There'd been a murder, a rarity, and she'd insisted on attending. A farmer, and a freeman, had been killed by his neighbour, also a freeman. An argument had started between them over land and one had ended up dead. Aelfgifu was present to hear the summary, for the man had already been interviewed and his guilt proven beyond any doubt. She'd left Sweyn to watch the court in Nidaros; her son was happy to be left to his own devices for a while, as he craved a chance to prove himself, both to her, Canute and the country. And he didn't like to roam far from the court and its protection, another good reason to keep him there.

She and her own council were seated at the head of the room.

"Leiv Bjornsson, you freely admit your guilt?"

A middle-aged man stood before the local council table. He was sturdy, dressed in rough brown linen trousers and tunic with a worn dark green cloak.

"Yes, my lords."

A second man on the council spoke. "You confess to the killing of Halvor Mannes?"

Leiv's words were quiet and he spoke with a lowered head. "Yes, it's true."

The councilman addressed the crowd: villagers who had gathered to watch the proceedings. "Who brings this man to trial?"

A young man stepped forward, followed by two women, one young, the other much older. Aelfgifu guessed that this was the dead man's family: his wife, son and daughter. "We do, my lords."

"And you'll abide by the council's decision and let any thought of a blood feud between you and the guilty man and his family forever perish?"

"We will, my lords."

Aelfgifu watched as the local council turned to each other. She could hear whispers and soon saw heads nodding. They turned back to the waiting family. "We declare the punishment to be fifty shillings to the dead man's family, to be paid by the guilty party, Leiv Bjornsson."

There was sorrow and shock on the faces of the dead man's family, plus something else. Resignation? Aelfgifu watched as the hall began to empty, all accepting the judgement of the council. Indignation and shame for Halvor's family rose and she suddenly stood.

"Wait!" Everyone stopped and looked back. "I wish to speak."

One of the local council turned. "My lady?"

Her anger was fuelled by the surprised look on the man's face, as if he was shocked that she'd spoken. "I'll speak. Now." Aelfgifu waited until everyone had returned to their seats, including her own council, who all carried puzzled looks. Standing and addressing the local council she cleared her throat and spoke. "Why was the amount of fifty shillings chosen?" When she received no reply she continued. "The price for slaying a freeman is typically two hundred shillings."

"Where you're from perhaps."

The sneer on the speaker's face was unmistakable and unhidden, taunting her.

"The guilty man will pay the correct amount to the dead man's family, two hundred shillings." She looked over at a man standing in the crowd. "You. What's used as a shilling here?"

The poor man, surprised at being addressed, spoke quietly. "My lady, the value of one sheep."

Aelfgifu faced the guilty man. "Then you'll pay the family of Halvor Mannes the value of two hundred sheep."

The room erupted in noise around Aelfgifu, something she was not only getting used to but that she'd begun to find boring, for she felt she'd said nothing to warrant such a reaction.

One of the local council spoke. "My lady, you can't!"

"I can and I will. From now on the correct wergeld will be paid. Those found guilty will also pay their wite."

"But my lady . . . "

Aelfgifu interrupted him. "Those who commit crimes

must pay a fine to the crown to atone for their deed. Their wite WILL be paid."

"But my lady, many can't afford the payment!"

"Then they shouldn't have committed a crime." There was further noise but thankfully less than before; she hoped people were accepting her edict. "Would you rather pay a victim less than they're owed and risk a blood feud or pay what they deserve, and is the lawful amount, and maintain the peace? A peace that surely benefits all?"

"But so much to the crown?"

Aelfgifu turned on the man who had spoken, not caring that her emotions showed. Good! Let them see her anger!

"The crown has lost a hard-working freeman, one who would've paid taxes and grown food for the country. That's a great loss to the king and therefore the entire country. Compensation must be paid."

There was still murmuring in the hall, exasperating Aelfgifu. "I'll have people treated fairly in this country! This is my final word!" She stepped away from her chair and, signalling to her court, walked away with as much dignity and ease as her anger would allow. Turning as she reached the door, she addressed the hall once more.

"There shall be severe penalties should these rules be ignored!"

Months had gone by since Aelfgifu passed her rule on stricter penalties for serious crimes and still she was dealing with problems with the council. She was in her rooms, having just returned from a walk around the court when Sweyn burst in. She barely noticed his behaviour anymore; it was one of many habits she'd given up on his ever breaking.

He threw himself down on a bench and grabbed an apple from a nearby dish. "I've heard they're asking the old king's illegitimate son, Magnus, back to rule Norway." She watched him bite into the apple and wipe his beard; the motion reminded her so much of Canute, who did the same thing when eating. "They're saying they want a Norwegian ruling Norway and not a Dane and his savage wife and son."

Another unfortunate habit of Sweyn's was to blurt out news such as this, with little thought to how it should be delivered. "You know how I feel about rumours."

"Yes but . . ."

"No! There are always rumours! Stories and lies. We're at court, how is it possible you haven't learned this?" She continued folding a dress, exasperated by her son yet again.

Sweyn sat silently, chewing, before throwing the mostly uneaten apple into a corner of the room. Aelfgifu turned and saw her son's face, the growing red and the scowl that accompanied it. "Perhaps this will convince you then, mother: the rumours come directly from your own council!"

There was no time to write to Canute and ask for his advice; Aelfgifu would have to make this decision on her own, and quickly. She waited a few weeks after Sweyn's revelation about her council, hoping the stories were false, but eventually had to admit to herself that even she could feel a change in the atmosphere of the court: the dark looks from all around her, the frowns from previously content workers. Even the council had begun to actively avoid her.

Sweyn provided further details. "Men are missing from the village around the court, as well as a few carls, those who were here before us." Behind his bravado she could sense a hint of desperation. "They have gone to fight for Magnus."

That was the final detail, the last bit of information she needed to force her decision: they would leave the court at Nidaros and move to a more secure location. After consulting with her private carls, those who had come over with her from England, she ordered that her son, Lufu, Wulfred and his men pack what belongings they needed; they were leaving as soon as possible, heading south to the fortified castle at Hamarr.

They travelled for many days, riding hard. Aelfgifu was relieved when they finally arrived at the castle but still, it was difficult for her to know who to trust at their new home. She felt safer in the large building but couldn't keep it manned with just her own supporters, there were far too few. Dismissing as many of those who were at the building when they arrived as she dared, she couldn't help but keep a few servants. Aelfgifu hoped these people wouldn't make trouble, had perhaps not yet heard any of the rumours from Nidaros.

It only took a few days for Aelfgifu to realise how wrong she'd been. The news she hoped had passed by this part of the country had not only arrived but had infiltrated the castle. The same dark looks and whispers followed her every movement here, as it had at the northern court. More often than not she turned to find Lufu following closely behind, wary of every movement and sound. They couldn't live like this, it was impossible! A decision would have to be made and she only hoped this time she would have the chance to write to Canute, asking for his advice.

Her hopes were soon dashed.

"My lady, there's news from the north." Wulfred lowered his head respectfully. He'd aged, as had they all, over the last few years.

"Sit." She pointed at a chair.

Aelfgifu waited until he was comfortable, seeing on his face that the news was bad. "My lady, Magnus, the son of old King Olaf, has taken the north. He has control of Nidaros and is fully supported by the council. He's declared himself king and swears that no foreigner will remain in his land."

Swearing under her breath she began to pace the room,

her hand grasping her pendant for strength. "Damn these people! Don't they understand what they've done?"

Wulfred nodded his agreement but remained silent until she stopped and sat. "It's too dangerous for you now. You must flee from here."

Her first instinct made her shake her head. No, they couldn't, they wouldn't flee. Run away like cowards? But Wulfred's words reached her.

"You've no support, my lady. There's no love for you or your son here. And we don't have men enough to fight."

He spoke the truth, but what he said next chilled her.

"There's no time left, no time to write to the king and ask for his help. We must flee. Now. Tonight."

This time she nodded, understanding this was their only hope of remaining safe. She was certain that, should Magnus Olafsson capture them, he'd deal with them fairly but she shuddered to think that he might be persuaded by other members of the Norwegian court, those whom she'd never managed to win over.

"Inform your men to ready themselves. And send a messenger you trust ahead with a letter to my husband, informing him of these events."

Wulfred nodded, his unruly grey brows knitted together in worry. As he left, Aelfgifu remained motionless, almost paralysed by the task ahead of them. After a moment she recovered herself and summoned Lufu; they had much to do and very little time.

The manor was quiet when the group fled: Aelfgifu and Lufu followed closely behind Wulfred and his men, the same two men who had travelled with him to Norway five years ago. Wulfred helped Aelfgifu into the saddle. With a last look back at the manor she urged her mount to a run, following the others into the darkness.

Chapter Twenty-Three

Norway, Denmark

As they trekked across the countryside the smell of the pine trees they brushed past reminded Aelfgifu of happier times. Reodfeld was surrounded by evergreens and the scent brought back memories of her childhood, when her father was still alive and her brother was whole and happy. That life seemed like it belonged to someone else, a story she'd been told.

The winter had been milder than usual. Mild or not, it was still cold and she shivered, pulling her fur cloak closer. Wulfred had forbidden a fire, knowing the light would attract unnecessary attention.

She was more exhausted than she could ever remember being; even the birth of her sons hadn't taken this much from her. Yet her senses were keen and she found herself constantly listening, alert to any danger. Even with Wulfred, his men, and their heightened diligence, Aelfgifu found it difficult to sleep.

The food they'd brought with them was plain and grew stale quickly: cheese, hard bread and old fruit that had been stored in the court cellars. They travelled in the dark and rested during the light. After a few days their food began to run low. Wulfred's men snuck into farms at night and stole what they could, something that shamed Aelfgifu. She felt for the farmers and their families, hard-working people who didn't deserve to have their winter stores raided. But there was nothing they could do, they needed to survive. All the same, Aelfgifu found she ate less, whether because of the guilt of stealing or the exhaustion from their flight she couldn't say. Sweyn on the other hand ate as much as he ever did, more than once complaining about the lack.

"Why shouldn't we take what we need? We rule this country after all." Sweyn's voice betrayed his frustration.

"Yes, we who are sneaking around in the dead of night and hiding during the day." Aelfgifu didn't even try to keep the sarcasm from her tone.

"Surely there are those who still support us?"

Aelfgifu shook her head. "There aren't. The council doesn't, they invited Magnus back. We no longer have allies."

Watching him shrug, she was surprised that he could still be so blasé about their situation. "Still, we're high born and important. We must take what we need."

She tried to explain that the families needed the supplies as much as Sweyn did but her son's own exhaustion made him unreasonable.

Lufu ate less than Aelfgifu, which worried her, as did her friend's silence. The woman had barely spoken since the night they'd fled, answering questions with only a 'yes' or 'no.' Aelfgifu had also seen her shivering, and had traded cloaks with her maid. She was grateful for the horses, and even if they couldn't ride them all night, the respite they granted was welcome.

They travelled east then south through Sweden and west again towards Denmark. The route had been Wulfred's idea; he believed sailing from Norway would be dangerous, with Magnus's men looking for them. Better to travel overland to Denmark where there would be less chance of discovery or of them being recognised. There would be no forgiveness from Magnus; his reputation was that of a hard, calculating man and it was said that he was filled with vengeance for the way his father had been treated by his own people. They followed the coast, the cold damp air causing Aelfgifu's knees and shoulders to ache. Lufu was also suffering but there was nothing to be done about it.

One morning, after they'd been travelling for a few days,

Aelfgifu had had enough.

"We must stop here."

"My lady . . ."

"I insist." She threw up her hands. "Look at me! My dress is torn and dirty, my hair is more unkempt than when I was a child and I am filthy with the efforts of our flight."

Wulfred and Sweyn both frowned. "We must keep going, we can't afford any delays." Wulfred's voice was calm, soothing.

But his tone did nothing to change her mind. "Just a few minutes. I just can't go on like this."

Wulfred looked at his men and after a moment's hesitation nodded. "We'll stop but you must be quick. We'll keep watch, you'll have some privacy."

Leaning over the stream she shivered as the ice cold water splashed on her face and neck and quickly reached for her cloak to dry herself. It was at that moment she became aware she wasn't alone.

"Hello."

A small boy, she guessed six or seven years old, was watching her from a short distance downstream.

"Hello." Aelfgifu raised an eyebrow; this boy was not surprised at all to see her there, viewing her as if she was the most natural thing in the world. She was aware of her appearance and was certain that she smelled as bad as the men.

The boy cocked his head. "Are you a beggar?"

She almost laughed; it was an honest mistake to make. "No, I'm not a beggar, I'm a . . . " What was she exactly? She felt abandoned and hopeless but, at this moment, delighted for this distraction. "I'm travelling." Aelfgifu suddenly became aware of the danger she was potentially inviting in, talking to this child. "And I don't wish to bother anyone." She watched him considering her words, saw the patched state of his own clothing and the wear of his boots. This was temporary for her, at least she believed, but the boy lived like this all the time. Her heart went out to him and she quickly searched the pouch on her belt, hoping to find some trinket to present to the child. But she'd nothing. Then an idea struck her. "Will you help me?"

The child hesitated then nodded, creeping closer. "Yes."

Aelfgifu smiled and pulled a ring from her little finger. It was an old ring, one that she'd worn for many years, a gift from her aunt Brihtwyn. The outside was engraved with a leafy pattern all around and on the inside was her name in small, delicate letters. She wasn't worried that the child could read but she was concerned that he may be discovered with the ring and be forced to reveal where he got it; she had to stop that happening. The ring was a bribe; the prize was the story the child would tell.

"Here's a gift." She stretched her arm and held out the ring, feeling like she was trying to tempt an exotic animal to take food from her hand. After a few moments the boy cautiously crept forward, reaching out his own hand to snatch the ring away.

"You may have the ring but you must promise me something. Will you do that?" The boy nodded. "Good. You must never tell anyone of our meeting. And you must never show anyone the ring, it is your reward for keeping my secret. Do you understand?"

The boy nodded once more, finally gathering the courage to speak. "Yes."

"And if anyone should see the ring, you are to tell them you found it. Far from here. Can you remember that?"

"Yes." He had the ring clasped tightly in his small fist. "I found it."

A noise from beyond a wooded field caught the child's attention and he scurried off, as sure footed as some small animal.

She said nothing of the boy as she re-joined the others,

mounted her horse and continued on the journey. The rhythmic sound of their hooves lulled her to dozing a number of times and she found herself mentally going over the words of songs from her childhood to keep awake. When the light grew bright enough for them to be discovered, they stopped.

"We'll camp here until night." Wulfred posted his men while Sweyn and Aelfgifu unloaded the few belongings they had from the horses. They had arranged their camp and led the still unspeaking Lufu to a sleeping roll when Wulfred joined them.

"We're almost out of food." Aelfgifu said, gnawing at a hardened crust.

"So we'll just go and take what we need again," Sweyn replied.

Aelfgifu was almost too exhausted to argue with her son. Wulfred interrupted the potential dispute.

"One of my men knows of a town less than a day's ride from here. He says the people are friendly to Canute."

"How can he possibly know this?" Her voice was hoarse.

"He has an uncle who lives there, his mother's brother. We can stay a day, perhaps two. Have the horses tended. Eat, sleep safely."

"To sleep in a bed again, it sounds too good."

Wulfred leaned in. "You can see if anyone can help your maid." He nodded his head in Lufu's direction. She was pale and silent, her arms grasping her legs, rocking slowly back and forth.

His last comment made Aelfgifu's mind up for her. She herself, despite her complaints, could stand another night outside. But to see her friend suffering so, it would be hurtful and selfish to not get Lufu the help she obviously needed. She nodded to Wulfred and gathered her cloak around her, sleeping better than she had for days, despite the cold.

They set off early that morning after eating the last of the hardened cheese. Once all had heard of their destination the mood lightened, if only a little. There was nothing, however, that could be done about the tediousness of their journey. They travelled for hours in silence until Wulfred trotted up beside her.

"My Lady, we are a short distance from the town we spoke of. You'll soon be warm and fed."

She smiled at him gratefully, still tired. Knowing that they were nearly there did little to help. Aelfgifu found her concentration fading and, almost asleep in her saddle, she imagined she heard yelling.

"My lady, we're discovered. Ride!"

Suddenly alert, Aelfgifu realised that the shouts she thought she'd dreamt were real; riders were coming in their direction. She urged her horse to a fast run but she was unfamiliar with the land and thus at a great disadvantage. Their horses were also hindering them, for the poor beasts were hungry and tired, sorely in need of tending. Instead of trying to outride their followers, they found a dense copse of trees and hid, hoping the horse's snorting and puffing didn't give them away. Their hopes were dashed however when they saw the torches coming toward them, the lights not only illuminating the faces of their pursuers but also the badge they wore, that of Harthacanute.

There was no struggle, for what would be the point? Although they were armed, Wulfred had far fewer men with him than in Harthacanute's band and even if her carls had slept and eaten recently there would still be no match; they were outnumbered. And it was obvious by the drawn swords and the general demeanour of these men that there was no chance of escape. Aelfgifu caught Sweyn's eye and nodded to him as reassurance.

"Why have you followed us? Why are we being detained? We're travellers, going to my cousin's farm."

One of Harthacanute's men stepped forward and in the torchlight held up the ring she'd given to the young boy. As her hand went to her mouth Aelfgifu saw Sweyn's eyes widen as he looked at her, his face questioning. Lufu's face showed nothing and Aelfgifu wasn't sure if it was exhaustion or shock that masked her friend's true emotions.

The soldier who held her ring spoke. "A young boy said a stranger gave him this ring. He described a woman who looks like you. How did you get this?"

"It's mine." Aelfgifu said, defiant by habit.

"That's doubtful. Who gave it to you?"

She didn't want to reveal too much for it seemed that these men hadn't discovered her identity. "It belonged to my mother. When she died she bequeathed it to me."

The man's eyes shone as he moved the torch around. "And these men who travel with you?"

Aelfgifu saw his gaze linger on the carl's weapons. "They're here to protect me. A woman can't travel alone."

"And why would you travel in the dead of night?"

She was growing weary of the man's questions. "How or when I travel is my business."

Watching his face Aelfgifu felt a small flame of hope for it seemed that he might believe her. Then she saw his look change and, heartbroken, saw a smirk on the man's face.

"You'll accompany us. There's someone who wants to speak with you." He bowed mockingly. "My Lady Aelfgifu."

It took many days to finally reach their destination, a southern manor belonging to the crown in Gram. Harthacanute's soldiers joked and laughed amongst themselves but greeted any questions from Aelfgifu or Wulfred with threats. Aelfgifu still held some hope that Harthacanute's men were being overzealous in their duties, and that Harthacanute himself would be more gracious.

They did have Canute in common and Harthacanute had been away from his mother, Emma, for many years now. Perhaps her influence over her son had waned? As they rode over the crest of a hill and saw the manor below them, Aelfgifu decided she would appeal to his sense of duty as a ruler by sharing her tale of being chased from Norway and hoped it would gain her some sympathy. All she'd ask of him was a boat and some men to take her back home to Canute.

They arrived at the town of Gram and were taken to the manor. A tall thin man met them at the gate, his great beard showing no signs of age. Aelfgifu guessed he was one of Harthacanute's carls.

"My lady, you and your son are to accompany me." He stepped aside to usher her into the building. She frowned, not trusting herself. Was the man fooling with her by showing false courtesy, or did she hear genuine respect? She just couldn't tell, but she had little time to think about it.

"What of my men?" Aelfgifu turned back towards the main gate.

Instead of a reply she felt a large arm guide her back to facing the door. She heard Wulfred's loud protests and Lufu's screams as Sweyn and she were led down the hall and up a flight of stairs. At the top of the stairs they were shown into a small room, the door bolted after them. Aelfgifu turned and looked at Sweyn, his own face reflecting all the emotions she herself felt.

Unsure of what to do, she began to explore the room, leaving her son with his puzzled expression. There were no other doors, only the one which had just been locked behind them. A small table sat by the hearth, where a meagre fire burned. The heat from the fire was welcome and she drew closer, holding out her hands. Looking over her shoulder she saw Sweyn was still standing where she'd left him. "Sweyn, come to the fire."

Her son joined her and together they warmed up as best

they could. She continued surveying the room. The floor was a dark wood, rough and barely finished. So not a bedroom then. There were small holes and rough boards where a shelf had been torn from the wall. A storage space perhaps? Breathing deeply she could smell stale onions with a sharp hint of spoiled apples. The room had definitely been used to store food.

Aelfgifu felt the ache in her legs getting worse and shifted her weight from foot to foot.

"You must sit, mother." It was the first he'd spoken since they'd been put here and his voice filled the entire room. She looked around once more. "There are no chairs. You'll have to sit on the floor." And then, as if to reassure her, he added, "no one will care. We're both beyond appearances now, aren't we?"

She sighed. He was right. Her dress was torn and dirty, her cloak covered in burrs and, she was certain, her hair loose and unkempt as a peasant's. Did it really matter if she sat on the floor? Using the wall to guide herself down, she was grateful for the rest, despite the hardness of her seat.

Aelfgifu lost track of time; there were no windows here for her to count the hours by the sun's passing. A noise from the door startled her and she was surprised to find that she'd dozed off. She looked up and saw a young girl enter the room, carrying a tray. Beyond her the door stood open. The maid walked quickly to the table, placed the tray down and walked back to the door.

"What's going on? Why are we being held here?" Aelfgifu's words were ignored. Wide awake, her anger fuelling her, she leapt up and ran after the girl but was stopped by a guard who stepped into view. He looked into the room then directly at her, before slamming the door. She heard the bolt thrust home again and footsteps getting fainter as the maid descended the stairs. Grabbing the door, Aelfgifu pushed and shook but it was solid. Frustration made her stop; it was a fruitless exercise.

"Mother, there's food here." Sweyn's voice again echoed in the room but his words were welcome; she hadn't realised how hungry she was. On the tray was bread and cold beef, along with a pitcher of ale. At least they were being fed, she thought. At least . . . At least . . . How dare they? How dare they treat her and her son in this manner! Her anger began to grow but as she ate, she stopped herself. There was no use in getting angry; it did nothing to improve their situation.

They ate in silence and returned to their positions on the floor, again losing track of time. Aelfgifu sensed rather than saw the sunset; there was a cooling in the room and the pressure in her head eased. She sat up. Surely we cannot have been here for a whole night and day? As if in response to this realisation the door opened once more, allowing the same maid to enter and deliver more food. Another maid accompanied the first, carrying furs and candles. She silently placed them near the table and both hurried from the room. Again the door slammed, the bolt sliding home.

"I hate that sound." Sweyn had stood and was walking around, his long legs taking in the entire room in three strides.

"Come and eat. Our host has provided food and we'll take it." Aelfgifu carefully stood, her neck and shoulders aching and her knees trembling as she regained her balance. There was more ale and bland food, but it was edible and they'd be foolish not to eat.

Their meal was interrupted by a visitor.

"Harthacanute, you . . . " Sweyn struggled to speak. "You *kamphundr!*"

"Sweyn!"

Harthacanute waved her away. "It's fine, I expected nothing less from my half-brother." She watched him walk around the room, a satisfied smile on his face. Seeing the ale, he poured himself a cup, finishing the jug.

"What do you think you're doing? Why have we been locked in like this?" Sweyn spat the words.

"Sit." He pointed at a corner of the room. "Down boy."

Aelfgifu grabbed Sweyn's arm just as her son tried to rush. "Harthacanute, what's going on?"

"What's going on, *my lord*."

She clenched her jaw and barely managed to get the words out. "My lord, why have you locked us away? What have we done to deserve this treatment? When your father hears of this . . . "

"Canute is dead."

Aelfgifu heard the words but when she tried to process them she felt a pain in her chest as though someone had kicked her hard and taken her air. The darkest night descended and she remembered nothing more.

Chapter Twenty-Four

Denmark

Aelfgifu woke in the same room and found herself on a pallet surrounded by furs and cushions. The noise of her movements as she became conscious attracted her son's attention.

"Mother, you're finally awake."

Awake. Yes, she was. Aelfgifu shook her head, trying to rid herself of the disorientation she felt. She searched through the dark cloud that was stopping her thoughts. Then the memories came back like a knife sliding into her belly. She felt like she might be ill and gulped in the cool air, holding her stomach tight, forcing it to be steady. When the nausea passed, she struggled to sit up, her body aching.

"Is it true?" Then, before Sweyn could reply, she shook her head. "No, it isn't true. It can't be. But why? Why would he say such a thing?"

"He spoke the truth. Father is dead."

Moving to the edge of the pallet, Aelfgifu gathered her dress around her and rose, swaying a bit as she stood. "No! He lies!"

Sweyn looked at her and for the first time she couldn't read his emotions, so flat was his manner. "He showed me the letter from Godwin, signed also by the Archbishop of Canterbury."

Aelfgifu began to pace the room, shaking her head. "I just ... I don't ... " She turned and faced her son. "How? What lies does this letter say?"

Sweyn sat on a small wooden stool beside the fire. Another was opposite, as well as a few other pieces of furniture that been placed in the room while she'd been insensible. "He was wounded and it became infected. And then he died."

"What wound? He's not at war." Her voice was hoarse, barely above a whisper but he heard her well enough.

"My half-brother was only too happy to divulge the details, even though the man was his father also." She could hear the venom in his words. "At first it was a minor wound, a sliver from a stable wall. He ignored it but it grew worse. The physicians did all they could, they even . . . "

She saw the hesitation in his eyes. "Tell me."

He sighed. "They cut off his finger, thinking to stop the poison. But it was too late, the disease had spread. Father protested but they also removed his arm." Aelfgifu's hand flew to her mouth, tears burning her eyes with the thought of Canute suffering and her so far away. She wondered if Sweyn was enjoying telling her these details, some sort of punishment for the way things had gone. Or perhaps it was just his usual way of speaking, direct and blunt. "He grew worse and became delirious." Aelfgifu saw that her son was just as upset as she; his voice now betrayed his true feelings. "Father fell unconscious and remained that way for three days. Godwin finished by saying he died in his sleep."

Aelfgifu sat, silently staring at her son. He lowered his head, unable to meet her gaze. "No. I must see for myself. There's some mischief here, I'm certain. We must get out."

Sweyn looked back up, shaking his head. "We can't. Now that father is gone my *brother* has decided we'll remain here."

She flew from her chair. "This is Emma's doing!"

He nodded. "What are we to do?"

Aelfgifu stopped, her eyes fixed on her son. "I don't know. But I swear I'll make that woman pay!"

They lived like this for many weeks, their routine that of sleeping, waking and eating. A few times a day the same maid brought food and took away their old dishes and waste bucket. At first Aelfgifu was grateful for the interruptions that accompanied the maid, for it was a break in their monotonous day. But after some time even the girl's visit became part of the monotony, so regular was she in her work. Pallets had been brought in, with flat pillows and thin blankets so they didn't have to sleep on the bare wooden floor. They spoke little for what was there to talk about? Escape? They'd made plans, devised ways of fleeing but each was flawed and so they remained captive. Aelfgifu watched and waited, knowing a chance would surely reveal itself. But so far nothing had been discovered.

During the first few weeks, as they lay on their own pallets, waiting for sleep to overtake them, Sweyn and she would speak of his childhood in England, and of his brother Harold. It became obvious to Aelfgifu that Sweyn missed his brother, despite the fighting their differences had brought about. After a while though Sweyn stopped speaking and she grew worried. He became thin and pale, drawn, not the man who stood with her against the Norwegian council only a few months past.

They were sitting near the fire when the door opened. Startled, as it wasn't the time for the maid to visit, Aelfgifu turned to see Harthacanute enter the room, dressed in the finery he was fond of. He looked around the room, his nose wrinkling slightly. Finally he simply looked at them, hand on his hips.

"I see you're both well."

"*Well*? We're trapped here with little food and warmth and with nothing to do each day. And you call us well?"

She cringed as Harthacanute laughed. "You're still alive, what have you to complain of?"

There was no point arguing with him, she'd tried before and it had gained her nothing. "What do you want?"

"Oh, such disrespect lady, not an enviable trait."

Aelfgifu started to rise, her hands clenched but felt

Sweyn's hand on her arm. Glancing over at her son she saw the look on his face, warning her to show caution. Relaxing back onto the stool, she forced a smile. "My lord, forgive me for my rudeness. What brings you to us today?" The words made her feel ill.

Harthacanute smiled, triumph in the grin. "That's better. You see, I can be generous. If treated correctly." He waved a hand in the air. "I've come to tell you of my father's funeral."

This time she did stand. "What?"

"Yes, Canute was buried in the old minster at Winchester a few weeks past. I've only just received news. When I found out I hurried here, knowing you'd want to be told." He shrugged, looked around the room again and turned, his task performed.

Aelfgifu stopped him. "What are you going to do with us, my lord?"

Harthacanute turned back and faced his prisoners. "Why, nothing. I will let my mother decide your fates. She'll be here in two days."

Aelfgifu held herself up until the door had closed, before collapsing onto the floor, her worn dress pooling around her. Her knees ached but she didn't care, so overwhelming was her grief and fear, renewed by Harthacanute's words.

"He wouldn't let me attend my husband's funeral. He keeps us here and doesn't allow me to mourn." She looked up at Sweyn and saw the misery in his face. "Allow *us* to mourn. Nor to say the prayers that must be said over his body." She put her arms around herself and rocked back and forth, barely able to stay the whimpering that accompanied her breathing. Something changed deep within her. She felt it rising, spreading from her heart to her head and throughout her body. It was a hardness she'd never felt before, an instinct; any softness she had left was gone. It was only her and her sons now, and Aelfgifu would do everything in her power to protect them.

Two nights after she'd received the news of Canute's funeral and Emma's pending arrival, Aelfgifu was lying on her pallet, unable to sleep. She'd taken a nap that afternoon; she found she grew tired more easily, even more so trapped with nothing to take her mind off their situation. During her sleep she'd dreamed of Canute but had been woken by the scrape of the chair Sweyn was moving. She was instantly furious with her son for taking her away from her husband, and saddened when she remembered he was no longer around; her only contact through her dreams.

As she lay there she listened to the noises in the room. A week ago something had moved into the walls around their prison and had found a way to enter the room. Tonight she heard the scurrying sound it made. If the creature, whatever it was, had appeared before her in the daylight hours, she might have been less disturbed, but here, in the darkness, she didn't want to see what made the noise.

Aelfgifu lost track of time and hadn't realised she'd fallen asleep again when another sound woke her. A knocking. The door? Had Emma arrived? What would she do with them? She quickly looked at Sweyn's pallet and saw that her son was fast asleep. There, again, soft knocking. Hurrying from her own bed she crept to the door.

"My lady?" A soft whisper from beyond the locked barrier. Then again. "My lady?"

"I'm here." She took the tone of the voice she heard as a guide and followed in kind.

"Stand back, be silent." The dreaded key sound scraped the lock on the door and it opened a crack. A small pale face appeared. "My lady, I'm here to rescue you."

Aelfgifu's hand flew to the door and she pulled it open. There stood the maid who had delivered their food and served them as best she could. "Quickly, come with me." She beckoned with her finger then pointed back down the stairs beside the room.

Sweyn had heard the door and had thankfully woken already. "Mother?"

"Sweyn, come, now." He was beside her so fast she barely saw him rise. As they'd no other clothing to wear to sleep, they'd gotten used to retiring fully dressed so there was nothing to do but follow the girl. Glancing down the hall as they entered the staircase Aelfgifu could see there were no guards outside their door.

The maid noticed. "My father fought with Canute and hates to see you treated thus. And he has no love for Queen Emma. He purchased ale tonight for all of the guards . . . " She stopped, lowering her voice once more. "And I added something extra to their drink, something my mother taught me aids in sleep."

As they hurried down the stairs and through the manor Aelfgifu saw that the maid spoke true, for no guards were there to stop them and a quick glance into the main hall as they passed presented her with a roomful of sleeping men. But this was no time to linger and wonder at the stupidity of their guards. They made it to the front door and out into the courtyard. Just beyond the gate, Aelfgifu saw Wulfred and Lufu, waiting with horses. "My father found only one of your men, and your maid." The girl lowered her head. "It was all we could do."

Aelfgifu rushed toward the gate and embraced her friend, looking over at Wulfred gratefully as she did so. He nodded his greeting in return, the urgency of their situation alive on his face. She went back to the maid. "I don't know yet how I can repay your kindness but I'll find a way."

The girl shook her head, embarrassed. "It's my father's wish to see you away safely, returned to your home. He loved the king." Nodding, she embraced the girl, feeling how thin she was under her furs. The maid struggled from Aelfgifu's arms. "My lady, time is short, you must flee. Your carl has horses and supplies, including cloaks for you and your son.

And he has instructions on where to go, everything's been arranged. I wish you a safe journey, may the All Father help you on your way."

Aelfgifu bowed to the maid and turned to leave. But a sudden thought stopped her and she turned back. "What's your name?"

"Sigrid, my lady. My name is Sigrid. After King Canute's mother."

She nodded. It was a good omen.

"Lufu, Wulfred, are you well enough to travel?"

Wulfred's smile was his answer. "Always." Even Lufu managed a weary smile. Her friend had not been treated as well as they, such as their treatment was. Lufu had grown thinner than Sweyn and the dirt on her face and torn clothing spoke volumes.

"We've horses and cloaks, food and a few coins." Wulfred took her arm and led Aelfgifu to a saddled horse. She gratefully accepted his help in climbing onto the beast but was startled by a noise from inside the manor. "Quickly, my lady, we must go now."

The clamour was growing louder. Distinct shouts could be heard and it was obvious their escape had been noticed. Cursing under her breath, Aelfgifu urged her horse to a run, following Wulfred who had jumped onto his own horse and started galloping in one smooth movement. She wanted to ask about Wulfred's men but guessed the news wasn't good and held her questions. They rode hard, Wulfred at the head of their small group, leading them. The noise behind grew louder and she heard a swishing noise, like a horse's tail flicking a fly away, then a shout. She turned in her saddle to see Sweyn, riding just behind her, his eyes as wide as his panicked horse. He was also glancing behind him, trying to control his mount but keep ahead of their pursuers.

Time slowed; Aelfgifu saw everything, she felt detached, an observer only, feeling nothing, neither fear nor anger. She heard the same sound as before and watched as Sweyn's body jerked forward, slumping onto the pommel of his saddle. Then she was back on her horse, fully aware of all around her: the smell of the horses' sweat and the metallic tinge of the winter air, the puffs of breath all around them as the horses, now mad with panic, struggled to breathe. She saw the snow falling, flakes lingering on her horse's mane for a moment before disappearing. And she saw the patch of red on her son's back, growing larger, spreading around the base of an arrow that protruded at an odd angle from his shoulder.

But they couldn't stop. "My lady, ride straight, keep going, I'll join you." Wulfred turned his horse and rode back towards their pursuers, using the trees for cover. She'd barely enough time to see him draw his axe and ready himself before losing sight of him. It was up to her to lead Lufu and her son and she rode, her body aching, the horse's hooves hitting the frozen ground hard. Aelfgifu didn't know how much time had passed but the noise behind had lessened. In fact there was only a single rider now, bearing down on them fast. She knew they couldn't outrun this man, he was too close, so she led the others into the trees, hoping to hide while the horseman rode past. She held her breath and waited, hearing the rider slow to a walk. "My lady?"

Relief made her body sag, she hadn't even been aware of how stiffly she was sitting. "Wulfred."

"My lady, it's safe. We're no longer being followed."

Aelfgifu was about to ask for more information but saw the blood dripping from the man's axe and remained silent. They rode until the sky turned from deep black to purple then became yellow-blue, before deciding it was safe to rest. Both they and their horses needed it; the poor beasts were nearly dropping from their exertion, foam heavy around their mouths. They found an abandoned barn and huddled in their cloaks. But before resting, Sweyn's wound had to be tended.

"Is it bad?"

Wulfred had managed to remove the arrow but the wound it left was red and ragged. Sweyn was much colder than he should have been. She did the best she could, using a strip from her dress to bind her son's arm to his body so that there would be less movement, but without her herbs there was little else she could do.

"I've seen worse," she said.

This seemed to satisfy her son and he lay back on the cold ground. Aelfgifu wrapped her cloak around him before leaning on a wall a short distance away. She was grateful when Wulfred leaned over and surrendered his own cloak. Surprising herself, Aelfgifu found that sleep came easily, despite the aches and pains, and she spent a few dreamless hours.

When she woke she checked on her son and found him worse. But he wouldn't admit to any pain. "Of course I'm able to ride, what do you take me for, a child?"

"You're badly injured."

"Then what'll you do? Leave me here? Tell me to ride behind Wulfred on his horse, like a woman?" He spat the words and she saw that the cold air had revived him. A blessing in disguise? Aelfgifu chose to see it that way.

They rode again, all of them stiff with the cold and the exhaustion. Lufu said little but Aelfgifu was pleased to see her friend keeping a close eye on Sweyn. Perhaps between the two of them he would be all right. Perhaps they would soon be free of this nightmare. She grasped her Mjölnir pendant and said a silent prayer. Perhaps the gods would help them. Perhaps.

They rode to the coast, as Sigrid had instructed, and there sought out the man who'd lend them a ship. Wulfred went ahead and asked the questions, leaving Aelfgifu, Lufu and Sweyn hiding just outside of the town for fear that one of them would be recognised and their presence reported.

"This is Sigrid's family friend." Wulfred had found the man. He knew who they were but would offer no information about himself.

"Thank you for your help, I'll see that you're rewarded for your efforts."

The man waved a hand. "Nay, lady, I fought alongside your husband many times, he was a good man and it's my duty to give aid to his family."

She thanked him again and they quickly boarded the ship. It was smaller than a longship, perhaps four men in length with a small mast and sail, places for oars along each side. Used for trading, Aelfgifu guessed, but easily managed. Two of the owner's men would accompany them, then sail the ship back to Denmark once Aelfgifu and her group were safely delivered to England. It was an arrangement that suited her, for Sweyn's injury had grown worse and she wished to concentrate on nothing but him.

They set sail and were once again blessed with calm waters, but Aelfgifu still couldn't breathe freely, not while her son was in such a dire condition. They sailed in silence, grateful for the wind, particularly as it made their journey shorter. As they slept, Aelfgifu was woken by Sweyn's moans, and found the next morning that his wound had festered. With no herbs there was nothing she could do for him save help him to drink some of the wine the ship's owner had supplied for their crossing.

A few days later Aelfgifu was woken by a shout. It was land. England. Placing her hand on Sweyn's chest, ready to rouse him to deliver the good news, her excitement fled.

"Sweyn!"

Her son opened his eyes and tried to speak, blood flowing from his mouth. "Mother." The word was accompanied by more blood.

"Don't speak. Lie still. We are home."

Sweyn struggled to sit up. Tears filled Aelfgifu's eyes as she watched him give up. For a moment she could see his wound. The patch of red on his shoulder had grown almost black.

"Home," he said.

"Yes. Home. You're safe at home. We'll find the best healers to treat you, you'll get well. You'll see your brother soon."

He nodded weakly while she caressed his hair, tears running unimpeded down her face. She looked up at the horizon, at the low clouds that hung there, showing them the way. When she looked down again, he was gone.

Chapter Twenty-Five
England

The moment she set foot on her home soil, Aelfgifu forced her grief aside in order to see to the practical matters of their return. The first thing she did was to send a messenger to Reodfeld from Sandwich, where they had landed, to deliver word to Harold. She wrote of the events in Norway, of their imprisonment by Harold's half-brother Harthacanute and of Sweyn's death. Sweyn's body was taken by Wulfred and wrapped, waiting for burial. She and Lufu took rooms at a local inn where clothes were ordered and bathing equipment supplied. A local seamstress was contacted in order to modify some dresses to fit them. Although not new, they were far better than what Aelfgifu and Lufu were wearing.

The rooms were comfortable, and after a decent meal Aelfgifu slept better than she had for months. The next morning, after she'd washed and dressed she went to the window, opening it and breathing in the cold English air, letting the familiar smells wash over her. She'd scrubbed the weeks of grime from her skin but her mind was still a mess, and the air of her homeland went some way towards calming her. Lufu lingered in the room behind her; she hadn't left Aelfgifu's side since they'd arrived back in England, insisting on moving a bed into her room so that she was never left alone.

"My lady, are you well?"

Aelfgifu shook her head, forcing herself back to the present and the things that needed to be done. "I'm fine, Lufu. Just enjoying the fresh air." The words she spoke meant nothing, they were just sounds made to reassure another, but as she spoke them she realised she was on the edge of hysteria, her heart telling her to scream but her mind insisting she continue the pretence. She turned to look at her friend. Focussing on Lufu distracted her from her grief, if only for a few moments.

It was clear her friend had suffered. The woman had been brought up at court and had been expected to marry a wealthy or important man and bring further glory to their family. Instead she'd devoted her life to Aelfgifu, eschewing marriage, and this is what she'd been forced to endure. Aelfgifu's heart broke and she felt tears stinging her eyes. This was her fault, the life this woman had led. Hers and Emma's. The sudden thought of Emma strengthened her resolve and she wiped her eyes. "What did they do to you?"

Lufu looked away, unable to meet Aelfgifu's gaze. "It's not something I wish to speak of, my lady. We're here now, that's all that matters."

Aelfgifu nodded. Whatever horrors her friend had suffered, it was the woman's right to keep those secrets to herself, no matter how terrible. A knock on the door interrupted their conversation. Wulfred was there. "My lady, we're ready."

She caught Lufu's eye and together they went outside, following Wulfred. Her carl had arranged for Sweyn's burial to take place in a small churchyard to the north of the village. They couldn't send him to the gods in the way that she wished but Aelfgifu would ensure that he was buried with all he would need in the next life, even if he was being interred in Christian ground. Her cautiousness had returned to her and she was aware that Emma's spies were probably watching them, were more than likely aware they'd returned from Norway. But she didn't care; it was because of Emma her son was dead, the woman wasn't going to deprive her of her right to see Sweyn laid to rest. There were only three of them: Aelfgifu, Lufu and Wulfred, plus a priest to say words over the dead body of her son. After he'd finished speaking Aelfgifu placed Sweyn's sword into the grave, as well as a goblet she'd bought. Then, reaching behind her neck, she undid the Mjölnir pendant Canute had given her and placed it on her son's chest.

"Go quickly to your ancestors, my son. Your father awaits you. Tell him of my love for him and that I'll see him again soon."

Wulfred leaned over the grave and spoke in a low voice so that she couldn't hear what he said. She was grateful to the man for his constant support and for the care he'd taken with her firstborn. In fact she suspected that he had feelings for her, a truth the man would never admit to. She nodded her thanks to him and left the gravedigger to finish his work.

They had little to pack save for a few new items they'd purchased when they arrived at Lowestoft and so were able to travel to Aelfgifu's manor with only themselves and the horses Wulfred had procured, no wagons were needed. Aelfgifu shivered and tried to pull her cloak closer. She'd been cold since fleeing Harthacanute and couldn't quite rid herself of the chill of their prison. The aches she'd sometimes felt had grown worse while they were trapped in the small room and were now a constant companion. But the hard ride was worth the discomfort for her heart jumped when they arrived at Reodfeld and she saw Harold.

"Mother, you're here, finally!"

Aelfgifu, ignoring all those standing around them in the courtyard, rushed to her son and embraced him.

"Sweyn . . . "She held him tighter.

"He's gone to meet our ancestors. We sent him off as well as we could." Feeling his body stiffen, she fought back her tears and held her son until he relaxed slightly. Releasing him, she stared into his eyes. "Come, there's much to talk about."

Aelfgifu revelled in the familiar sights, smells and sounds of Reodfeld. It'd been years since she was last here and nothing had changed. A huge fire blazed in the hearth of the main hall and they'd shared a meal together. She'd sent Lufu to bed; her poor friend was exhausted and wasn't needed and now Aelfgifu sat with Harold, Wulfred and Canute's old friend, Oswulf, who'd been left behind in England to watch over her son. She was grateful to the man for he'd done an excellent job of keeping both her properties and her son safe.

"Tell me everything that happened." So far they hadn't spoken of Canute's death, but it was obvious to all in the room what information Aelfgifu sought.

Oswulf cleared his throat. "My lady, I was with the king. He'd cut himself but the wound grew infected. The physicians did all they could, they even ... " The carl stopped himself, looking down.

"It's all right, Oswulf, I know the details, you need not repeat them." A part of her thought it silly that a man of war such as Oswulf would be squeamish about sharing details of injuries with a woman.

He nodded his thanks. "The king fell senseless after a meal, fell from his chair. He was carried to his bed but he never woke." He stopped to take a drink before continuing. "The king uttered strange words before collapsing but I don't know what they meant or if they were even words."

"Where did this happen?" If Harthacanute knew these details, he'd kept them to himself.

"We were in the main hall at the manor in Shaftesbury; Canute was meeting with his thegns over matters of running the region." She nodded for him to continue. "He remained senseless for three days before all signs of life departed and he was declared dead."

"And was ... " She didn't want to ask but needed to know.

"Emma wasn't with us but she took control of the king's

burial, her and the archbishop. Both declared him the most Christian of kings and insisted that any signs of the old religion be forbidden." He leaned in toward her. "But fear not, my lady, for many of Canute's supporters were in possession of relics and most said the old prayers to the All Father for him. He was surely welcomed to Valhalla."

She reached across and took the man's huge hands in hers, squeezing her thanks. "Please go on."

Oswulf leaned back in his chair and continued. "The king was taken to Winchester with great ceremony and placed in the minster. Emma remains there still, living at the palace. She had the entire treasury moved to her rooms, all of the king's gold and plate, the seals of the country, his ring, all under her protection."

Harold, who'd been listening intently, interrupted. "Does she think England will be attacked? Who does she protect the treasure from?"

Aelfgifu glanced at Oswulf, then at Wulfred. It was clear they all thought the same thing.

Looking at her son, she spoke the words aloud for the first time. "She protects the treasure from you." She saw the confused look on Harold's face and elaborated. "Emma fears you, Harold."

Later, when they were alone in her chambers, Harold finally spoke. "Me? Why me?"

Aelfgifu threw up her hands in exasperation. "Because you'll be king! And Emma knows it!"

"But what about Harthacanute?"

She drew her son to her side, pulling his chair toward her. "We must act quickly. He won't sail until the weather is better. In the meantime, we must persuade the council that *you* are the better choice to rule."

Aelfgifu watched her son, his face revealing his emotions.

"Surely you've considered this?"

"Yes, but . . . "

"But you didn't think to see the day?" He nodded at her, making her smile. "My son, the day has come. Now we must act, else it will be too late."

Aelfgifu started the new year by sending letters to the council, first among them Godwin. A few weeks after she'd written, a letter arrived back. She was disappointed he hadn't come in person but was glad he'd replied so quickly.

It started with the usual wishes for her health and prayer on her behalf to the gods, then:

"My lady, I'm dearly sorry I'm unable to attend you in person but I dare not leave the south at present for there is much to see to and watch over."

She took this to mean Emma, for Canute had often used the excuse that he wouldn't dare leave the woman alone. His next words brought a smile to her face:

"But while I'm unable to present myself in person I declare to you now that I'll wholeheartedly support your son Harold in his bid to rule."

Her spirits soared, for here was the first proof her son was indeed meant to be king, that it was his wyrd. Aelfgifu continued to write, to send missives of friendship and promises all over the country. The determination she felt, the single-mindedness of her purpose, led her to neglect her own comfort. She was so engrossed in composing yet another letter she didn't hear the announcement of a visitor.

Leofric strode into the room, the earl's rich cloak swirling around him. He stopped before her and bowed.

"My Lady Aelfgifu."

"My lord, what a surprise, I hadn't expected to see you here." She stood and brushed the wrinkles from her dress and, seeing that ink had seeped into her sleeve, rolled it back quickly. Waving at a chair, she bid her visitor sit.

"I can't stay long, my lady. Emma is already suspicious of any councillors who leave court save on her business."

She nodded and wondered how Emma got any sleep at night, so deep ran her suspicions; the woman saw conspiracy everywhere. "I understand."

Leofric paused before speaking next, which could've been mistaken as natural except Aelfgifu knew this man.

"What is it?"

The earl turned red. "My lady, it's Emma."

Of course it was. Sighing, she closed her eyes. "What has she done now?"

"She knows of your effort to see Harold on the throne over Harthacanute." He hesitated and Aelfgifu wondered what could be so terrible that a powerful man like Leofric was afraid to speak the words. "My lady, I hate to be the one to tell you these things, but Emma has begun to spread rumours about your son and his . . . " the earl looked away before continuing, "his legitimacy."

Aelfgifu, despite her shock, was too tired to stand. "What? What has she said?"

"Emma claims Canute isn't Harold's true father, rather that you had a," he searched for the right word, "liaison with a shoemaker . . . "

It was too much. "How dare she? Where does she get the nerve to accuse me of such actions? And to say Canute isn't Harold's true father?" Aelfgifu felt sick and ordered a maid to fetch bread to calm her stomach, a trick she'd been using more often lately.

Leofric remained silent while she ate and she was grateful for his kindness. Only when she had finished did he speak again. "My lady, be assured that myself and all of Harold's supporters deny these malicious rumours whenever we hear them."

Aelfgifu nodded her thanks at him, still feeling nauseated

by this latest news. It sickened her that anyone should think, even in passing, that she had been anything but loving and loyal to Canute. She would take care of this, along with everything else she'd been doing, and Emma would pay.

"I won't waste your time with more about Emma. It's obvious by her actions that she fears Harold and my efforts to see him crowned. You'll support my son?"

"Yes, lady, fully. And I'll work with Godwin to convince the others. But . . ."

"Yes, my lord?"

"It will take more than words to persuade many of these men, especially the younger ones, those newly important and who already believe Emma's story."

Aelfgifu shook her head. "I suspected as much. Let me know what is needed, it'll be arranged." She said a silent prayer of thanks to the gods that she still held all of her own lands, and had her own wealth.

Earl Leofric left the next day and all she need do now was wait for the seeds she'd sown to grow.

A few weeks later her work bore fruit: the council wrote, declaring that Harold would rule until Harthacanute returned. It wasn't what she wanted, but it was a start, and revealed that Emma didn't always get her own way.

By late spring there was still no sign of Harthacanute and Aelfgifu was unable to find the reason for his delay. Godwin arrived, the first she'd seen of him since their escape from Norway and he brought news.

"Harthacanute isn't coming."

She nearly dropped her wine. "What?"

"He says he has too much to do in Denmark, apparently some discontent has arisen and he must remain there."

Aelfgifu put her cup down and clapped her hands. "But that's it then! Harold is truly king!" Bringing her arms back in, she stopped. There was a nervous look on his face, more to be said. Then a thought came to her. "Emma must surely be furious, but she wouldn't . . . "

"Aye, she would and she has. She's written to her sons by Aethelred, Edward and Alfred, who both reside in Normandy, and demanded that the eldest, Edward, return and seize the crown." Her eyes widened at the news. Godwin continued. "Emma has remained in the palace at Winchester. She has no more power but is still fearsome enough that no one dares oppose her for the belief is that Edward will return and to anger Emma is to invite penalty from her son when this happens."

"But her sons hate her! I hear that Edward wishes only to be a monk, a holy man left alone to pray!"

"Yes, but her youngest, Alfred, wants just the opposite."

Aelfgifu was indignant, even though the emotion made no sense here. "He can't rule, he's second-born. The council won't allow it."

Godwin nodded. "Yet Emma still tries."

Aelfgifu stared at the earl before replying. "She can't force the eldest to take the crown, no matter how hard she cajoles in her letters, no matter how manipulative she is. If Edward decides to abandon his claim there is nothing anyone can do, not even a mother. My hope is that it'll all come to naught." Hope flared in her breast, but a vine of fear tangled itself around her heart. She addressed the emotion directly. "We must show Emma who rules England and put an end to her."

With the news that Harthacanute wouldn't be returning anytime soon the country grew used to Harold's rule. Or Aelfgifu's rule, she sometimes thought, for while he was enthusiastic and growing into the role he was still a young man of eighteen and didn't have the experience she possessed. Had they had more time for Harold to settle into his rule, perhaps she would have backed away. But the country needed someone to make decisions and rulings, things that couldn't wait. Despite the fact that Harold had been officially recognised as king by the witan, she stepped in to take her son's place as ruler until he was ready.

Aelfgifu was in Northampton and Harold had gone south to deal with yet another council squabble when Godwin arrived once again. Now that Harold ruled she'd been having regular meetings with the earl, both him and Leofric. She preferred to reside in the north, her home, thus the men had to travel up from London to meet with her.

Godwin was announced and shown into the hall where she was reviewing land charters that Harold would need to sign, some of which were transfers of her own land to the southern nobles, those whose support needed to be strengthened. She looked up, immediately noticing that he hadn't changed from his travel clothes, having come directly from the stable. The news, whatever it was, had to be important. She did not have long to wait.

"The Atheling Arthur is dead."

"What? How?"

Godwin sat and waved for ale. There was no pretence between them; Aelfgifu valued his opinion and presence and allowed him indulgences others were denied.

"No one is certain." He took the cup of ale and downed it, holding it out to be filled again. The servant poured, then stood back, waiting. Godwin's love of ale was well-known at Reodfeld. But despite this, he never lost control of his wits. "His body was discovered on the Isle of Ely." Another drink and swipe of his beard by his massive hand. "His eyes had been put out and his body beaten."

Aelfgifu's gasp was audible and automatic. "Like my father and brother! They'll think I had something to do with this!"

He shook his head. "You needn't worry on that account, the gods are with us. I overheard some men talking in a tavern. They'd just come from meeting with another group nearby. They didn't recognise me as anyone of importance." Godwin waved his hand over his simple clothing. When he travelled he shunned the ornaments that were his due as an earl. This was a trait they had in common and Aelfgifu liked to believe she'd influenced him in this habit.

"And?" Feeling cold and ill, she was anxious to hear anything that would mean she, and Harold by association, wouldn't be blamed for this.

"They spoke of killing a king and laughed. One man placed a bag of coins on the table and ordered the best wine for them all, along with a fine roast dinner."

"And you think these men killed Arthur?"

"Yes."

She frowned. "Why didn't you question them? Have them arrested?"

Godwin paused and Aelfgifu's stomach lurched. Finally he spoke. "They wore Emma's badge."

Her illness grew worse with this news, the feeling not for herself but for the horror she felt. "Why? Why would she have her own child murdered?"

"I've been thinking about that. The only reason I can see is to force the elder son back to England."

"He didn't return to England with his brother?"

"No, Edward remained in Normandy. He believed his brother would take his place as king, leaving him free to join the church."

Aelfgifu felt the dizziness that had accompanied her the past few days grow worse. She hadn't eaten much that day, despite Lufu's constant hovering. "But if he doesn't come home, then . . . " A feeling of joy flooded through her and she would've danced around the room had her breath suddenly not become short. She tried to breathe, but couldn't. She clawed at her throat, trying to release the invisible restriction and it was the last thing she remembered before falling to the ground, blackness enveloping her.

"Harold?" She woke in bed, Lufu sitting on a chair beside her, picking at her sewing.

"He's not here, my lady." Aelfgifu felt a cup against her lips and drank, thankful that Lufu wasn't making a fuss of her. She tried to sit up but became breathless. "Lay back, my lady. You've been too busy and barely eating. Rest a while."

Aelfgifu was surprised by the authority in Lufu's voice and reluctantly agreed, but only if her documents and letters be brought to her bedchamber. Lufu sighed and said she would deliver the papers later. Sinking back into the covers, Aelfgifu had to admit she was grateful for the chance to lie here and sleep. Her life over the past year had been filled with banquets, bequests and outright bribes, anything she could think to do to help her son to the throne. She'd lost count of the number of meetings she'd had. And when she was home there were the letters and charters to attend to, for if she left them for even a week the piles could easily be knocked over by an errant elbow or dress sleeve, they were so high.

After a week of living in bed Aelfgifu rose and continued to rule on behalf of her son. She found that Harold had been taking over more and more duties, hers included, and was turning out to be a successful and admired ruler. Although she had some trouble giving up some of her responsibilities, she was pleased that Harold continued to include her in his most important decisions. The months passed and soon it was the new year, with the entire country giving thanks for the peace and prosperity they'd experienced recently. There was no war, no enemy to be paid off, no foreign campaign to plan, and even the weather had been blessed and there was

304

excess food throughout the country. Many praised the Christian god, but Aelfgifu knew that there were still those, few as they were, who credited the good fortune to the All Father and his children. And fewer still who thanked Aelfgifu. All was well, but there was one thing still left to do.

"How are the talks going with the Welsh?" Harold helped himself to early potatoes.

Aelfgifu washed her beef down with wine. "Slowly. The Welsh lords demand much." She took another slice of beef from the wooden tray. "But I'm confident we'll come to a favourable arrangement."

They spoke on all topics, matters of rule as well as those that affected Reodfeld, his home. As a servant cleared their plates Aelfgifu looked at Harold, as if noticing for the first time that her son was a grown man. And how like Canute he looked. It almost tore at her heart to watch him. "There is one last thing you must do."

Harold's attention, focussed on the departing food, was now on Aelfgifu. He recognised her tone, had heard it before. "And what is that?"

"You must gather your most trusted warriors and march on Winchester." She raised a hand to stop Harold's interruption. "You must take the treasury."

"What?!" He stood, banging his hand on the table. One of his carls appeared in the doorway and was waved away by Aelfgifu.

"Sit. Listen to what I have to say." She waited until he was settled again and poured him wine before speaking. "The treasury is yours by right. It was your father's and contains many of his personal items. Having it will strengthen your claim to the throne." Draining her cup she continued. "It will also give you power, for he who controls the purse controls the country. Power over everything." She was satisfied that Harold listened to her, she had at least taught him that value.

After a few thoughtful moments Harold spoke, his voice even and considered. "If I control the treasury, I control it all. The lords, the church, the country. All will be loyal to me."

"Loyalty is a negotiable virtue and paid for in gold." Aelfgifu sighed.

"And Emma?"

"She will no longer be a threat. To either of us." She spit out the words.

It took little planning for there were many loyal to Harold. He left Aelfgifu at Reodfeld and marched south to Winchester.

"My lord, more townspeople up ahead." Harold's carl Gest rode back to meet him.

"Go see what they want. We must keep riding, these interruptions are only causing delays." Harold was getting impatient; once he made up his mind about a course of action, he was immediately ready to act. And they kept encountering people on their trek south who wanted to join them.

Gest spoke to the group, all men and armed. Harold could see they were farmers by their dress. His carl rode back to him. "They want to join us, show their support."

Harold sighed. He was grateful, but he and his men really did not need any more help. Together they were a group of the finest warriors in the land and he trusted their fighting skills completely. "Thank them, tell them their offer to join us is appreciated but the best way they can help is to go back to their homes and watch over their fields."

They rode quickly, giving every group who offered to join them the same answer, and arrived in Winchester to find the gates barred. "Did you think it would be easy?" Another of his men, Jorunn, smiled grimly.

"No, but I admit a small part of me hoped." He grinned at his men. "Ready?" They had come prepared with a battering ram and after a few attempts the cracking of the splintered gate could be heard both outside and inside the town. "Here we go!" Harold rode first, heading for the palace, running down anything in his way. Again, they found their way blocked. Harold's frustration grew. They brought forth the battering ram again. As the palace gate fell, arrows began to rain down on them.

"Shield wall!" His men gathered around him, each protecting the other from the barrage. Together they moved, as a single unit, towards the main door, hacking at any of Emma's soldiers who tried to stop them. When they were through the door they broke up, pairs of men breaking off to rampage. Screams echoed through the halls as more and more of Emma's carls succumbed to the attack.

"Here. This is the room." Harold pounded the hilt of his sword on the ancient wood. "Locked."

"Let me." Gest stepped past Harold and with a powerful thrust of his leg kicked the door open. Harold entered the room, sword drawn, Gest following close behind.

"I might have guessed you'd do something like this." Emma's icy voice came from the shadows. With a rustling she emerged from a dark corner. "Pathetically determined, just like your whore of a mother."

Harold stepped forward, his anger surging. Gest's hand on his shoulder stayed him. "My lord, she's not worth it. They are only words."

He brushed the hand from his shoulder. "My lady. The treasury is mine. You will be relieved of your 'responsibility' for it, I thank you for your service in keeping it for me."

By now more of his men had arrived. "Take this woman to her rooms and see that she doesn't leave. I want someone posted outside her door at all times while I decide what to do with her."

Two carls stepped forward and took Emma by the arms.
"You'll pay for this," she said, her voice venomous.
He could hear a tremor under the words. "No, lady, I will not. For you have nothing left to bargain with." He turned to watch her being led from the room. "Nothing." As he surveyed the room, the chests of gold goblets and plate, coin and jewels and swords of all shapes and sizes, he spoke. "Send a letter to my mother, informing her of what happened here today."

Aelfgifu was sitting outside at the back of the manor on a patch of moss, propped up by pillows when a messenger arrived. There was so much correspondence in and out of her home these days that one more messenger was barely worth the notice. Lufu delivered the note and it was only as she began to read that Aelfgifu understood that this wasn't just any letter.
"They've done it! They've finally agreed!"
"Agreed to what, my lady? Who?" Lufu was sitting nearby, had placed herself there after delivering the note.
"The council! That group of children have finally come to a sensible decision: they have agreed to formally crown Harold as King of England!"
Lufu clapped her hands, openly exhibiting the excitement that Aelfgifu felt. "My lady, this is wonderful news!"
Aelfgifu smiled, unable to contain herself. She lay back and looked up at the summer sky, letting the sun warm her pained joints. It was excitement she felt, excitement and pride and happiness and a hundred other emotions she couldn't put a name to. But the most powerful feeling she had, the one she cherished most, and the one she wouldn't share with anyone, was the feeling of triumph. Emma's supporters had abandoned her, the lies she told had not

been believed and her son hated her. Aelfgifu wrapped her arms around herself, enjoying the feeling of perfect peace that flowed through every part of her. She had won.

Kelly Evans

ABOUT THE AUTHOR

Born in Canada of Scottish extraction, Kelly Evans graduated in History and English from McMaster University in Hamilton, Ontario.

After graduation Kelly moved to the UK where she worked in the financial sector. While in London she continued her studies in history, focussing on Medieval England and the Icelandic Sagas.

Kelly now lives in Toronto, Ontario with her husband Max and two rescue cats. The Northern Queen is her first novel.

BIBLIOGRAPHY

Barlow, Frank. The Godwin's. Harlow: Pearson Education Limited, 2003.

Barnes, Michael. An Introduction to Old Norse. London: Viking Society for Northern Research, University College London, 1999.

Blair, John. The Anglo-Saxon Age: A Very Short Introduction. Oxford: Oxford University Press, 1984.

Blair, Peter Hunter. An Introduction to Anglo-Saxon England. Cambridge: Cambridge University Press, 2003.

Cameron, M.L. Anglo-Saxon Medicine. Cambridge: Cambridge University Press, 2006.

Campbell, Alistair, ed. Encomium Emmae Regina. Cambridge: Cambridge University Press, 1998

Campbell, James. The Anglo-Saxons. London: Hambledon Press, 1986.

Collins, Roger and McClure, Judith, ed. Bede: Ecclesiastical History of the English Nation. Oxford: Oxford University Press, 1999.

Danziger, Danny and Lacey, Robert. The Year 1000. Great Britain: Little, Brown and Company, 1999.

Ferguson, Robert. The Hammer and the Cross. London: Penguin, 2010.

Fjalldal, Magnus. Anglo-Saxon England in Icelandic Medieval Texts. Toronto: University of Toronto Press, 2005.

Fleming, Robin. Britain After Rome. London: Penguin, 2011.

Haywood, John. The Penguin Historical Atlas of the Vikings. London: Penguin, 1995.

Holland, Tom. Millennium. Great Britain: Abacus, 2009.

Hrisoulas, Jim. The Complete Bladesmith: Forging Your Way to Perfection. Colorado: Paladin Press, 1987.

Lunde, Paul and Stone, Caroline, ed. Ibn Fadlan and the Land of Darkness. London: Penguin Classics, 2012.

Martin, Prof. G.H. and Williams, Dr. Ann, ed. Domesday Book: A Complete Translation. London: Penguin, 1992.

McGillivray, Murry. A Gentle Introduction to Old English. Canada: Broadview Press, 2011.

McGillvray, Murray, ed. Select Historical Documents of the Ninth and Tenth Century. Cambridge: Cambridge University Press, 1914.

O'Brien, Harriet. Queen Emma: A History of Power, Love and Greed in Eleventh Century England. London: Bloomsbury Publishing Company London, 2006.

Richards, Julian. Blood of the Vikings. Great Britain: Hodder and Stoughton, 2001.

Scott, R.A. Basilica. London: Penguin, 2007.

Stafford, Pauline. Queen Emma and Queen Edith: Queenship and Women's Power in Eleventh Century England. Oxford: Blackwell Publishers Inc., 2004.

Stenton, Frank. Anglo-Saxon England. Oxford: Oxford

University Press, 2001.

Strachan, Isabella. Emma: The Twice-Crowned Queen: England in the Viking Age. London: Peter Owen Publishers, 2004.

Swanton, Michael, ed. The Anglo-Saxon Chronicles. Great Britain: Phoenix Press, 2000.

Thorsson, Ornolfur, ed. Saga of the Icelanders. London: Penguin, 2000.

Whitelock, Dorothy, ed. Anglo-Saxon Wills. Cambridge: Cambridge University Press, 1930.

Wilson, Sir David M. The Bayeux Tapestry. New York: Thames and Hudson, 2004.

Wood, Michael. In Search of the Dark Ages. London: BBC Books, 2005.

NORDLAND PUBLISHING

Follow the North Road.

nordlandpublishing.com
facebook.com/nordlandpublishing
nordlandpublishing.tumblr.com

NORDLAND

www.nordlandpublishing.com

29048552R00201

Made in the USA
San Bernardino, CA
14 January 2016